T0339812

THE PYRAMID AGE

THE PYRAMID AGE

Vol. 2 in the series
Ages in Alignment

Emmet Sweeney

Algora Publishing
New York

ISBN-13: 978-0-87586-566-9 (trade paper)
ISBN-13: 978-0-87586-567-6 (hard cover)
ISBN-13: 978-0-87586-568-3 (ebook)

Library of Congress Cataloging-in-Publication Data —

Sweeney, Emmet John.
   The Pyramid Age / Emmet Sweeney.
      p. cm. — (Ages in alignment ; v. 2)
   Includes bibliographical references and index.
   ISBN 978-0-87586-566-9 (trade paper: alk. paper) — ISBN 978-0-87586-567-6 (hard
cover: alk. paper) — ISBN 978-0-87586-568-3 (ebook) 1. Egypt—History—To 332 B.C. 2.
Egypt—History—Errors, inventions, etc. I. Title.

   DT83.S942 2007
   932—dc22
                                    2006038650

Printed in the United States

Table of Contents

Introduction

The works of Egypt's pyramid-building kings, the pharaohs of the Fourth, Fifth and Sixth Dynasties, are perhaps the most celebrated of all ancient monuments. Countless volumes have been written about the pyramids, particularly those at Giza, and about the mysterious and godlike kings who raised them. Yet still there is little that can be said with certainty about either the monuments or their builders. Neither Cheops (Khufu), who erected the Great Pyramid, nor his successor Chephren (Khafre), who raised an equally impressive monument nearby, bequeathed to posterity much in the way of inscriptions. Fundamental questions remain unanswered. The very purpose of the buildings, and the method of their construction, remain mysterious.

Modern investigators using the scientific and mathematical tools of the age have disclosed facts about the Giza pyramids that can only be described as astonishing. The result has been a proliferation of books making sensational claims, which have only served to discredit their publishers and cause profound confusion amongst the general public.

Yet, as we shall see in the course of the present volume, the "alternative" writers are not solely to blame. The scholarly establishment itself, by burying its head in the sand and refusing to consider uncomfortable facts, has been largely responsible for leaving the field wide open to these outlandish hypotheses that now fill the "Egyptology" shelves in libraries and bookshops.

To the ancients however there was little mystery. The pyramids of Giza, they said, were built by three generations of pharaohs, Khufu, Khafre and Menkaure, who intended them to be funerary monuments, though they were never actually buried there. Nevertheless, even in antiquity there was some controversy or contention over the age of the pyramids, over the question of when Khufu and Khafre had lived. Herodotus, the Greek "Father of History", provides the earliest reference (outside Egyptian sources) to Khufu and Khafre — whom he names Cheops and Chephren. According to him, these kings lived at a comparatively late date; just before the Ethiopian pharaohs, as a matter of fact. But the Ethiopians kings, it is accepted by all, reigned at the end of the eighth and the beginning of the seventh centuries BC; which of course then implies that the Father of History placed the pyramid-builders some time in the eighth century. Such a proposition is now held to be outrageous, because modern Egyptology places these kings in the third millennium BC — almost two thousand years earlier!

It has long been the fashion to castigate Herodotus for his apparently absurd chronology. Manetho, the Hellenistic Egyptian chronicler, upon whose ideas modern Egyptology is largely based, placed the pyramid-builders near the beginning of Egyptian history; Herodotus apparently placed them nearer the end. How could the Greek writer, who visited Egypt, and who claimed to derive his account from native source material, have been so wrong? One solution has been to suggest that the order of Herodotus's history is corrupt, and that those passages concerning the pyramid-builders were misplaced by a later editor. Flinders Petrie, for example, suggested such a solution. However, the sense of comfort derived from this answer is a false one, and has resulted in the concealment or suppression (almost unconsciously) of a vast body of evidence, which, had it been properly examined, would have provided powerful support for Herodotus.

In some ways, the work that follows may be regarded as a vindication of Herodotus. It is also, however, a vindication of the much-maligned Immanuel Velikovsky, whose epoch-making *Ages in Chaos* (1952), first called scholarship's attention to the dramatic errors upon which ancient chronology is built. In *Ages in Chaos*, Velikovsky called for subtracting five to seven centuries from the length of Egypt's history, and argued that the imperial Eighteenth Dynasty be placed early in the first millennium BC, rather than the middle of the second. Though derided at the time, especially for his catastrophist views, Velikovsky's work has stood the test of time, and slowly but surely the need for a radical reconstruction of ancient history is gaining acceptance.

Perhaps the most impressive chronological work in recent years has come from the pen of Professor Gunnar Heinsohn. In his *Sumerer gab es nicht* (1988), Dr. Heinsohn revealed how Mesopotamian history had been distorted in a way that made the distortion of Egyptian history uncovered by Velikovsky pale into insignificance. Chimerical empires and civilizations were created by historians, and placed up to 2000 years before any literate civilization even existed in Mesopotamia. According to Heinsohn, Mesopotamian civilization only began at the start of the first millennium BC, and the great civilizations of the third millennium — namely the Sumerians and Akkadians — were actually alter-egos of the great civilizations of the early first millennium — the Chaldaeans and Assyrians. Now, it is known that the Akkadians and Sumerians were contemporary with the pharaohs of Egypt's Old Kingdom, and for this reason it became obvious that, should Heinsohn be on the right track, Egyptian history would need to be shortened in a way comparable to that of Mesopotamia.

The immense amount of material brought forward by Heinsohn (some of which will be examined in the pages to follow) leaves no doubt that his proposals, astonishing though they may have appeared initially, are essentially correct; and that a full two thousand years needs to be subtracted from the histories of both Mesopotamia and Egypt.

Our investigation of the Pyramid Age begins however with a general look at the whole phenomenon of pyramid-building. The pyramid is revealed to be a sacred temple dedicated to the celestial deities, and inspired by awesome natural events occurring early in the first millennium BC. The pyramids of Giza are shown to be little more than part of a world-wide *genre* of megalithic ("Great Stone") structures, whose range included both occident and orient. The age of megalith-building saw the erection of Stonehenge, the great mound-tomb of Newgrange in Ireland, the cyclopean monuments of Mycenaean Greece, and the ziggurats of Mesopotamia. The question as to why pyramids, or pyramid-type structures, are found in almost every corner of the globe (a question rarely broached by orthodox academia) is revealed to have a sinister answer.

We move on from there to examine the history of the Pyramid Age; for in that history we find important clues to a correct chronology. For example, the lives and careers of many of the pharaohs of the Fourth, Fifth and Sixth Dynasties seem to connect in strange ways with events described in the early books of the Bible. On the other hand, much of the literature of the Pyramid Age seems to have its closest parallels in material found not in Genesis and Exodus, but in the supposedly much later biblical books of the Prophets.

The next chapter takes a general look at the Pyramid Age and its achievements. The pyramid-builders made abundant use of iron tools (though this is generally denied in mainstream academic works) to carve the hard granite so much used in these structures. Their knowledge of glass-making was not at all inferior to that of the craftsmen of the Eighteenth Dynasty, whilst their scientific and mathematical achievements were not far behind those of classical Greece. Even more to the point, the Pyramid Age is revealed as an epoch of astonishing moral development, with evidence of a philosophical movement towards monotheism; all of which, of course, is totally inexplicable in the third millennium BC.

Chapter 4 takes an in-depth look at how the chronology of the ancient Near East was formulated. There we find that far from having any firm scientific basis, the timescales of Egypt and Mesopotamia, the twin pillars upon which the history of early civilization rests, depend almost entirely for their validity upon venerated literary tradition, specifically from biblical tradition, and from a fundamentalist interpretation of it to boot. It was the 4th-century Christian chronicler Eusebius who outlined the Egyptian chronology that is still, with only minor amendments, accepted by scholarship. In his mistaken attempts to "prove" the Book of Genesis, Eusebius made Manetho's Egyptian history conform to the chronology of the Old Testament, and therefore followed earlier Jewish historians in tying Menes, the first pharaoh, to Adam. The end result was a history that commenced around 3700 BC (the date for Adam most favored in Jewish circles). The great irony is that, properly understood, Egyptian history would have supplied a great deal of verification for the Old Testament; but, having been put together wrongly, we now find ourselves in the situation where it is claimed than none of the great Hebrew characters whose lives were supposed to have impinged on Egypt (as for example Abraham, Joseph and Moses), are even mentioned by the Egyptians. Yet we shall find that all of these personalities do indeed figure in Egyptian tradition: they have been missed because scholars looked for them in the wrong places. One of the most startling and far-reaching discoveries we shall make is the extent to which the great events of Egyptian history are in fact very precisely reflected in the contents of Genesis, Exodus and Judges.

Another claim now made by Egyptologists is that "modern" dating methods, such as radiocarbon analysis, have served to verify textbook chronology. Yet we shall find that the proponents of such methods have been no more scholarly in their approach, and they have, almost unwittingly, selectively manipulated data with the aim of upholding the ultimately fundamentalist status quo.

Chapter 5 takes us to the start of the 8th century, when Assyrian might reached the borders of Egypt. The Assyrian rulers, who carried the shepherd's crook as their royal symbol, are identified from the Egyptian records and king-lists, and their relationship with the Hyksos Shepherd Kings clarified. Here we also examine the multiplicity of dynasties that arose in Egypt in the immediate aftermath of the Assyrian conquest, and these are revealed to be the "Middle Kingdom" pharaohs (Dynasties 11 to 13), who ruled a fragmented nation under the auspices of the Asiatic invaders, and who were known to classical tradition as the Dodecarchs.

The final chapters examine Pyramid Age Egypt's relationship with two other antique nations of the region, Israel and Greece. There we find an abundance of evidence to show that the Israelite Exodus was contemporary with the very beginnings of the Pyramid Age, whilst Greece's Heroic or Mycenaean epoch commenced at the same point in time. There are some exciting moments. We shall discover, for example, the identity of the pharaoh drowned in the Sea of Passage, as well as the name of his successor, who restored order in the kingdom after the departure of the Israelites. We shall find too the identity of Egypt's rulers during the Trojan War, and how Greek warriors fresh from the sack of Ilion participated in the wars which established Egypt's greatest royal dynasty in power.

As might be expected, the sources used in the present work have been diverse. Since a major aim of the book has been to expand and build upon the work of reconstruction already begun by Velikovsky, I have made liberal use of his writings and ideas. *Ages in Chaos* and *Peoples of the Sea* were most influential in determining the course of my thought, and other writers of the Velikovsky school have had their impact. The work of Gunnar Heinsohn in particular has helped to inspire the complete overhaul of Egyptian chronology that is attempted in the following pages. Had his radical reconstruction of Mesopotamian chronology not appeared, it is doubtful if Old and Middle Kingdom Egyptian chronology would ever have been effectively challenged. Of the older school of Egyptology, I have found the works of Gaston Maspero, Flinders Petrie, and James Henry Breasted most valuable. No serious work on Egyptian history could ever hope to proceed without the support of these men's truly Herculean efforts. In addition to these, and a host of other scholars of the 20th century, I have drawn freely on the writings of the classical authors (a most essential, though sadly neglected, source) as well as on the hieroglyphic records of Egypt herself.

It must be admitted that the use of such divergent and apparently unrelated source material has turned the writing of this work into a highly interdisciplinary exercise. I would argue, however, that this is not a weakness but a strength, since it was largely the myopia caused by over-specialization that brought about the intransigent adherence to a patently absurd chronology that we now witness on the part of orthodox scholarship.

It would of course be foolish to claim that the reconstruction presented in these pages is anything approaching definitive. What we have is little more than a skeletal outline. Further research must subject the identifications made to ever closer scrutiny. If mistakes have been made, and they surely must, then they will have to be identified and corrected. The author however holds that such errors as have been committed are of a relatively minor nature; and that the overall picture presented here will stand any amount of cross examination. What is being proposed is not nearly as radical as it might first appear. On the contrary, I would argue, it is the modern "histories" of Egypt and Mesopotamia, which reject most of the revered traditions of these lands, that are radical. What the reader will find in the pages that follow, I suggest, is a picture of ancient history more or less in line with how the ancients themselves saw it.

Chapter 1. Walls Raised by the Hands of Giants

Glimpses of a Bygone Age

Egypt's glorious Third Dynasty came to a sudden and dramatic end. Amidst scenes of natural disaster, slave rebellion and foreign invasion, the great line of kings which had raised the world's first monuments in stone was no more. In the ensuing chaos, a commoner seized the reins of power. This man, whom history would know as Sneferu, repelled marauding invaders from the desert lands to the east, restored order in the Nile Valley and had himself proclaimed pharaoh. To legitimize his position, he married Hetepheres, daughter of the previous ruler Huni, last pharaoh of the Third Dynasty.

Sneferu was to become one of the best-loved of all Egyptian kings. He inaugurated an age of peace and prosperity which was to see the art and culture of Egypt reach unprecedented and never repeated heights of achievement. During his time and that of his immediate successors, Cheops and Chephren, the craftsmen and architects of Egypt raised monuments that would astonish the world; architectural masterpieces which survive to this day and which even the modern visitor to the Land of the Nile views with awe. With Sneferu began the Pyramid Age.

Yet although Sneferu and his successors launched a veritable Golden Age, historians of our time claim to know little of him and his epoch. It is not known why the Egyptians began suddenly to raise such massive structures as the Giza pyramids, and the whole phenomenon of pyramid-building and the culture attached to it is said to be an enigma. Such explanations as are offered, for instance that the pyramids were royal tombs prepared for god-like kings, beg more questions than they answer. Why, for example, would any people exert such effort in raising vast tombs for mere men of flesh and blood, mortals like themselves? And if we counter that the pharaoh was not regarded as a mere mortal but as an incarnation of the deity himself, we must then enquire about the source of such a strange idea.

Along with the mystery of pyramid-building comes the mystery of the rise to power of Sneferu's dynasty. How a commoner could seize the throne of the Two Lands, marry into the royal family, and make himself pharaoh, is by no means understood. The scenes described in our opening paragraph are not found in conventional textbooks. These volumes, which fill the libraries and bookshops of the world, know of no natural catastrophes in Sneferu's time. They do not speak of a dramatic end to the Third Dynasty. They know of no slave rebellions and no foreign invasions — though they do admit that Sneferu confronted and overcame the desert tribes in the Sinai Peninsula. Admitting that he was regarded by later generations of Egyptians as a great warrior, they nevertheless say nothing of Sneferu defeating invaders within the borders of Egypt herself.

Whence then come the confident assertions of our opening paragraph? How do I know that the Third Dynasty ended in a natural cataclysm? From what source also do I know of a slave rebellion, of the breakdown of law in the land, and of an invasion of Egypt by desert tribes? In addition to these questions, it may be asked how I explain the pyramid-building mania inaugurated by Sneferu, and what relevance this might have to the other questions posed.

The truth about the Pyramid Age is far stranger than anything that has yet appeared in fiction.

A Worldwide Phenomenon

Modern readers are all too familiar with the plethora of wild speculations about the pyramids which seem to be churned out in ever-increasing numbers every year by certain publishing houses. Why should these structures elicit such outlandish theorizing? Some of the pyramids, it is true, are impressive enough monuments. The Great Pyramid is very impressive. But it is not supernatural; raising such a building was not beyond the abilities of ancient man. It would very definitely not be beyond the capabilities (as has been seriously suggested) of modern human beings. The cathedrals of medieval Europe, some of whose spires rise almost to the same altitude as the Great Pyramid, are much more impressive structures, and there is no question that the Egyptians would have been unable to raise anything comparable. Yet no one suggests that the cathedrals were built by aliens or Atlanteans. Why pick on the pyramids?

To this there is a comparatively straightforward answer: The field has been left wide open because the conventional explanation of the pyramids, found in countless learned textbooks, is simply not satisfactory. The pyramids *are* a great mystery, and it is eminently clear that attempts to explain the Egyptian monuments, for example, as a local phenomenon which evolved solely as a result of economic conditions in the Nile valley, just does not stand up to scrutiny. It is quite wrong, and totally misleading, to see pyramid-building as something peculiar to Egypt. Pyramids, or pyramid-like structures, as the proponents of the various "alternative" theories never tire of repeating, are found in almost every corner of the globe. Recent discoveries have shown substantial pyramids in China, and the various pagoda-style temples still standing throughout southern and eastern Asia are rather obviously medieval descendants of an ancient pyramidal architectural form. All these can now be placed alongside the ziggurats of Mesopotamia, the pyramids of southern and central America, the megalithic tumuli of Europe and various mound-structures throughout North America and Asia. At the moment, the only areas without pyramids are sub-Saharan Africa and Australia, but this may change as our knowledge of the archaeology of these areas improves.

Any attempt therefore to explain pyramids as isolated local phenomena, without taking into consideration the broader picture, is immediately ignoring a crucial piece of evidence. Yet mainstream scholarship rarely, if ever, looks at pyramid-building in this way. Very occasionally, a historian may ponder the conundrum of the pyramids and mounds of the Near East and of adjacent cultures. That there is a genuine mystery is readily admitted, though generally speaking no explanation is proffered.

> For reasons that are still largely obscure peoples with no apparent contact with each other, separated by enormous distances and with totally unrelated cultural traditions began, early in the third millennium, to build more and more complex structures in which to house the remains of their chiefs and Kings and, increasingly, a substantial part of the community's moveable wealth. Often these monuments were enclosed in mounds, or were themselves mound-like in structure, though built of stone [i.e. pyramids]. In the history of human obsessions the practice represents a curious chapter. From the Orkney islands in the most remote north-west, across Europe, through Egypt and Mesopotamia, down the coastlands and islands of the Arabian Gulf, in Oman, and away into the Indian subcontinent and beyond, elaborate tombs of this type were constructed at this time. In the Arabian Gulf, for example, an extraordinary concentration of mound burials is to be found on the principal Bahrain island where it is estimated that some 170,000 tumuli are to be seen still, the vast majority dating from the late third to the early second millennia. Examples of similar mound fields can be

found in eastern Arabia: Oman has its own, even earlier type of mound, constructed often from finely made ashlar blocks of brilliant white limestone. The
pyramids, stupendous though they may seem to later generations, must be seen
against the backcloth of the long development of Egyptian funerary monuments
on the one hand and, on the other, of the much more varied range of tomb structures devised for the great ones of a substantial part of the ancient world during
the third millennium. Even the pyramids [of Egypt], incidentally, contain the
more simple tumulus or mound, as do the great mastabas of the early Kings; it
obviously had a profound and pervasive significance.[1]

The writer of the above words, whilst recognizing the mystery of mound- and
pyramid-building, nevertheless conceals from the reader the true extent of the
puzzle: for all the cultures he mentions could conceivably have exerted a mutual
influence. Some of them are reasonably far apart, but the distances are not insurmountable. He did not dare to include among them the peoples of the Americas;
for here the question of cultural diffusion is virtually a non-starter. Nevertheless,
the writer would probably have justified the omission of the Mexicans and Pe-
ruvians on the grounds that these folk are known to have commenced tumulus-
building only around 1000 BC — roughly two thousand years after the supposed
commencement of pyramid-building in the Old World. But the mystery would be
infinitely more profound were it to be shown that pyramid-building commenced
in the Old and New Worlds at exactly the same time.

As we proceed through the present work, powerful evidence will be presented to show that there was no gap between the rise of the mound-building
civilizations of the Old and New Worlds. All of these began shortly before 1000
BC. Leaving aside however for one minute the question of chronology, it is still
evident, even whilst considering only the mound- and pyramid-building cultures
of the Old World, that something truly extraordinary, something quite beyond
the ken of modern archaeological theory, must be called upon to explain the phenomenon. What then could it have been? Why were the pyramids built? Viewed
in this way, the various alien and Atlantean speculations begin to seem less absurd than at first glance. Yet such ideas are unnecessary; for the pyramid-builders
themselves have told us, in the most straightforward way possible, why the monuments were built. The only problem is that scholars have not been listening.

The last pyramids to be actually used, so far as we know, were those of Mexico, and what the Spanish *conquistadors* witnessed at these monuments is entirely
in accordance with the literary testimony from ancient Mesopotamia, where
evidence shows the ziggurats were used as high altars upon which were performed blood sacrifices. Evidence from almost every corner of the globe makes it
clear that pyramids were cult edifices of a world-wide stellar religion, a religion
which viewed the heavenly bodies, especially the sun, moon and planets, as gods,

1 Michael Rice, *Egypt's Making* (1990) p.171

and which regarded the offering of blood-sacrifices to these deities as vital to the wellbeing of the whole community. Indeed it was seen as vital to the wellbeing of all creation.

The pyramids of Egypt, it is true, were not employed as high altars, though more ancient structures (now demolished) from the Early Dynastic epoch may well have been used for sacrifice. Certainly human and animal sacrifice was common in Early Dynastic Egypt, and, as was the case everywhere else, these blood offerings would have been dedicated on some high place or other. The later pyramids — those of the Fourth, Fifth and Sixth Dynasties — although not used as altars, were very definitely sacred monuments of a sky religion. The Pyramid Texts which were inscribed on the inner chambers of these structures leave no doubt that they were dedicated to the same stellar gods as those of Mexico and Mesopotamia.

The very universality of the ancient stellar religion has led most scholars to conclude, quite erroneously, that the worship of the sun, moon and planets was somehow instinctive to humanity. The warmth and light of the sun, it is surmised, led early humans naturally to honor this life-giving body. The worship accorded to the sun would in course of time have been extended to the moon and planets.

Yet such a conclusion, accepted by almost every contemporary authority, is entirely mistaken. For there was a time when neither sun, moon nor planets figured, or at least seemed to figure, in the religious ideas of mankind. We possess very substantial evidence from the artwork of the Paleolithic (Old Stone) epoch, particularly from the Magdalenian culture, to show that religious beliefs at the time were almost entirely concerned with ancestor-worship, sympathetic magic, and the honoring of a mother-goddess. In all the artifacts, artwork and cult-objects of the Paleolithic, there is no evidence of a stellar religion, or even that folk were in any way interested in the heavenly bodies. The sky-gods appear everywhere quite suddenly after the end of the Paleolithic, which coincides with the end of the Pleistocene, a break-off point which, significantly, saw the extinction of an estimated two-thirds of all land animal species.

The evidence shows that the appearance of the sky-gods immediately after the Pleistocene extinctions is not merely coincidental.

THE DRAGON OF CHAOS

Along with the worship of sun, moon and planets, the early Neolithic (New Stone Age) peoples also honored a dragon or serpent figure, a motif which appears, along with planetary deities, with an apparent suddenness, at the close of the Paleolithic epoch. In every corner of the planet, from orient to occident, from north to south, this cosmic serpent is invariably linked to a cataclysmic disaster that devastated the world and wiped out most of humanity.

Like the sky-gods, the cosmic serpent or dragon is closely associated with pyramids, and it is evident that many of the sacrifices offered atop these sacred mountains were dedicated to this strange god. Indeed in a very real sense pyramids were altars of the cosmic serpent. The mystery of the pyramids is inextricably connected with the mystery of the dragon.

For centuries scholars have pondered the meaning of this creature, so universally important to early humanity. The modern consensus is that the serpent or dragon (the two are identical) is a metaphor for concepts and ideas important to primitive man, such as rebirth (the serpent sloughing its skin) and sexuality. Yet such explanations ignore a great deal of what the myths say in very graphic terms, and we might wonder whether, especially in the latter case, scholars have attributed to early man concerns which are more their own. In Egypt, Mesopotamia, India, China, Mexico and elsewhere, the cosmic serpent unleashes cataclysmic floods, as well as titanic convulsions of the earth, and frequently breathes fire and brimstone upon the terrestrial sphere. Frequently the dragon is portrayed as battling against the heavenly gods (the planets), and threatening to destroy the world. In Egypt, the dragon monster was named Apop or Apep, a much-feared deity who had in the past attempted to plunge the whole universe into primeval chaos. Apop was almost certainly originally identified with the evil Set, whose battles with his brother Horus occupy much of Egyptian sacred literature. We are told that, "In Egyptian belief the ship of the sun-god Re made a journey through the skies above by day and the skies below by night. Every night, this ship faced the peril of destruction from a demon lurking in the underworld, Apophis. An important part of the ritual of Egyptian temples was the repulsing of this dragon."[2] In Mesopotamia the cosmic serpent was known as Tiamat, and a huge collection of prayers and poems describe this dragon's assault on the heavenly gods and her attempt to destroy the universe.

Everywhere, whether among the Aztecs, Babylonians, Chinese, Celts, Greeks or Scandinavians, the dragon is linked to water and to the sea. And frequently the monster unleashes mountainous waves against the land. These ancient accounts leave no doubt whatsoever that some form of natural cataclysm or other is being described. Whilst it would be possible to quote literally hundreds of such legends, one or two accounts from Mesopotamia and Greece should be enough to illustrate the point.

The dragon-monster *par excellence* of ancient Mesopotamia was known as Tiamat, a name apparently linked to Hebrew *Tehom*, the personified watery abyss. But

2 J.A. Wilson, in J. Pritchard *ANET* p.6

the Babylonian Tiamat was a terrifying serpent demon that actually dwelt in the watery abyss who, along with her offspring, eleven "raging monsters" — "sharp-toothed serpents" and "fierce dragons", sought to bring creation to an end. The story of the ensuing battle with the gods (who are led by Marduk, the Babylonian Jupiter), is dramatically told in the Creation Epic also known as the *Enuma Elish*.

With the whole universe in danger of destruction, the gods appeal to Marduk to destroy Tiamat. This he agrees to do, subject to the condition that the others proclaim him the Supreme God. Armed with his powerful weapons, a bow, lightning, the flooding storm, the four winds and a net, and clad in a "fearsome halo", he mounted his "storm-chariot" and set his course for the raging Tiamat. Marduk launched his terrible storm wind at the monster, and

> Tiamat opened her mouth to swallow it,
> And he [Marduk] forced in the *imhillu*-wind
> so that she could not close her lips.
> Fierce winds distended her belly;
> Her insides were constipated and she stretched her mouth wide.
> He shot an arrow which pierced her belly,
> Split her down the middle and slit her heart,
> Vanquished her and extinguished her life.[3]

Having slain Tiamat, Marduk fashioned a new heaven and a new earth from her smashed skull, and it is evident that the ancients regarded this as a titanic encounter, a battle of planet-sized dimensions.

> He [Marduk] sliced her in half like a fish for drying:
> Half of her he put up to roof the sky,
> Drew a bolt across and made a guard hold it.
> Her waters he arranged so that they could not escape.

Other Babylonian sources make it very clear that these battles among the gods, the Annunaki, had devastating consequences upon the earth. In the Gilgamesh Epic we read;

> The Annunaki lifted up their torches;
> setting the land ablaze with their flare;
> Stunned shock over Adad's deeds overtook the heavens
> And turned to blackness all that had been light.
> The [...] land shattered like a [...] pot.
> All day long the South Wind blew [...],
> blowing fast, submerging the mountain in water,
> overwhelming the people like an attack.
> No one could see his fellow,
> they could not recognise each other in the torrent.

---

3 S. Dalley, *Myths from Mesopotamia* (Oxford, 1989) pp.253,255

> The gods were frightened by the Flood,
> Retreated, ascending to the heaven of Anu.
> The gods were cowering like dogs, crouching by the outer wall.
> Ishtar shrieked like a woman in childbirth,
> The sweet-voiced Mistress of the Gods wailed:
> 'The olden days have alas turned to clay,
>   because I said evil things in the Assembly of the Gods!
> How could I say evil things in the Assembly of the Gods,
>   Ordering a catastrophe to destroy my people?!
> No sooner have I given birth to my dear people
> Than they fill the sea like so many fish!'
> The gods — those of the Annunaki — were weeping with her,
> The gods humbly sat weeping, sobbing with grief(?),
> Their lips burning, parched with thirst.
> Six days and seven nights
> Came the wind and flood, the storm flattening the land.
> When the seventh day arrived, the storm was pounding,
> The flood was a war — struggling with itself
> like a woman writhing (in labour).[4]

These Mesopotamian descriptions of cataclysms have their parallels in all ancient traditions. In Greek mythology, for example, equal prominence is given to the cosmic serpent, most famously under his guise of Typhon, the titan-demon who led a revolt against the Olympians which threatened to destroy creation. The account of this battle given by Hesiod, where he has Zeus (the Greek equivalent of Marduk) delivering the *coup de grace* to the monster, is strikingly similar to the Babylonian account of the contendings of Marduk and Tiamat. Typhon was "half man, half snake", and his head "knocked against the stars". From his shoulders a hundred serpent heads "all flashing fiery tongues" came out. Zeus however attacked the monster with his thunderbolt, and fire "burst over the dark sea". The ocean "boiled" and "towering waves beat upon all the promontories". The whole earth quaked. Again Zeus hurled the lightning bolt. This time Typhon crashed to the earth, and much of the world was consumed by fire. The flames were so hot that "much of the earth dissolved". Finally the mighty king of the gods hurled the flaming victim "into gaping Tartarus — whence to this day there pour forth from his titan form all those winds that blow terribly across seas and bring to mortal men distress."[5]

What then was this destructive deity that flew through the sky and assaulted the earth as well as the planetary gods? If we take the myths and legends at face value, we have to conclude that the dragon-serpent was a comet. This is spelled out in traditions from all corners of the globe. In the Americas, for example, there is an abundance of legends which speak of the "star that smoked" or the "feath-

4 M.G. Kovacs, *The Epic of Gilgamesh* (Stanford, 1989) pp.100f.

5 Hesiod, *Theogony* 823-880

ered star", or the "bearded star" that sought to destroy the earth and brought the Flood. The Greeks were no less forthright in their explanation of the serpent. According to the Roman Pliny, whose sources included both Greek and Egyptian material, the Typhon monster was a comet:

> There was a dreadful one [comet] observed by the Ethiopians and the Egyptians, to which Typhon, a king of that period, gave his own name; it had a fiery appearance and was twisted like a spiral; its aspect was hideous, nor was it like a star, but rather like a ball of fire.[6]

Other traditions identified Typhon as the name of the king who ruled in Egypt during the Exodus, when Moses led the children of Israel to freedom, and insisted that it was during this incident that the terrible comet made its appearance.[7] Evidently then these myths and legends are not dealing with events in the distant past, but within the period of recorded human history, no more perhaps than three or four thousand years.

In full accordance with Pliny's testimony, comets have always been regarded as harbingers of evil and their appearance greeted with the greatest apprehension, if not outright terror. But this in itself is now seen as a mystery, since comets are now regarded as harmless, if not rather beautiful, cosmic phenomena. Pliny however clearly suggests that Typhon, the serpent-demon who in Greek myth threatened to overturn creation, was in reality a "dreadful" comet, and that it was this cosmic body that wrought the destruction recalled in the myth. Is Pliny's explanation the correct one? If he were the only source connecting the cosmic serpent with a comet then perhaps there would be room for doubt; yet in legends from every part of the globe the cosmic serpent is invariably linked with, or identified as, a comet. And indeed the cometary nature of the dragon, a creature with a long tail that flies through the sky and breathes fire on the earth, is obvious enough.

DARK SECRETS OF THE PYRAMIDS

At this stage we must ask a question: Could it really be, as the evidence seems to suggest, that all pyramids (and mounds) are cult edifices of the stellar and dragon-worshipping religion; and that their purpose originally was to serve as high altars upon which human victims were immolated? Could it be also that all ancient cultures regarded these sacrifices as vital to the survival of creation, as offerings intended to avert the wrath of a cosmic serpent or dragon?

---

6 Pliny, *Natural History* ii,23

7 See the vast amount of evidence on this subject collated by Immanuel Velikovsky in *Worlds in Collision* (1950)

The mythology and cosmology of the pyramid-building peoples offers abundant evidence to support this view.

The Aztecs, whose human hecatombs to Huitzilopochtli and the Feathered Serpent Quetzalcoatl so horrified the Spaniards, assured Cortes and his followers that these terrible offerings were essential to ensure that the sun would continue to rise and that the end of the world would be averted:

> It was supposed that the luminary [the sun] rejoiced in offerings of blood, and that it constituted the only food which would render him sufficiently vigorous to undertake his daily journey through the heavens.... The sun must fare well if he was to continue to give life, light, and heat to mankind.

> The Mexicans ... believed that the luminary they knew had been preceded by others, each of which had been quenched by some awful cataclysm of nature. Eternity had, in fact, been broken up into epochs, marked by the destruction of successive suns. In the period preceding that in which they lived, a mighty deluge had deprived the sun of life, and some such catastrophe was apprehended at the end of every "sheaf" of fifty-two years. The old suns were dead, and the current sun was no more immortal than they....

> It was therefore necessary to sustain the sun by the daily food of human sacrifice, for by a tithe of human life alone would he be satisfied.[8]

From Mesopotamia we learn that the bloody offerings dedicated atop the ziggurats — in the House of the God — were all that stood between creation and a renewed assault by the serpent monster Tiamat. The Creation Epic itself tells us how immediately after destroying Tiamat, Marduk orders the building of the first ziggurat:

> "I shall make a house to be a luxurious dwelling for myself
> And shall found his [Marduk's] cult centre within it ..."

In gratitude for saving the universe from Tiamat, the other gods offer to build Marduk's home for him; at which point,

> His face lit up greatly, like daylight.
> "Create Babylon, whose construction you requested!
> Let its mud bricks be moulded, and build high the shrine."

For an entire year the gods manufacture bricks and by the end of the second year they have built the great shrine and ziggurat of Esagila. Another well-known Mesopotamian text, "The Deluge", is equally specific in connecting the establishment of cult centers (temples) to the aftermath of a cosmic catastrophe;

> My mankind, in its destruction I will ...

8 Lewis Spence, *Mexico and Peru: Myths and Legends* (1920) p.98

> I will return the people to their settlements
> After the ... of kingship had been lowered from heaven,
> After the exalted tiara and the throne of kingship
> had been lowered from heaven,
> He perfected the rites and the exalted divine laws ...,
> Founded the five cities in ... pure places,
> Called their names, apportioned them as cult centres.[9]

The Mesopotamian sources therefore connect not only the establishment of religious customs, but the very idea of priest-kingship, to the aftermath of some cataclysmic disaster. We shall presently see that the concept of kingship was everywhere initially inseparable from priesthood, and that all the early kings were at the same time High Priests, one of whose major functions was the offering of blood sacrifices on high altars.

We recall at this point how in Egypt one of the most important parts of the ritual of Egyptian temples was the repulsing of the deadly dragon Apop.[10] The Egyptian pyramids of Dynasties 4, 5 and 6 were not employed as high altars, but the temples of this epoch and still later had within them an altar placed at a higher elevation than the rest of the building, upon which victims were slaughtered. Yet the true Egyptian equivalents of the Mexican and Mesopotamian pyramids were the stepped pyramids of the Early Dynastic Age; and this epoch in the country's history was the period *par excellence* of human sacrifice.

It is commonly believed, and so it is stated in one authoritative publication after another, that the Step Pyramid of King Djoser (Dynasty 3) was the first such structure ever raised in Egypt. Yet an abundance of evidence suggests that pyramids were being built right from the beginning of the First Dynasty, and that the only distinguishing feature of Djoser's monument was its height and the fact that it was fashioned of stone, whereas the others were of mud-brick. (Manetho agrees that Djoser and Imhotep were the first to build in stone, but does not say they were the first to construct a pyramid). Sure enough, an inscription from Sakkara reports that King Djet of the First Dynasty also built a pyramid there,[11] whilst it has been demonstrated that the "mastaba" tombs of Dynasties 1 and 2 (as well as Dyn. 3) were constructed over mounds of earth which were sometimes given a stepped appearance.[12] Reisner believed that the superstructures of

---

9 S.N. Kramer, *History Begins at Sumer: Thirty-Nine Firsts in Man's Recorded History* (Pennsylvania, 1981) p.149

10 J.A. Wilson, in Pritchard *ANET* p.6

11 See *Egyptian Archaeology* No.6 (1995) pp.26-7

12 M. Rice, *Egypt's Making* (1990) p.118

the "tombs" of Djer and Djet rose by two and three steps respectively to a flat summit about eight and twelve meters in height.[13]

All in all, the evidence suggests that large numbers of stepped pyramids, mainly of brick, but also (after Djoser's reign) of stone were erected throughout Egypt in the Early Dynastic period, but that all of these, with the exception of Djoser's monument, have been ruined and lost.

How these monuments came to be destroyed, we shall presently see, is significant in itself.

The Egyptians seem to have regarded Djoser's pyramid as the Stairway to Heaven, a term which is loaded with symbolic significance. The stepped pyramids of other cultures were of course also stairways to heaven — especially for the sacrificial victims who were put to death on their summits. It would seem then that these Egyptian step pyramids were also high altars devoted to human sacrifice. Certainly there is no shortage of evidence of human sacrifice in the Early Dynastic Age; sacrifice which is, moreover, closely associated with the mastaba-mounds. Thus a large mastaba-tomb at Giza, Mastaba V, almost certainly dating from the reign of the First Dynasty King Djet, was surrounded by the graves of 56 retainers.[14] At Abydos and Abu Rawash there are clear indications of prisoners being sacrificed.[15] According to one authority, "In spite of the insufficiency of evidence to show the extent of the practice of human sacrifice during the Early Dynastic Period, the fact of its existence cannot be questioned. If the number of subsidiary graves bear any relation, as is probable, to the number of persons sacrificed, the custom reached its peak under Djer, whose two 'tomb' complexes at Abydos contained more than 590 subsidiary graves."[16]

The Early Dynastic era then was the age of sacrifice; and astonishingly enough the Early Dynastic Age of Mesopotamia (contemporary with that of Egypt) was noted for precisely the same thing. The vast scale of Mesopotamian human sacrifice in this epoch was brought to the modern world's attention when Sir Leonard Woolley opened the notorious Grave Pits at Ur, where the bodies of literally hundreds of servants who had been forced to accompany their masters to the Underworld were discovered. Scholars are agreed that in Mesopotamia the practice of human sacrifice began at the start of Early Dynastic II (contemporary with the first ziggurats) and ended towards the close of Early Dynastic III (the end of

---

13 I.E.S. Edwards, "The Early Dynastic Period in Egypt" in *CAH* Vol.1 part 2 (3rd ed.) p.65
14 I. Shaw and P. Nicholson, *British Museum Dictionary of Ancient Egypt* pp.109-10
15 I.E.S. Edwards, loc. cit. p.58
16 Ibid. p.59

the Early Dynastic period).[17] But here again there is precise correspondence with the situation in Egypt. For here too human sacrifice apparently comes to a rather abrupt end with the close of the Early Dynastic Age, at the end of Dynasty 3. The pyramids of the Fourth, Fifth and Sixth Dynasties were very definitely *not* used for sacrifice, human or otherwise. On the contrary, the prevailing mood of this later epoch was one of pronounced humanitarianism. What could have prompted such a radical departure from norms that were so recently accepted by all?

We shall show that the age of Cheops and Chephren saw the inauguration of a religious revolution that was directly prompted by events in the cosmos itself.

THE CULT OF THE PHOENIX

What has come in Egypt to be known as the Pyramid Age, the period spanning Dynasties 4 to 6, was an epoch marked by revolutionary changes in all areas of life, an epoch moreover that appears to have been launched by some catastrophic upheaval of nature.

There is no question that the giant smooth-sided pyramids of this later age of pyramid-building were in direct line of descent from the stepped structures of their Early Dynastic predecessors. But something remarkable had happened. These new pyramid-builders no longer offered hecatombs of human victims to their deities. Almost overnight, the rulers of the Nile Valley became paragons of wisdom and moderation. The new pyramids were not raised to kill people; they were designed simply and solely to honor the celestial beings. It was, to all intents and purposes, as if a New Age, or, more accurately, a new World Age, had begun.

The Egyptians of the period themselves saw their epoch as a new age; and central to the whole cult of these later pyramids was the myth of that mystical bird of legend, the phoenix. The phoenix, it was said, appeared at the top of the primordial hill when Atum first emerged from the Nun, the watery abyss. In the words of Jaroslav Cerny, "There were several such primordial hills in Egypt. In Heliopolis its image in historic times was the 'sand-hill' with a stone of conical shape, the prototype of the later obelisk, on the top of which Atum appeared first when he emerged from the Nun, according to one tale in the form of a mythical bird, the Phoenix."[18]

Since the primordial hill was apparently the prototype of the pyramid, it seems clear that the pyramid-building of the Fourth, Fifth and Sixth Dynasties

---

17 Sir Max Mallowan, "The Early Dynastic Period in Mesopotamia" in *CAH* Vol.1 part 2 (3rd ed.) p.286

18 J. Cerny, *Ancient Egyptian Religion* (London, 1952) p.44

cannot be dissociated from the cult and legend of the phoenix. The Egyptians knew the phoenix as the *benu*-bird, and the capstone at the top of each of the giant smooth-sided pyramids was known as the *benben*. All accounts of the phoenix story identified Heliopolis (On), the site of the pyramids of Cheops, Chephren and Mycerinus, as the home of the miraculous bird. The priests of Heliopolis boasted that their city was actually located on the first ground created by Atum; and in the city there existed a Temple of the Phoenix which housed a sacred conical-shaped stone known as the "Benben Stone". This sacred object, the original pyramid capstone, was reputed to have fallen from the sky, and was therefore almost certainly a meteorite.

In this age of obsessive sky-watching and planet-worship meteorites were everywhere, in every culture, regarded as supremely sacred. Temples were erected round them, and these became centers of pilgrimage. But was the benben stone of Heliopolis, a simple meteorite, the source of the phoenix (benu-bird) legend; or did the myth have an altogether grander meaning? In fact, the unique holiness of this particular meteorite had probably more to do with its shape than anything else. It is known that some meteorites, in their heated encounter with the earth's atmosphere, can assume a conical, pyramidal form. These extra-terrestrial objects are thus shaped like miniature hills or pyramids. So the benben stone of Heliopolis was a model of the sacred hill, the Nun, given directly by the gods to man. But the original phoenix was a celestial body of much grander proportions, a body which gave birth to the meteorites that bombarded the earth in this epoch.

By any reckoning the phoenix legend is one of the strangest myths of antiquity. Classical sources say that this bird was the only one of its kind, that it inhabited the Arabian Desert, and that every thousand, or in some accounts every five hundred years (in addition to various other intervals), the creature returned to Egypt, to the city of Heliopolis. There it built itself a nest wherein it rested and was duly consumed by fire. From the ashes of the old phoenix a new one arose, fated to live the same number of years as its predecessor.[19]

From the testimony of other classical writers there seem to be good grounds for believing that the phoenix, a winged deity that was consumed by fire, is analogous to Phaethon, a character who, in Greek legend, tried to drive the solar chariot through the firmament. He was unable to control the wild steeds, however, and the chariot veered off course, causing a conflagration that engulfed the whole earth. Phaethon himself was struck dead by a thunderbolt.

In his *Timaeus*, Plato has an Egyptian priest explain the meaning of the Phaethon myth to Solon of Athens:

---

19 Ovid, *Metamorphoses* xv, 931-400

> You [Greeks] are all young ... you have no belief rooted in old tradition and no knowledge hoary with age. And the reason is this. There have been and will be many different calamities to destroy mankind, the greatest of them by fire and water, lesser ones by countless other means. Your own story of how Phaethon, child of the sun, harnessed his father's chariot, but was unable to guide it along his father's course and so burnt up things on earth and was himself destroyed by a thunderbolt, is a mythical version of the truth that there is at long intervals a variation in the course of the heavenly bodies and a consequent widespread destruction by fire of things on the earth.[20]

The phoenix or benu-bird is thus in part at least an allegorical deity who personifies what the Egyptians saw as the cyclic process of world destruction and rebirth. The whole concept of World Ages was central to ancient man's understanding of the universe, and, like the dragon-cult and pyramids, is universal. The myths consistently tell us how at the close of each World Age there would be a great destruction, followed by a great rebirth and renewal. Very often, a new sun would appear in the sky and a new race of men would appear on the earth.

Yet the phoenix, like Phaethon, is more than purely allegorical. Actual pyramid-capstones, benbens, like the famous one of Amenemhet III, portray what is almost certainly the original phoenix, or benu-bird. And here the creature is clearly shown as a winged-disc — a comet. Ancient legend insists that the comet-monster, the cosmic serpent which had brought the flood, was also responsible for bringing World Ages to their conclusion. After the cataclysm a new order appears in the firmament. The stars have been moved from their accustomed positions and all (even lengths of years, months and days) has changed.

This linking of pyramids with chaos in the firmament followed by renewal was recalled even in the Middle Ages, when the Arab scholar Masoudi quoted a legend said to be derived from native Coptic tradition:

> Surid, Ben Shaluk, Ben Sermuni, Ben Termidun, Ben Tedresan, Ben Sal, one of the kings of Egypt before the flood, built two great pyramids; and, notwithstanding, they were subsequently named after a person called Shaddad Ben Ad ... they were not built by the Adites, who could not conquer Egypt, on account of their powers, which the Egyptians possessed by means of enchantment ... the reason for the building of the pyramids was the following dream, which happened to Surid three hundred years previous to the flood. It appeared to him that the earth was overthrown, and that the inhabitants were laid prostrate upon it, that the stars wandered confusedly from their courses, and clashed together with tremendous noise. The king though greatly affected by this vision, did not disclose it to any person, but was conscious that some great event was about to take place...[21]

---

20 Plato, *Timaeus* 22

21 L. Cottrell, *The Mountains of Pharaoh* (London, 1956)

Later, however, Surid did disclose his dream to a gathering of Egypt's chief priests. These men informed him that a great catastrophe would strike the earth, but that afterwards it would again become fruitful.

Evidently in Egypt so strong was the association of pyramid-building with cosmic upheavals and catastrophic inauguration of new world ages that the tradition survived into the medieval period.

The appearance of the new firmament, apparently in the time of Sneferu, marked the dawn of the new World Age. The sun and the cosmos were reborn, just like the phoenix, rising from its own ashes. The Great Pyramid, we are told, was originally encased in smooth limestone, and its capstone, the benben, was covered in gold leaf. As the sun rose above the horizon every morning, its rays would have first touched the golden benben of Cheops's monument, and these beams would have shone throughout the twilit land of Egypt like the beacon of a lighthouse. Ra's reawakening in the morning was gloriously announced to all the subjects of pharaoh.

In a number of senses then these pyramids of the Fourth Dynasty were symbolic of rebirth: the rebirth of the universe at the beginning of a new world cycle; the rebirth of the sun-god every morning; and the rebirth of human beings after death. Atum, the god of the setting sun, is endlessly praised in the Pyramid Texts, whilst the empty sarcophagus at the core of Cheops's pyramid is there as the symbolic home of Osiris, Lord of the Underworld, and thus of human rebirth.

THE THEORY OF CATASTROPHES

For centuries human beings accepted as given fact that the great upheavals of nature recalled in the mythologies of Greeks, Romans, Celts, Germans, as well as in the Bible, had actually occurred more or less as they were described. With the rebirth of classical learning during the Renaissance, European scholars began, for the first time, to cast a critical eye on the Bible. Efforts were made to discover what truth might lie behind the stories of miraculous events described in the Old Testament, as well as to integrate Hebrew history and tradition with that of Greece and Rome. William Whiston, the renowned astronomer and student of Isaac Newton, was one of many scholars of this time to suggest that the Deluge of Noah had been caused, not by perpetual rain as the Book of Genesis implies but by devastating tidal effects resulting from a close encounter between the earth and a giant comet.[22]

By the middle of the 18th century attempts at a scientific classification of geological strata was well under way. The savants of the time soon came to real-

---

22 W. Whiston, *New Theory of the Earth* (1696)

ize that earlier geological ages had seen the earth inhabited by vast numbers of creatures no longer in existence. The new science of paleontology was concerned not just with the discovery and classification of these species, but with trying to discover why they became extinct. Georges Cuvier, the greatest of the early paleontologists, was convinced that the extinct genera had been wiped out by a cataclysm or rather series of cataclysms. This concept, which came to be known as "catastrophism", was shared by almost all earth scientists until the second half of the 19th century. Contrasting the superficially tranquil appearance of the earth's surface with the evidence for cataclysmic destruction beneath, Cuvier mused on how the observer,

> ... is not led to suspect that Nature ... had her intestine wars, and that the surface of the globe has been broken up by revolution and catastrophes. But his ideas change as soon as he digs into the soil which presents so peaceful an aspect.[23]

In his numerous publications Cuvier made it very plain that he regarded these upheavals of nature as world-wide events. Whilst he never explicitly endorsed the then widely-held view that such cataclysms had to be the result of collisions with other cosmic bodies, neither did he rule such events out. Yet this catastrophist explanation of mythology and paleontology was overturned in the latter years of the 19th century, when the "uniformitarian" concepts of Darwin's friend, the solicitor Charles Lyell, gained the upper hand. So complete was the victory that by the early years of the 20th century textbooks were being written which decreed that the cataclysms described in ancient myth were entirely fabulous, and that the catastrophist ideas of such great thinkers as Whiston and Cuvier belonged to the "lunatic fringe", alongside the works of the Flat Earth Society.

How this epoch-making shift in opinion occurred is a question beyond the scope of the present work. Suffice to say that catastrophism was not abandoned for lack of evidence: On the contrary, it was Lyell's uniformitarianism (the theory that only forces now operating could have operated in the past) that strikes one as unscientific and based more on faith than anything else (the equivalent of saying, "world wars are not happening now, therefore they could not have happened in the past"). In fact, research before and since Lyell has only multiplied the proofs that world-wide catastrophes did take place; and some of this evidence is now again, belatedly, being given due recognition by mainstream academia. The debate was spectacularly reignited in 1950, just when it seemed that the whole theory of catastrophism was about to become as extinct as the mammoths or

---

23 G. Cuvier, *Essay on the Theory of the Earth* 5th ed. (1827) p.240. English translation of "Discours sur les révolutions de la surface du globe, et sur les changements qu'elles ont produits dans la règne animal."

the dinosaurs. In his intensely controversial *Worlds in Collision*, the Russian/Israeli doctor Immanuel Velikovsky explored a multitude of ancient myths to demonstrate his thesis that immense natural catastrophes, involving the members of the solar system, had occurred within the period of recorded human history. Around 1450 BC, Velikovsky claimed, a great comet had given the earth a near miss, devastating our planet with giant tidal waves, showers of meteorites, and massive seismic convulsions. It was this comet, said Velikovsky, that gave rise to the legend of the dragon.

Velikovsky's ideas provoked a storm of controversy almost as violent as the events he described in his book, and repeated attempts were made to have his work suppressed. Yet by the 1980s, much of what he said in *Worlds in Collision*, and which had seemed so outrageous at the time, was beginning to be taken quietly on board by the scholarly establishment. Thus for example it became clear, following the researches of Luis Alvarez, that the Cretaceous dinosaurs had been wiped out by some form of asteroid or comet impact, and in 1984 two of the most respected of British astronomers, Victor Clube and Bill Napier, published a book entitled *The Cosmic Serpent: A Catastrophist View of Earth History*, which more or less endorsed much of what Velikovsky had said in *Worlds in Collision*.

One of the most important criticisms levelled at Velikovsky during the 1950s concerned dates and dating-systems. How could he claim an earth-shattering event occurred around 1450 BC, if the great civilizations of the time made no mention of it? Egyptologists, for example, claimed that they knew the very coronation-date of the pharaoh who sat on the throne of Egypt in 1450 BC. In addition, monuments such as the pyramids, which they confidently dated to the third millennium BC, would surely have been levelled to the ground by events of the magnitude described by Velikovsky. Furthermore, since Velikovsky was postulating real alterations in the make-up of the Solar System, we should certainly not expect these structures to remain aligned to the earth's cardinal points as they stand. Yet the Giza pyramids, and those that came after them, are aligned precisely with the cardinal points (though those of the Early Dynastic Age are very definitely not so aligned — a fact to which we shall return presently).

Early in his researches, and well before the publication of *Worlds in Collision*, Velikovsky had become convinced that there was something fundamentally wrong with the chronologies of the ancient civilizations, and he commenced work on a series of books entitled *Ages in Chaos*, whose purpose was to demonstrate the need for a drastic reduction in the length of Near Eastern pre-Christian chronology. Velikovsky died in 1979, before he could complete *Ages in Chaos*, but the work he began has continued till the present day. My own researches, which have been greatly influenced by the work of Professor Gunnar Heinsohn of Bremen and Dr. Heribert Illig of Munich, have led me to conclude that the reduction of ancient chronology proposed by Velikovsky was inadequate. Right to the end, he adhered to the conventional idea that the Near Eastern civilizations commenced in the third millennium BC, a full two thousand years earlier than those of the Americas and the Far East. Believing that the ziggurats of Mesopotamia and the pyramids of Egypt predated the tumuli of the Americas and China by 2,000 years, Velikovsky was unable to fully comprehend the significance of the phenomenon.

But Egypt and Mesopotamia had no 2,000 year head start. All early civilizations (as I intend to demonstrate in the pages to follow) commenced simultaneously in various parts of the Globe around 1000 BC — and these civilizations, with their priest-kings and blood sacrifices, came into being as a direct result of the catastrophes so recently witnessed by humanity. The traumatized survivors of Velikovsky's first comet-catastrophe (which probably occurred around 1300 or 1250 BC) sought, by means of ritualized violence, to control events over which they had, in reality, no control whatsoever.[24] The gods who lived in the sky, it seemed, delighted in death and destruction. What if they were voluntarily offered victims? Perhaps they might leave the world in peace! High places, altars (Latin *altus*), usually on mountain-tops, were sought out, and upon these victims were offered to the dragon. When people once again settled in low-lying regions artificial mountains, or pyramids, upon which the sacrifices could be performed, began to be erected.

Thus, by quirk of fate, was literate civilization born. The erection of the sacred hills needed organization: it needed building skills: it needed record-keeping skills: and the close watch kept on the night skies delivered to mankind the science of astronomy.

For five centuries or so the comet, the dragon-monster, hung over the earth like the proverbial Sword of Damocles, threatening, with its apparently erratic elliptical solar orbit, to repeat the carnage it had wrought upon the earth in the second half of the second millennium BC. However, around 800 BC, or shortly before, the comet came on a collision course with another member of the solar system (the planet Mars, according to Velikovsky) and was removed as a threat.

The peoples of the earth rejoiced. They thanked the gods for deliverance. The Age of Sacrifice (as Hindu tradition rightly names it) was over. The dragon-monster of chaos had been slain, and the great heroes of the time are recalled as having put an end to human sacrifice. Thus in Greek tradition Perseus and Hercu-

---

24 For a discussion of this topic see Gunnar Heinsohn, "The Rise of Blood Sacrifice and Priest-Kingship in Mesopotamia: A 'Cosmic Decree'?" *Religion* (1992) 22, 109-134

les were dragon-slaying heroes who rescued many victims destined for sacrifice to the beast. All over the earth great structures were raised in commemoration. These "megaliths" were frequently fashioned from enormous tight-fitting blocks of stone, and were designed specifically to be earthquake-proof. The tectonic convulsions which had so recently gripped the planet had not yet fully subsided, though mankind was now confident that they eventually would.

The truth then is that the pyramids do hold a great secret in their massive structures, a secret infinitely more dramatic and certainly more terrible than anything imagined by the purveyors of most "alternative" pyramid theories. As they stand, they are mute witnesses to a time when chaos reigned in the heavens, when the members of the solar system could not necessarily be relied upon to maintain their accustomed paths through the firmament. These great monuments, from the infancy of civilization, speak to us of mankind's escape, in the not too distant past, from a very real Armageddon.

An Age of Megaliths and Heroes

According to Professor Heinsohn, whose work has been most influential in the debate over the true antiquity of pyramid-building, the Fourth Dynasty monuments at Giza epitomized the mood of the 8th century BC, the age that marked the definitive end of the cosmic upheavals that had punctuated the previous half millennium. Having been freed from the Sword of Damocles that had hung over the earth throughout the Early Bronze Age, men built these monuments as an expression of new-found confidence and optimism. "It is no surprise," says Heinsohn, "that Cheops is not only renowned for his Pyramid but also famous (or infamous) for 'preventing' the sacrifices by which the people of the Bronze Age attempted to restore equilibrium to their catastrophe-scarred psyches. These constructions, built tall but at the same time particularly stable against all eventualities, became the expression of calm in the heavens and in part observation posts for their astronomical surveillance. Celestial deities could now be forgotten and their temples closed — and it is just this that Cheops and Chephren are accused of."[25]

The present writer concurs with Heinsohn's assessment. The 9th/8th century saw the birth of a new religion; a religion whose idea of divinity was infinitely less material and infinitely more moral. We even witness, in the Pyramid Texts, the first tentative movements towards a limited monotheism. Nevertheless, it is not true to say that the ancients immediately abandoned the worship of celestial

---

25 Gunnar Heinsohn, "Egyptian Chronology: A Solution to the Hyksos Problem" *Aeon* Vol.1 (1988) no.6 p.7

gods. The later pyramids of Egypt and the contemporary ziggurats of Mesopotamia, as well as the equally contemporary megalithic structures of Western Europe, were still built with an eye to the heavens; they were still intended to honor the celestial bodies. But these gods had now adopted a much more moral aspect. They no longer demanded hecatombs of human beings to feed their appetites. Indeed the dragon-slaying deity, the most loved and celebrated god of the epoch, positively abhorred human sacrifice. In Greece, the dragon-slayer *par excellence* was Hercules (Herakles), and a wide range of stories told how he had traversed the earth putting a stop to this barbarous practice and saving victims from the dragon-monster.[26] So profoundly did Hercules make his mark on the epoch that it was named, apparently in his honor, the Age of Heroes. The Heroic Age was viewed as a semi-mythical epoch situated between the earlier *mythikon,* or age of myths and the later *historikon,* or age of history. The transition from myth to history occurred gradually, and three or four generations of the Heroic Age were enumerated during which the gods still interacted directly with mortals, but not on the level hitherto prevailing.

The precise moment in time marking the end of *mythikon* and the beginning of *historikon* was for the Greeks the establishment of the Olympic Games, by Hercules incidentally, an event traditionally dated to the year 776 BC.[27]

The Heroic (or Mycenaean) Age of Greece, we will find, falls in after this date, and the mighty monuments built by the Achaean lords of the time, with their huge tight-fitting polygonal stones, Homer's walls "raised by the hand of giants", were contemporary with the great megalithic structures of Egypt's Fourth and Fifth Dynasties, though in conventional chronology they are separated from each other by a thousand years. These "megaliths", found in virtually every quarter of the globe, were of course built to withstand the mighty earth tremors which still afflicted the planet — even in lands that are today not associated with earthquake activity. Thus the megalithic lintels of Stonehenge are secured to the uprights by mortise and tenon joints, joints that are nowadays completely redundant, but which would have been essential if the British Isles were being devastated by the terrible earthquakes that Irish and Welsh traditions vividly recall.

Careful comparison of the architectural styles and techniques of Old Kingdom Egypt, Mycenaean Greece and Megalithic Britain reveals striking parallels. Thus the megalithic Passage Graves of Western Europe, with their central burial-chambers covered by mounds and approached by long passageways, are essentially identical in concept to the Mycenaean tholos tombs and the Fourth and Fifth Dynasty pyramids. All three building techniques also employ corbelling to

---

26 R. Graves, *The Greek Myths* Vol.2 (1955) p.384

27 Ibid.

roof either the central burial chamber or passageways, and it is evident that some form of cultural interaction is indicated.

At a later stage we shall see how the entire cultural and historical *milieu* of Mycenaean Greece matches very precisely that of Pyramid Age Egypt, and we shall see how the legends, myths and traditions of the two lands display very clearly an active cross-fertilization at this early age.

One very interesting tradition, which we shall examine here, illustrates these links and is for us additionally important in that it recalls the precise point at which human sacrifice in Egypt was abolished. From other evidence we know that this occurred at the start of the Fourth Dynasty, yet this Greek legend says that the deed was performed by Hercules. Upon his arrival in Egypt Hercules was seized by the king Busiris, whose custom it was to sacrifice one foreigner every year to Zeus (i.e. Amon). The great hero was bound and placed upon an altar, and the king was about to deliver the death-blow when Hercules broke his bonds and slew the entire company.[28]

It is interesting to note that the name Busiris means "grave of Osiris",[29] a fact which makes us recall that pyramid-building was intimately connected with the cult of Osiris, lord of the dead. Now one of the Egyptian equivalents of Hercules was Horus (Hor), son of Osiris, whose prolonged battle with the evil Set restored peace and equilibrium to the world. Prior to this victory, so the story goes, Set had ruled the world, and his reign was an epoch marked by violence and lawlessness.

It was from the 9th/8th century BC then, the Age of Hercules, that human sacrifice began to be abandoned. From then on the quarrelling, treacherous and thoroughly amoral gods of earlier times began to disappear. An age of Sage Kings, seers and prophets was inaugurated: Moses and the Judges in Israel, Ptahotep and Mycerinus in Egypt; Zoroaster in Persia; Krishna in India, and the Tao sages in China. Nor would the epoch of prophecy end with the 8th century. The new ideas developed at the time would continue to inspire religious leaders and thinkers throughout the 7th and even 6th centuries BC. Men like Amos and Isaiah in Israel, Buddha in India and the Seven Sages (including Thales and Pythagoras) in Greece, mark this as an Age of Prophecy. It was with the age of demi-gods and megalith-building sage kings that all the great civilizations of mankind were launched.

---

28 Apollodorus, ii, 5, 11
29 R. Graves, loc. cit. p.384

Chapter 2. God-Like Kings of Old

The Demise of Early Dynastic Egypt

We have argued that the epoch now known as the Pyramid Age was inaugurated by some natural catastrophe. Certainly there is a clear break-off between the almost mythical Early Dynastic Age, the age of Menes and Djoser, and the epoch of the Fourth Dynasty. The earlier rulers may only vaguely be said to belong to the historical age; those from the Fourth Dynasty onwards certainly do. Indeed, we may be justified in asserting that in Egypt the age of history, properly speaking, begins with this line of kings. Compared with the monuments and relics of the Fourth, Fifth and Sixth Dynasties, almost nothing of the legendary rulers of Dynasties 1 to 3 has survived. This was a fact noted first by Flinders Petrie,[30] and confirmed repeatedly since then. True, there is the Step Pyramid of Djoser at Sakkara, together with its attendant magnificent funerary monument. But the funerary temple was reconstructed extensively during the Late Period, with large parts fashioned from reused blocks of Eighteenth Dynasty material (so thoroughly reconstructed in fact that for some time there was serious debate as to whether the entire monument might not be an original Late Period — perhaps Persian

---

30 F. Petrie, *A History of Egypt* Vol.1 (1894) p.27 "If we cannot find a fiftieth of the proportion of tombs before the IVth dynasty that we find so soon as dated monuments arise, the inference is that there never existed any much greater number."

age — construction),[31] and it is certain that the Step Pyramid too was extensively rebuilt by Djoser's pious successors of the New Kingdom and later. According to Petrie, "the step pyramid of Sakkara has certainly been largely altered, and new passages made in it, probably more than once; the glazed tiles of the doorway in it are also considered by some to be late in date...."[32]

Other monuments of the Early Dynastic Age, including various pyramids (as for example that of Sekhemkhet at Sakkara), are now thoroughly shattered, and it seems that this destruction was wrought very soon after their construction.[33] Something extraordinary, it appears, brought the Third Dynasty to a definitive conclusion. There are few clearly-demarcated stratigraphies in Egypt, so it is difficult to assess exactly what the record in the ground says. But such is not the case in Mesopotamia, where numerous well-stratified sites have been excavated and explored. And here, without any question, the Early Dynastic Age is brought to a dramatic and catastrophic end. At Ur for example a layer of destruction terminated Early Dynastic 3a. This destruction-layer, evident also at Kish and virtually all the other sites in the region, was the last of the so-called "Flood Layers" which had periodically afflicted Mesopotamia since the end of the Chalcolithic period. The last destruction-stratum in the region more or less coincides with the demise of the Early Dynastic Sumerians and their civilization. Following the last disaster, after a short period of Sumerian recovery, the mighty Akkadian Empire rose to dominate the Land of the Two Rivers.

But this catastrophe was by no means confined to Mesopotamia — though to read some reports one would imagine that to be the case. On the contrary, the devastation ranged throughout the Fertile Crescent, Anatolia, the Aegean region, Iran and India. Yet in these areas there is a problem. Syria and Palestine, for example, display abundant evidence of catastrophic destruction; yet the stratigraphies of these areas, as I demonstrate in detail in *The Genesis of Israel and Egypt* (1997), the first volume of the Ages in Alignment series, are not accurately aligned to those of Mesopotamia. They are "out of sync" by roughly a thousand years, and the stratum which in Mesopotamia is termed Early Bronze 2 is in Syria/Palestine termed Middle Bronze 1. So, if we seek evidence of the cataclysm which brought

---

31 Leonard Cotterell, *The Mountains of Pharaoh* (1955) pp.152-3 "The columned gallery was most probably made by the Saites more than two thousand years after the Step Pyramid was built. In building it they used a fragment of an Eighteenth-Dynasty tomb to support one of the pillars."

32 Petrie, loc. cit. p.58

33 Djoser's funerary monument was apparently a ruin in the time of the 5th Dynasty, for king Unas used blocks from the temple enclosure to build the Causeway leading to his own pyramid. (See e.g. I.E.S. Edwards *The Pyramids of Egypt* p.188)

Mesopotamia's Early Dynastic Age to an end, we must in Syria/Palestine look to Middle Bronze 1.

We should therefore seek evidence of the same disaster in the Palestinian Early Bronze 3/Middle Bronze 1 interchange. We are told that at the end of the Early Bronze Age in Palestine (i.e. Early Bronze 3) there is evidence of "a complete and absolute break in Palestinian civilization."[34] So clear were the signs of nature's destructive power at this time that Claude Schaeffer devoted much of his *opus magnum*, *Stratigraphie comparée et chronologie de l'Asie occidentale* (1948), to an examination of the period. The destruction of the Palestinian cities was accompanied by a complete transformation of lifestyle. Urban life was abandoned and nomadism became the norm.[35] All in all, the archaeological reports read very much like a description of the region in the days of the Israelite Conquest, following the Exodus.

And this brings us to a conclusion of fundamental import, one explored at length in *The Genesis of Israel and Egypt*: Egypt's Early Dynastic Age is rightly contemporary with the Israelite Age of the Patriarchs; and Egypt's Imhotep is one and the same as Jacob's son Joseph. The catastrophe which terminated the Early Dynastic epoch can be shown to be identical to the cosmic upheaval so dramatically recounted in the Book of Exodus. Egypt's final Third Dynasty pharaoh, Huni/Ka-nefer-ra — Manetho's Keneferre — is therefore the Pharaoh of the Oppression drowned in the Sea of Passage, and his successor, king Sneferu, first ruler of the almost monotheistic Pyramid Age, is a contemporary of Moses, the Egyptian prince who threw in his lot with the Hebrew slaves and led them across the wilderness of Sinai. According to the Jewish writer Artapanus, the pharaoh of the Oppression was named Khenephres, though it is claimed that the latter was already dead when Moses led the Israelites to freedom. Possibly pharaoh Huni/Ka-nefer-ra died in the catastrophic disturbances which preceded the flight of the Israelites, and it was another royal prince who pursued the Hebrews into the Sea of Passage. In fact, the tomb of Huni, a huge brick mastaba, was discovered at Bet Khallaf. In a chamber at the bottom of a subterranean passage a skeleton, believed to be that of the king, was found. This proved to be "that of a massively built man, over six feet in height."[36] In the same chamber was discovered the "pulverized" remains of a coffin, along with various other — mostly shattered — trinkets.

---

34 K.M. Kenyon, "Syria and Palestine c.2160-1780 BC: The Archaeological Sites" in *CAH* Vol.1 part 2 (3rd ed.) p.567

35 Ibid.

36 Arthur Weigall, *A History of the Pharaohs: The First Eleven Dynasties* (London, 1925) p.154

Egypt's Pyramid Texts, which are full of catastrophic images involving the celestial gods, must allude to real events, but events in the recent, not the distant, past. These and other documents insist that the gods, or planets, were involved in effecting dramatic disturbances in the cosmic order. The movement and position of the sun (and by implication, the cardinal points) was affected. These assertions have been graphically illustrated by the strange alignment of the Early Dynastic monuments. From the start of the Fourth Dynasty onwards, the great monuments of the pharaohs were aligned very precisely on a north-south axis. But in each and every one of the structures left from the first three dynasties a very different alignment is observed. Typically, this follows an axis roughly north-northwest by south-southeast.[37] Since Velikovsky's theories of pole-shifts are universally derided in establishment circles, it is regarded as something of a mystery that the Egyptians of the period should have so consistently adopted this alignment; an alignment which nowadays has no obvious significance. From the Fourth Dynasty onwards religious structures are always aligned to the cardinal points. It was seen as essential that the entrance of the pyramid should face due north, in the direction of the "imperishable" circumpolar stars, so it seems hard to believe that religious structures of the earlier period were otherwise aligned. Essentially this means, astonishing though it may seem, that during the Early Dynastic epoch the north and south poles occupied positions significantly different to their present ones.

These disasters, it appears, truly were of cosmic dimensions.

In addition to the Pyramid Texts, which are only attested from the end of the Fifth Dynasty, there exists one important document which claims to date from the very beginning of the Fourth Dynasty, and which gives a rather graphic description of events exactly like those we claim terminated the Early Dynastic and launched the Pyramid Age. This is the famous "Prophecy of Neferty".

The "Prophecy of Neferty", said to have been written by Neferty the Lector Priest during the reign of Sneferu, is a dark and foreboding document, its flavor clearly placing it among Egypt's so-called "Pessimistic Literature", a body of compositions written during a time of disturbance and dealing with the dark side of life. The whole tone of the Pessimistic Literature shows that it dates from a period when upheavals of nature (floods, famines, etc.) led to a breakdown of social stability. Accordingly, the *genre* is normally dated to the First Intermediate Period (the epoch following the collapse of the Old Kingdom); and there is in fact strong evidence to show that most of the Pessimistic material does belong close to the Old Kingdom. But the question, of course, is: to what period of the Old Kingdom?

---

37 I.E.S. Edwards, *The Pyramids of Egypt* (1961 ed.) See illustrations on pp.40,44 and 81

The Prophecy of Neferty, in line with the rest of the Pessimistic Literature, portrays a world plunged in chaos:

> What was spoken by the Lector Neferrohu [Neferty], that wise man of the East, who belongs to Ubast in her rising ... as he was brooding over what should come to pass in the land, and conjuring up the condition of the East, when the Asiatics approach in their might and their hearts rage against those who are getting in the harvest.... And he said:

> Up, my heart, and bewail this land whence thou art sprung. He who is silent is a transgressor (??). Behold, the great one is fallen in the land whence thou art sprung. Be thou not weary. Behold, these things are before thee; rise up against what is in thy presence. Behold, princes hold sway in the land, things made are as though they had never been made. Day begins in falsehood (??). The land is utterly perished, and naught remains.[38]

We are thus presented with a picture of a land in ruin; but the evil of men is matched by the destructiveness of nature:

> The river is dry (even the river) of Egypt. Men cross over the water on foot.... Their course is become a sand-bank. And the sand-bank shall be stream.... The South Wind shall blow against the North wind, the sky shall not have one wind alone.

> A darkness descends over the land. Ra, the sun, removes himself from men.... None knoweth that midday is there; his shadow is not discerned.

The papyrus goes on to tell how the people, despoiled both by nature and by the enemies of Egypt — the Asiatics and Libyans — shall be rescued by a savior. A mighty leader called Ameny will arise in the south. He shall slay the Asiatics, the Libyans, and the bandits, and will erect the "Wall of the Prince" to keep them at bay.

The mention here of the king Ameny, who would expel the Asiatics, appears to be a fairly clear reference to Amenemhet I, of the so-called Twelfth Dynasty, an individual whom we shall identify as a contemporary of Ahmose, founder of the Eighteenth Dynasty, and expeller of the Asiatic Hyksos. Clearly then the prophecy, in the form that we now have it, could not possibly have been written by a priest in the time of Sneferu. Nevertheless, the catastrophic imagery contained in the work suggests that Sneferu's epoch was indeed an age associated with such events: And it could well be that seers and sages of the time, maybe even one called Neferty, were making predictions of repeat performances of the selfsame events.

In Chapter 3 of the present work we shall see that much of the literature of the Pyramid Age displays astonishing parallels with the works of the Hebrew prophets, and Neferty's prophecy in particular is strikingly similar to whole pas-

---

38 A.H. Gardiner, "New Literary Works from Egypt", *Journal of Egyptian Archaeology* 1 (1914) 100-16

sages in the Book of Amos, a document not older than the 6th or 7th century BC. The same forces that inspired the wise men of Egypt also inspired those of Israel, whilst the common desire for the coming of a savior, a Messiah, was rooted in the calamitous events of the 9th and 8th centuries BC, events which threatened to consign both gods and men to oblivion.

THE REIGN OF SNEFERU

If the foregoing is correct, the first pharaoh of the Pyramid Age, Sneferu, must have been a contemporary of the original and greatest of all the Hebrew prophets, Moses; and we might expect some of the events of his reign to reflect the happenings described in the Hebrew Scriptures.

Already we have seen that the catastrophe described so vividly by Sneferu's lector-priest Neferty, as well as by other "Pessimistic" writers such as Ipuwer (to be examined in the following chapter), provide fairly striking agreement with what we read of in the Book of Exodus. As might be expected, the correspondences between the words of Neferty and Ipuwer on the one and the Book of Exodus on the other were noted early by scholars; but once again the chronology, which placed the Egyptian scribes roughly seven centuries before Moses, forced the abandonment of any attempt to make them contemporary. Released from the straightjacket of that system, we can now, for the first time, begin to make sense of the period. Plunged into primeval chaos, with the ruling pharaoh and half his army drowned or otherwise slain, an able and gifted leader — known to posterity as Sneferu — seized his chance. In the chaotic weeks following Huni/Ka-nefer-ra's death, Sneferu took the reins of government, legitimizing his position by marrying Hetepheres, the daughter of Huni's chief wife.

As a contemporary of the Exodus, Sneferu cannot have been ruler of the quiescent and placid land so often portrayed in the textbooks; nor was he.

We are told that, "The founder of the Fourth Dynasty was ... a considerable warrior,"[39] and his martial exploits, evidently early in his reign, saw him engage the enemies of Egypt on all three frontiers. Nonetheless after what seems to have been a relatively short period of chaos and lawlessness the new pharaoh succeeded in restoring order. According to Velikovsky, the departure of the Hebrew slaves coincided with the arrival in Egypt of a horde of Amalekites from the Arabian Desert, uprooted by the same catastrophe. The Book of Exodus tells us how just two weeks or so after their departure from the Land of the Nile, the Amalekites, apparently moving in the opposite direction, attacked the Israelites

---

39 A.H. Gardiner, "New Literary Works from Egypt", *Journal of Egyptian Archaeology* 1 (1914) 100-16

at Rephidim.[40] This was the famous engagement during which the children of Israel were successful as long as Moses held his hands aloft (evidently a position of prayer). As he grew tired, his arms were said to have been supported by Aaron and Hur. This attack upon the traumatized Israelites gave rise to an enduring animosity between the two peoples.

Velikovsky believed the Amalekites, recognized by the Arabs as one of their tribes, to be the notorious and feared Hyksos, whose conquest of Egypt was long told and lamented. But the Amalekites were not the Hyksos. They did not conquer the Nile Kingdom.[41] They may well have entered Egypt to plunder. Certainly this is hinted in the Pessimistic Literature, but their sojourn was short-lived. They were quickly driven from the Delta by the new pharaoh and pushed eastwards across the desert. Sneferu himself records his victory on an inscription at Wadi Maghara, in the Sinai Peninsula.[42] Attempts by Nubians and Libyans to take advantage of Egypt's moment of weakness (mentioned also by Neferty) were met with equal vigor, as the Annals of Sneferu, recorded on the famous Palermo Stone, make clear.[43]

Probably within months peace and security was restored. But now all things were different. The very heavens themselves had changed. A new World Age had been inaugurated. The bloody rituals to appease the gods, which had hitherto been enacted atop the sacred mounds that formed the centerpiece of the mastabas, and quite possibly atop the stepped pyramids, were no longer required. Human sacrifice was a thing of the past. So Sneferu busied himself with raising a new type of pyramid; one with steep smooth sides. A new age required a new architecture for a new religion. Historians comment on the abandonment of star- and planet-worship at the time — to be replaced by an almost monotheistic adoration of the sun.[44] The epoch that now began was ever afterwards looked upon as a Golden Age, the classical period of Egyptian civilization; the epoch that all later generations sought to emulate. And the pattern was set by its first pharaoh. The Egyptians were tireless in their praise of Sneferu. He was famously regarded by subsequent generations as a paragon, a veritable Messiah (not incidentally unlike the way the Jews regarded the man we see as his contemporary, Moses). His exalted status was reflected in his royal titles; thus the name Sneferu itself

---

40 Exodus 17:8

41 Nevertheless, there is some evidence that the Arabian tribes did at least become allies of the Hyksos; for one of their kings, Khamudi, has a fairly obviously Arab name.

42 W. Stevenson Smith, loc. cit. p.167 These Arabian tribes are known simply as the "sand-dwellers".

43 Ibid.

44 Michael Rice, loc. cit. pp.195-6

means "the Gladdener", whilst his Horus name Neb-maat implies "Lord in Truth". Sneferu "was revered throughout the length of Egyptian history; his reign was always regarded as one of the high points of the Egyptian Golden Age. Virtually uniquely amongst the Kings of Egypt he was remembered by a sobriquet; he was 'the Beneficent King' and his cult was sustained down to Ptolemaic time.... His cult was practiced as far away as the mines of turquoise in Sinai, and as late as the Middle Kingdom a little shrine to his memory was maintained at Dahshur. A simple dish with the charcoal for an offering of incense was found still on the modest altar which was consecrated there to his memory".[45] Why Sneferu should have been recalled with such fondness is a mystery to conventional historians, though for us it would be a mystery were he not.

In keeping with his reputation for wisdom, Sneferu's reign coincided with the life of one of Egypt's greatest sages: this was the famous Kagemni, who is said to have addressed to his children a book of maxims which took its place as one of the classics of Egyptian literature.

> [Kagemni,] having become thoroughly acquainted with men's characters, sent for his children to come to him, and they came, full of wonder (as to why he had summoned them). Then he said to them: "Pay attention to everything that is written in this book, just as if I myself were telling it to you"; and his children thereupon laid themselves down on their faces (on the floor around him), and recited these maxims as they were written, and, in their opinion, these maxims were more beautiful than anything else in the whole land, and they continued to recite them both standing up and sitting down (all their life long). Then His Majesty King Huni died, and King Snofru became the gracious king of all this land, and Kegemni was made Prime Minister.[46]

Before moving on, one very interesting legend recounted on the Westcar Papyrus may well represent a distant echo of the parting of the Sea of Passage during the Exodus. The tale describes how a bored King Sneferu is persuaded by the magician Djadjaemankh to seek some diversion by sailing on the lake in the palace gardens. A crew of girls dressed in fishing nets is commissioned to row for the king, and one of these loses her hair-ornament in the water. Before the voyage can continue, therefore, the magician is required to turn back (or, one might say, part) the waters to reveal the ornament, a malachite fish-pendant, which is lying on a potsherd at the bottom of the lake.[47]

No one could pretend that the above is a precise Egyptian version of the story of the parting waters of *Yam Suf*. A much more exact rendering is found, as Ve-

---

45 Ibid. p.197

46 Arthur Weigall, loc. cit. p.155

47 W. Stevenson Smith, "The Old Kingdom in Egypt and the Beginning of the First Intermediate Period" in *CAH* Vol.1 part 2 (3rd ed.) p.168

likovsky demonstrated, on the El Arish shrine.[48] Nevertheless, it is clear that the wondrous event of the sea-waters parting could not but have been incorporated into Egyptian legend. Though the Egyptians did not benefit from the incident, as an unprecedented divine miracle it could scarcely be ignored. The boat which Sneferu uses is evidently symbolic of the vessel employed by Egypt's great gods, and the connection with the ship-like Ark of the Covenant, which the fleeing Israelites carried before them on their journeys after traversing the Sea of Passage, should not be ignored. The placing of the event in the time of Sneferu is precisely correct.

CHEOPS AND HIS SUCCESSORS

The reign of good king Sneferu is said to have endured twenty-four years, a period of peace and prosperity for the people. Next in line to the throne was Khnum-Khufu, better known by his Hellenized title Cheops. With him Egypt was about to enter an age of architectural and artistic grandeur unparalleled in world history. Sneferu had initiated the custom of raising colossal, smooth-sided pyramids. Cheops took the art-form to its logical conclusion.

We know little of the life and career of Cheops from the contemporary monuments. A tiny ivory statue is, ironically enough, the sole portrait of him to have survived. He is shown seated on his throne, wearing the crown of Egypt. Although the scale of the portrait is small, the king definitely has a "disagreeable" face, with an expression of "dyspeptic ill-temper". It would appear that he was not remembered fondly by the Egyptians, though for further information we must look to the classical writers. These invariably portray him as a cruel tyrant (a reputation, incidentally, which almost certainly explains the non-survival of any major portraits or representations of the king). The two most extensive descriptions of the pharaoh's life are found in Herodotus and Diodorus. According to the former "no crime was too great" for Cheops; he closed the nation's temples and subjected the populace to prolonged and backbreaking labor.[49] We have already explained this program of temple-closure as part of the religious revolution of the age. Yet there is ample evidence from throughout the pyramid-building age of continuous social and religious upheavals — upheavals which were the direct result of ongoing disturbances in the cosmic order.

---

48 See *Ages in Chaos* (1952) p. The Hebrew *Yam Suf* is almost certainly to be translated as Hurricane Sea (from Heb. *Suf, sufa* "hurricane"). This agrees with the Egyptian name for the Red Sea, *shari*, signifying Sea of Percussion, or Thundering. The attempt to translate *suf* as denoting "reeds" was first postulated by scholars who rejected the traditional interpretation of the Exodus, which saw it as a catastrophic episode.

49 Herodotus, ii,126

When money for his great pyramid began to run out, Cheops is said to have "sent his daughter to a bawdy-house with instructions to charge a certain sum."[50] It is interesting to note here that Herodotus also records a tradition among the Greeks of the Delta that the third Giza pyramid, that of Mycerinus, had been built by the courtesan Rhodopis, whom some traditions made a contemporary of pharaoh Amasis (560-525 BC).[51] Diodorus too mentions this tradition, which can only point to the custom of sacred prostitution, still alive in the time of Herodotus. It may be that the earnings of these prostitutes helped finance the construction of the pyramids.

According to both Herodotus and Diodorus, Chephren was the brother of Cheops, not his son; an opinion apparently contradicted by some inscriptional evidence, which places Redjedef, a son of Cheops, just before Chephren. This would imply that Redjedef was an elder brother of Chephren, who died after a very brief period on the throne. If our reconstruction is correct, the fifty-odd year reigns attributed to Cheops and Chephren by Herodotus can safely be ignored. It is doubtful whether their combined reigns could have exceeded fifty years. Hieroglyphic texts imply that Cheops reigned, like his father, for twenty-four years. Where then are these two monument builders to be placed, in terms of absolute chronology? For various reasons, we shall argue that Sneferu could not have ascended the throne much before circa 840 BC, which would then imply that Cheops's reign is to be dated from roughly 830 BC, or shortly thereafter. A combined reign of forty years for Cheops and Chephren would leave us around 790 BC, for the accession of Menkaure (Mycerinus). Since we shall date the rise to power of the Sixth Dynasty sometime near 780 BC, this gives us only a handful of years for the rest of the Fourth, as well as the entire Fifth Dynasty. The brevity of these reigns can be seen from the careers of a number of characters whose lives spanned most of the Fourth Dynasty and much of the Fifth. Thus, for example, an official named Netjerpunesut claimed to have enjoyed a position of favor during the reigns of Redjedef, Chephren, Mycerinus, Shepseskaf, Userkaf, and Sahura.[52]

The classical authors and the monuments agree that the immediate successor to Chephren was Mycerinus (Menkaure), who, although reputedly one of Egypt's wisest rulers, was accorded only a short reign by the gods:

> Mycerinus, reversing his father's policy of which he did not approve, reopened the temples and allowed his subjects, who had been brought into such abject slavery, to resume the practice of their religion and their normal work. Of

50 Ibid.

51 Ibid.

52 W. Stevenson Smith, "The Old Kingdom in Egypt and the Beginning of the First Intermediate Period" in *CAH* Vol.1 part 2 (3rd ed.) p.176

all the kings who ruled in Egypt he had the greatest reputation for justice in the decision of legal causes, and for this the Egyptians give him higher praise than any other monarch.[53]

But in spite of all his piety an oracle from Buto warned Mycerinus that he was destined to live only six more years — whereupon, it is said, the king angrily reproached the god, and attempted to prove the oracle wrong by lighting innumerable lamps, whose object was to turn night into day, thereby prolonging his life.[54] Diodorus agrees on the brevity of the pharaoh's life, informing us that he died before his pyramid, small though it was, could be completed.[55] There is in fact good evidence to suggest that all of the Fourth Dynasty monarchs, with the exceptions of Cheops and Chephren, occupied the throne for extremely short periods of time, and it is possible the combined reigns of Mycerinus and Shepseskaf, as well as the ephemeral Baka(re) did not exceed five or six years.

The monuments tell us that Cheops's line was replaced by a family of kings descended from the High Priest of Ra, a family known to us as the Fifth Dynasty. Yet the accounts given by Herodotus and Diodorus differ in a most controversial way from the monuments. According to Herodotus:

> The successor of Mycerinus, the priests told me, was Asychis, and he it was who added to the temple of Hephaestus its eastern entrance-gate, much the finest and biggest of the four....

> Wishing to go one better than his predecessors on the throne, Asychis built a pyramid of brick to commemorate his reign....

> Having no further achievements of this monarch to recount, I will now pass to the next. This was Anysis, a blind man who came from a city of the same name. During his reign Egypt was invaded in great force by the Ethiopians under Sabacos their king.[56]

The strange mention here of Sabakos (Shabaka) the Ethiopian pharaoh of the Twenty-Fifth Dynasty, will be discussed presently.

For the moment, we should note that Herodotus may not be too far removed from conventional ideas in one respect. It is tempting to identify his Asychis and Anysis with Isesi and Unas (Wenis), two of the latter pharaohs of Dynasty 5.

---

53 Herodotus, ii,127

54 Ibid. ii,133 This story probably contains a catastrophic message. The reference to day turning to night may well imply a disturbance in the cosmic order, or a change in the calendar, or both. The tale is paralleled by contemporary stories from Israel and from Greece.

55 Diodorus, i,64,7

56 Herodotus, ii,137

THE KINGS OF ELEPHANTINE

Towards the second half of the Fourth Dynasty the power and prestige of the quasi-monotheistic cult of Ra-Atum grew to such an extent that it appears to have destabilized the throne. The priests of Ra-Atum, it would appear, felt confident enough to challenge royal authority. Mycerinus's successor Shepseskaf attempted to curtail their power, and failed. That at least is how the Fourth Dynasty's demise is now most commonly explained:

> Although documentary records are lacking, the character of the political events which attended the close of the IVth Dynasty may be conjectured from a number of indirect indications. The three successors of Cheops — Djedefre, Chephren (Khaef-Re), and Mycerinus (Men-kau-Re) — had proclaimed their recognition of the Sun-god Re by forming their names of compounds with his name. There is some evidence also that Chephren and Mycerinus had adopted the title "Son of Re" — a royal title which figures regularly from the Vth Dynasty onwards.... At the end of the IVth Dynasty, however, Shepseskaf not only departed from the type of tomb built by his predecessors, but, so far as is known, did not follow their precedent by acknowledging unequivocally, either in name or title, his association with Re. Whether he was guided by motives of religious principle or political expediency cannot be deduced from the evidence available, but, in view of the caution and conservatism shown by the Egyptians at all times in matters appertaining to religion and the After-life, it is difficult to believe that Shepseskaf would have introduced such fundamental changes if he had not thought that the increasing power of the priesthood of Re directly menaced the authority and independence of the throne. Shepseskaf's struggle, which was perhaps passive and not waged with destructive bitterness, failed to achieve any permanent success, for his death, after a reign of little more than four years, led to the accession of a line of kings who raised the cult of Re to the position of the official state religion.[57]

This interpretation is partially confirmed, or at least not contradicted, by a well-known story recounted in the Westcar Papyrus. King Cheops, the papyrus informs us, was enjoying an idle hour with his sons, who told him stories of the great seers and wonder-workers of old. Prince Hordedef intervened in the discourse, enthusiastically proclaiming that there still lived a seer capable of performing similar feats. The wise man is promptly sent for, and, after displaying a few of his remarkable powers, reluctantly informs the king of the future of his dynasty. Three children, he says, are soon to be born to the wife of a priest of Ra, and these children, actually begotten of Ra himself, would all become kings of Egypt. These three, who are named Userkaf, Sahura and Kakai/Neferirkare (the first kings of Dynasty 5), would not rule immediately. The prophet tells Cheops that his own son and grandson would reign, then one of these children: "Thy son, his son, and one of them." The conclusion of the tale is lost, but it must have gone on to tell how the three children finally became pharaohs. Many wondrous

---

57 I.E.S. Edwards, *The Pyramids of Egypt* (1961 ed.) pp.170-1

prodigies are recorded in the tale, including how the three are born wearing the insignia of royalty.

The cult of Ra, or Ra-Atum, is in fact one of the defining characteristics of the Pyramid Age. In the famous Pyramid Texts, which were inscribed on the inner walls of the pyramids of the Fifth and Sixth Dynasty pharaohs, Ra-Atum is raised virtually to the level of the Supreme God. How this situation, bordering on a form of monotheism, arose, is one that we shall return to at a later stage; though for now we should recall that the Pyramid Age itself, with Sneferu, was inaugurated by a cataclysm which temporarily blotted out the sun; and we should recall too that the people of Mexico, who offered human sacrifices atop their pyramids, spoke of repeated cataclysms which saw the "death" or blotting out of the old sun, followed by the birth, or rebirth, of a new sun.

It is not clear how these sons of Ra attained to the kingship; yet it seems unlikely that the transition to the new dynasty could have been entirely peaceful. These things rarely are. It is possible that the tale told on the Westcar Papyrus was initially intended to provide legitimacy to the new line. One thing is certain, the pharaohs of the Fifth Dynasty, as the document makes abundantly clear, were peculiarly devoted to Ra-Atum, and it was during their epoch that the Pyramid Texts, which praise this deity in almost monotheistic terms, first appeared. Six pharaohs of this line built special Sun-temples in honor of Re, the design of which was later copied by Akhnaton.

Userkaf, the first of the new dynasty, may well have sprung from priestly stock, and it seems likely that he himself had held the office of High Priest of Re before ascending the throne. Whether he was a brother of Sahura and Neferirkare is not so certain, though there seem good grounds for believing the latter two to be brothers.[58] Certain hieroglyphic texts indicate this Ra-worshipping dynasty was of Elephantine origin, which in effect implies that they were Nubian. Deriving from this region, they may thus be regarded as Egypt's first "Ethiopian" dynasty; and this is a factor which will be mentioned again when we come to consider why Herodotus and later Diodorus placed the Nubian pharaohs of the Twenty-Fifth Dynasty (Shabaka, et al.) almost immediately after Cheops, Chephren and Mycerinus.

In point of fact, there are numerous similarities between the Fifth and Twenty-Fifth Dynasties, and it is by no means difficult to understand how they could have become confused. As in the later Ethiopian age, when kings like Shabaka and Tirhaka battled against Asiatic invaders and their clients in Lower Egypt, so it would appear that this earlier Ethiopian age was also a period of division and fragmentation. These kings too had to wage war against the princes of Lower

58 Ibid. p.171

Egypt in an attempt to unite the country; and furthermore, there is a strong hint that they were also in conflict with an invading Asiatic power. The Pyramid Texts of Unas, last of the Fifth Dynasty, tells of hostility between Upper and Lower Egypt. One passage praises a goddess with the words: "Thou hast placed terror of thee in the heart of the kings of Lower Egypt, dwelling in Buto."[59] King Unas is said to have conquered Lower Egypt; he had "eaten the Red"; the Red being the red crown of Lower Egypt.[60] Again, we read that "it is king Unis who binds with lilies the papyrus [binds the papyrus of Lower Egypt with the lily of Upper Egypt]; it is king Unis who reconciles the Two Lands; it is King Unis who unites the Two Lands."[61] According to Breasted, these texts were written at a time when "hostilities had not yet ceased [between Upper and Lower Egypt], but the kings of the South were nevertheless maintaining control of the North and preserving the united kingdom."[62]

But who were these enemies faced by Unas in Lower Egypt? The actual names of the Fifth Dynasty kings, as listed below:

> Userkaf
>
> Sahura
>
> Neferirkare
>
> Shepseskare
>
> Khaneferre
>
> Nyuserre
>
> Menkuhor
>
> Isesi
>
> Unas

— show striking parallels with the names of a few of the kings of the Asiatic dynasty commonly known as the Great Hyksos (a dynasty which, however, in conventional chronology is supposed to have reigned around seven hundred years after the 5th Dynasty). Thus Khaneferre and Neferirkare are virtually identical to Kaneferre (Kenephres), a popular Hyksos title; Isesi is very close to the Hyksos Assa, whilst Nyuserre (also read Userenre) looks very close to Se-userenre/Khyan, one of the greatest of the Hyksos rulers.

The Hyksos parallels are no coincidence, for the latter, whose most prominent kings were named Apepi (Apophis), are one and the same as the mighty Sixth Dynasty (whose prominent kings are named Pepi), which is agreed to have immediately followed the Sixth.

59 J.H. Breasted, *Development of Religion and Thought in Ancient Egypt* (London, 1912) p.86

60 Ibid. p.87

61 Ibid.

62 Ibid. p.87

It could be then that the kings of Lower Egypt, against whom Unas battled so long and hard, were vassals of the newly-arrived Hyksos invaders. Yet the naming of kings with Hyksos-style titles among the list of Fifth Dynasty pharaohs would suggest that there was no clear sequence from one to the other, from the Fifth Dynasty to the Sixth, but rather that for a substantial period there was conflict between the two lines for control of the country, and that the Fifth Dynasty kings with Hyksos names were really Hyksos pharaohs whose control of the Nile Valley at times extended right into the heart of Upper Egypt.

The advent of the Sixth Dynasty was a far cry from the peaceful transition to a new ruling family imagined in the textbooks. These kings were not native Egyptians, but a mighty nation of Asiatic warriors who employed revolutionary new weapons, and whose bloody march of conquest across the ancient East would be long recalled by generations to come.[63]

THE CHRONOLOGY OF HERODOTUS

It is a strange thing that whilst the facts highlighted above cause grave concern to modern scholars, they would not have troubled Herodotus, the Greek "Father of History" in the slightest. Herodotus visited Egypt himself and travelled extensively throughout the country, gathering material for his encyclopedic History, a work centered round the Persian invasion of Greece but incorporating the histories of the numerous nations then forming the Persian Empire. By good fortune, Herodotus provides us with a fairly detailed account of Egypt, which was brought under Persian rule by Cambyses in 525 BC. The writer claims to derive all the information he sets down from the Egyptians themselves, particularly from priests and temple officials, and the account he provides is the earliest systematic attempt to chronicle Egyptian history that we possess.

Herodotus begins his history fairly conventionally, with Menes (or Min, as he names him), the first pharaoh. Many years after Min, he tells us, there lived a queen called Nitokris, who "drowned hundreds of Egyptians," then threw herself into a roomful of ashes. Historians shy away from such mythic talk, and it is generally agreed that Nitokris is but a euhemerization of the goddess Neith. Following Nitokris there is another unspecified lapse of time, after which pharaoh Moeris took the throne. The latter king gave his name to the Faiyum Lake, and he raised numerous monuments in the area. Scholars are now generally agreed that Moeris represents one of the Twelfth Dynasty kings — probably Amenemhet I or

---

63 The discovery of two rich hoards of royal treasures belonging to the 5th Dynasty in Anatolia (namely the now lost "Dorak treasure" and the "Boston Hoard") almost certainly found their way to that far-off region as part of the loot taken from Egypt by the victorious Hyksos conquerors. These, as we find in Chapter 5, were identical to the Akkadians.

Senwosret I. Next in line after Moeris comes Sesostris, a mighty conqueror who led armies throughout Asia. The Egyptians boasted much to Herodotus about the deeds of Sesostris, clearly one of Egypt's most illustrious rulers. Numerous suggestions have been put forward in an attempt to identify this man, though there is a consensus amongst mainstream Egyptologists that he was yet another of the Twelfth Dynasty pharaohs — possibly Senwosret (or Usertasen) III, who made one or two minor expeditions into southern Palestine.

A more probable alter-ego of Herodotus's Sesostris is the biblical Shishak, who plundered Solomon's temple in Jerusalem. But since this identification raises profound problems for chronology, it has been rejected by most Egyptologists.

Following Sesostris, Herodotus lists a king Pheros, a man whose name simply means "pharaoh".

After Pheros there is a king Proteus, described as a contemporary of the Trojan War, and Rhampsinitus, who was famously rich, and whose story was linked to a decapitation legend, as well as a visit to the underworld. It is only after Rhampsinitus that Cheops comes into the story. Now even if we accept the impossibly high "traditional" date for the fall of Troy — 1184 BC — it is clear that that the chronology given by Herodotus places Cheops and the other pyramid-builders over a thousand years later than the date now given in the textbooks. However, the situation is made even worse when we go further through Herodotus's chronology: for there Mycerinus, last king of the Fourth Dynasty, is placed just two reigns before Shabaka, the Nubian king who conquered Egypt in the 8th century BC!

Since the rise of modern Egyptology over 150 years ago these passages of Herodotus have presented a perennial problem. Manetho, the Ptolemaic scholar, placed Cheops and the pyramid-builders near the beginning of Egypt's history; Herodotus seemed to place them nearer the end. Scholars trusted Manetho rather than Herodotus because Manetho was an Egyptian and because he appeared to be supported by certain king-lists dating from the Ramesside epoch. In time then Herodotus's version was gradually overshadowed, and scholars looked rather to Manetho, with his system of thirty dynasties, for a framework on which to work. As a final answer to the "problem" of Herodotus, it was suggested that the text was corrupt, and that the passages dealing with the Pyramid Age had been misplaced by a later editor.

There the matter has rested for many years. Yet even in the early days, discoveries were being made which seemed, in many strange ways, to support Herodotus. We have seen that much of the technology and artwork of the Pyramid Age looked incredibly modern, like products of the Iron Age. Even worse, it soon became apparent that the Nubian pharaohs of the 8th and 7th centuries BC were indeed great imitators and devotees of Cheops, Chephren and the rest — precisely as we would have expected from Herodotus. Thus it was found that the Nubians went to extraordinary lengths to copy the art and architecture of the pyramid-builders, whilst the religion and cult-practices of the age also displayed marked "archaizing" tendencies. Flinders Petrie, for example, noted the revival of the cults of Cheops and Chephren in the 7th century. Cheops's priests, whom Petrie lists, all belong to the Fourth and Fifth Dynasties, and after that to the Twenty-Sixth Dynasty.[64] Even Old Kingdom throne names were adopted. Thus the Nubian king Shabataka (c. 690-680 BC) was also called Dadkara, in apparent imitation of Dadkara-Isesi, of Dynasty 5; whilst Tefnakht (c. 720-715 BC) had a Nebti-name constructed precisely like those of the Sixth Dynasty pharaohs.[65] Furthermore, Tefnakht's Suten Bat name, Shepsesra, sounded very close to Shepseskaf, of Dynasty 4, and Shepseskara of Dynasty 5.

None of this is to suggest that these kings really did come immediately after the pyramid-builders, as Herodotus implied. But the parallels do suggest a reason why the Father of History, or his Egyptian informants, got the two epochs confused — a topic we shall return to at a later stage. Yet conventional scholarship requires us to believe that almost two thousand years elapsed between Cheops and Chephren and their Nubian admirers; a stretch of time that also stretches credulity. In fact, as the remainder of the present volume will show, Herodotus got it spectacularly right; the pyramid-builders really did flourish in the 8th century BC and the iron tools which Herodotus claimed they used to raise the structures were real enough. But their Nubian admirers, who were also pyramid-builders, reigned not in the 8th and 7th centuries, but in the 6th and 5th. They revived traditions two centuries old, not two millennia.

THE ETHIOPIAN PYRAMID-BUILDERS

From the time of the Fourth Dynasty onwards Egyptian cultural influence pushed its way further and further southwards, and, in time, an entirely separate civilization, an offshoot of the Egyptian, would flower in the Sudan. A powerful Nubian kingdom, with its capital at Napata, now emerged.

These later Nubian rulers, like their Fifth Dynasty predecessors, were also great devotees of the sun-god Ra — a fact hinted at even by Herodotus.[66] But it was not only in their religious practices that they resembled the earlier kings: for

---

64 F. Petrie, *A History of Egypt* Vol.1 (1894) p.186

65 J. Von Beckerath, *Handbuch der Aegyptischen Königsnamen* (Berlin, 1984) pp.184ff.

66 Herodotus iii, 20 refers to the Ethiopians' magical Table of the Sun, which provided them with an endless supply of food.

the Nubians of the Twenty-Fifth Dynasty were also great builders of pyramids. Large numbers of these distinctive latter-day pyramids, with their peculiarly steep sides, are still to be observed in and around Napata and the various other Nubian centers. Yet these pyramids, according to conventional ideas, are supposed to have been raised a thousand years after the custom of pyramid-building was finally abandoned by the Egyptians themselves!

Even worse, when the Nubians, in the 4th century BC, moved their capital further south to Meroe, they continued even then to erect pyramids, the last of which date from as recently as the 4th century AD!

Now there is no doubt that the Twenty-Fifth Dynasty kings were cultural conservatives, and quite deliberately so. They copied many of the forms of their illustrious Egyptian predecessors — particularly those of the Fourth and Fifth Dynasties. Yet in terms of style and appearance the steep-sided pyramids of the Nubians owe much more to the small steep-sided pyramidions of the Nineteenth Dynasty found at Deir el Medina. But even this line of kings is placed five hundred years before the Nubians. Elsewhere, I have demonstrated in some detail how the Nubians of the so-called Twenty-Fifth Dynasty actually come immediately after the Nineteenth Dynasty; and so it is no surprise that their pyramids resemble the smaller structures of the latter.[67] Yet there is no doubt that in terms of scale, the Nubian monuments are in direct line of descent from the mighty building of the Fourth, Fifth and Sixth Dynasties: And it surely stretches credulity almost to breaking point to accept that they would have revived a form of funerary monument which had been, according to accepted chronology, consigned to the dustbin of history almost a thousand years earlier. However, if the kings of the Fourth, Fifth and Sixth Dynasties lived in the 8th century BC, then the Nubian rulers of the Twenty-Fifth Dynasty — who we shall argue flourished in the 6th and 5th centuries — could easily have revived an architectural feature which had only recently (or perhaps had never completely) died out.

Much more worrying however than the pyramids themselves, from the point of view of orthodox chronology, are the mastaba-tombs they replaced. In the accepted scheme of things, mastabas very similar to those used in Egypt in the Early Dynastic epoch were the preferred type of funerary structure until Piankhy of the Twenty-Fifth Dynasty raised the first small pyramid just south of Napata.[68] The problem here, of course, is that mastabas were the funerary monument *par excellence* of Dynasties 1 to 3, though they continued to be used, in a limited way, until the end of the Middle Kingdom, supposedly around 1600 BC. Now, it is just possible that the Ethiopians, styling themselves as pharaohs, may have had

---

67 In my *Ramessides, Medes and Persians* (New York, 2001)

68 I.E.S. Edwards, loc. cit.

good motive for reviving after a long interval the majestic form of the pyramid, an architectural feature linked in people's minds to the semi-divine pharaohs of the Fourth and Fifth Dynasties. But why should the Ethiopian predecessors of Piankhy, who made no claim to being pharaohs, revive, after a gap of almost a thousand years, the humble form of the mastaba?

But the problem is illusory. The so-called "Middle Kingdom" of Egypt, the last period to employ the funerary mastaba, was largely contemporaneous with the New Kingdom, the mighty Eighteenth and Nineteenth Dynasties (the latter immediately preceding the rise of the Nubians). Such being the case, there was no need whatever for the Nubians to revive mastaba-building. It was in continual use from the very moment Egyptian influence first reached into the Sudan, sometime during the Fourth or Fifth Dynasties.

CONFUSED EPOCHS

Why, it has been asked again and again, did Herodotus make the Nubian Dynasty (Twenty-Fifth) immediately follow the Fourth? How could the Father of History have made such a monumental blunder? Was the fault really that of an editor, who misplaced entire passages and chapters? Or was the mistake committed by Herodotus himself?

This is a problem that has perplexed classicists for many generations. Yet it is a problem no more. The petty kings of the Twenty-Fourth Dynasty, as well as the more substantial rulers of the Twenty-Fifth, deliberately revived the customs, traditions and names of the Fourth and Fifth Dynasties. According to Breasted this "tendency to retrospect" first appears during the epoch of the Twenty-Fourth Dynasty, and by the time of the Twenty-Fifth Dynasty the revival of the past became an all-consuming passion. In the words of Breasted,

> The worship of the kings who had ruled at Memphis ... was revived and the ritual of their mortuary services maintained and endowed. Their pyramids were even extensively restored and repaired. The archaic titles and the long array of dignities worn by the lords at the court and the government of the pyramid-builders were again brought into requisition, and in the externals of government everything possible was done to clothe it in the appearance of remote antiquity.[69]

Not only court officials, but kings too began to copy the archaic titles of the pyramid age. Thus Tefnakht, the first Twenty-Fourth Dynasty "pharaoh", employed the prenomen Shepsesra, clearly recalling Shepseskaf of Dynasty 4: whilst Tefnakht's successor Bocchoris (Bokenranef), had a name easily confused with another prince of the Fourth Dynasty, Baka, or Bakare. Manetho, whose Fourth

---

69 J.H. Breasted, *A History of Egypt* (2nd ed. 1951) p.510

Dynasty is comprised of eight kings, lists a man named Bicheris as the penultimate ruler of the line. Whilst the royal title Bicheris (Bakare) has not actually been found on the monuments, a prince by the name Baka does occur, and it is surmised that he later added the royal "re" after ascending the throne.[70]

The Ethiopians of the Twenty-Fifth Dynasty were even more enthusiastic revivers of Old Kingdom culture. They deliberately copied the names and titles of their pyramid-building predecessors, and were particularly fond of the Fourth and Fifth Dynasties in this regard. Thus Shabataka of Dynasty 25 used the same Suten Bat name (Dadkara) as Isesi of Dynasty 5, whilst his artists made great efforts to duplicate the styles of his Fifth Dynasty namesake: the result being that even modern archaeologists are frequently confused as to the true ownership of a number of monuments bearing the name.[71]

Indeed the conservatism of the Ethiopians has meant that much of their artwork is virtually indistinguishable from that of the Old Kingdom. The tomb of Mentuemhet, for example, High Priest of Amon during the reign of Tirhaka, is decorated precisely in the style of the Fifth Dynasty, and only the appearance of Tirhaka's name enables us to date it to his reign. In particular, the Ethiopians were almost unbounded in their devotion to Cheops and Chephren. Amenardis, a priestess of the time, dedicated at least one inscription to Cheops, whilst Flinders Petrie was dismayed by the difficulties involved in trying to determine the true ownership of a large body of work dedicated to these kings. He remarked, for example, that one statue of Shabataka bore "a resemblance to some of the statues of Khafra [Chephren]."[72] He could not, of course, explain this; though he recorded one opinion frequently expressed by archaeologists that "such statues of Khafra are all of late date."[73] One much-discussed example of this tendency is a battle-scene in one of Tirhaka's temples depicting a campaign against the Libyans. In every way this scene is identical to one of Sahura (Dyn. 5), and the accompanying inscription repeated that of Sahura line for line, even down to the names of the wife and sons of the enemy Libyan chief.[74]

If modern scholarship finds it so difficult to tell apart the work of the Pyramid Age and the Twenty-Fifth Dynasty, it is little wonder that Herodotus's informants had the same problem. An "Ethiopian" dynasty, the Fifth, did indeed

---

70 Artefacts bearing the name Bakare, or Wakare, have actually been discovered in Greece and southern Italy. However, because these (a scarab and a situla) occur in a Late Geometric (c.700 BC.) context, it is assumed they belong to Bocchoris (Bokenranef) of the 24th Dynasty. See N.J. *Coldstream Greek Geometric Pottery* (London, 1968) pp.316-7

71 F. Petrie, *A History of Egypt* Vol.1 (1894) p.80

72 Ibid.

73 Ibid.

74 C. Aldred, *Egypt to the End of the Old Kingdom* (London, 1965) p.102

immediately follow the line of Cheops and Chephren, but since their names and monuments were so closely copied by the Twenty-Fifth Dynasty, it is obvious that even by the Father of History's time some Egyptian scribes had the two thoroughly confused.

There was one other factor or element contributing to the confusion. The original successors to Cheops's line, the kings of the Fifth Dynasty, had been faced by an invasion from Asia, an invasion by a people known to the Egyptians as Hyksos, "Shepherd Kings", but also understood, as we shall see, to be Assyrians. Yet the Ethiopians of the Twenty-Fifth Dynasty also faced invaders from Asia, and these too bore apparently Assyrian names. One of these, Sennacherib, is actually mentioned by Herodotus. Yet, as I have demonstrated elsewhere, these enemies of the Twenty-Fifth Dynasty were not Assyrians but Persians, and their Ethiopian opponents, Shabaka and Tirhaka, lived not in the 8th and 7th centuries, but in the 6th and 5th.[75]

As a semi-Egyptian dynasty claiming descent off the mighty pharaohs of the past, the Ethiopians saw themselves as defenders of Egypt's heritage, a heritage threatened by the savagery of the Persians in their repeated military incursions into the Nile Valley. Small wonder then the Ethiopians did all they could to revive the culture of Egypt's own classical age.

---

75 In my *Ramessides, Medes and Persians* (New York, 2001)

Chapter 3. When Was the Pyramid Age?

Science and Technology of the Pyramid-Builders

The first two chapters of the present study made two very dramatic assertions about the Egyptian Pyramid Age. First and foremost, the pyramids were inspired by catastrophic events on the earth and the cosmos, events experienced by the whole of humanity. Second, we have asserted that these events occurred at a much more recent age than is normally believed. Indeed, we have claimed that the Pyramid Age should rightly be placed in the 9th and 8th centuries BC, a period of time normally designated as the early Iron Age.

As a corollary to all of this, we have stated that the beginning of the Pyramid Age proper, during the reign of King Sneferu, corresponds precisely with the event known to biblical history as the Exodus, an event placed by us sometime near the middle of the 9th century BC.

If all of this is true, it will be necessary above all to justify our dramatic chronological adjustment in far greater detail. We shall need to show, for example, how the art, culture, science, technology and religion of the Pyramid Age fits into such a recent epoch.

Can this be accomplished?

The methods employed by Egypt's pyramid builders rank among the great mysteries of the ancient world. It is held that colossal monuments such as the pyramids of Cheops (Khufu) and Chephren (Khafre) at Giza were constructed near the middle of the third millennium BC by masons whose only tools were of stone and copper. To erect the pyramids, blocks of granite and limestone were carved to size with mathematical precision; the angles and surfaces of the stones so true that not even a penknife blade can be inserted between them. Modern artisans, no matter how skilled, would certainly be incapable of such a feat without the aid of good-quality steel tools.

Investigation of the pyramids increases, rather than decreases, our admiration for the builders. These massive structures are aligned precisely with the cardinal points of the compass (or at least those from the Fourth Dynasty onwards are), displaying only an infinitesimal margin of error. So impressed were early archaeologists by these structures that they openly questioned whether they should be assigned to a remote antiquity at all. These men were struck by certain modern-looking features in the pyramids, pyramid-temples and artwork in general of the age. The arch, for example, which had not been used in Greece until the 7th century BC, was already being regularly employed in the temples and tombs of the pyramid-builders.[76] Because of such things many were inclined to believe that not all the work attributed to the "Old Kingdom" was genuine, and that the monuments of the time had been extensively renovated, and indeed modified, during the 8th and 7th centuries BC. Flinders Petrie noted these points, but rejected the idea because, "Not a hieroglyph, not a graffito, can be seen anywhere associated with these supposed reconstructions."[77] Thus these monuments were not reconstructions, though their general design looked in many ways incredibly modern.

Yet the techniques of modern surveying have revealed a science and technology in use by the pyramid-builders which seems truly astonishing. Thus according to Peter Tompkins, whose *Secrets of the Great Pyramid* is one of the most authoritative works to date, the builders of Cheops's monuments knew the value of π, the circumference of the earth, and the length of the year down to its 0.2422 fraction of a day.[78] Tompkins, as scientific a scholar as may be imagined, reached conclusions that were truly startling. The central burial chamber, for example, is said by him to have "incorporated the 'sacred' 3-4-5 and 2-5-3 triangles (a + b = c) which were to make Pythagoras famous, and which Plato in his *Timaeus* claimed as the building-blocks of the cosmos."[79]

Other writers, less rigorous than Tompkins (and there are many of them), have gone much further; and claims are regularly made that the design of the

76 F. Petrie, *Egyptian Architecture* (London, 1938) pp.71-2

77 F. Petrie, *A History of Egypt* Vol.1 (1894) p.60

78 P. Tompkins, *Secrets of the Great Pyramid* (London, 1977)

79 Ibid.

Great Pyramid is full of esoteric religious significance. "Decoding" the pyramids, especially the Great Pyramid, has now in fact become one of modern man's perennial hobbies. Some see Cheops's monument as a gigantic coded document, whose dimensions contain clues to a hidden or lost science. Although a modern obsession, such notions can in fact be traced to the medieval period, when a number of Arab treatises on the subject spoke of hidden chambers, wherein were to be found books on alchemy, science and magic.[80] But contemporary writers have gone much further, and it has even been claimed that the entire future of the earth is incorporated into the design of the pyramid. Whilst all such suggestions can be safely ignored, there is no doubt that the builders of the Great Pyramid did intend that the monument should serve some esoteric function. For example, it has now been established beyond reasonable doubt that no one was ever buried in the monument. Indeed, it is doubtful if a single intact body has ever been discovered in any pyramid. In most of them, it is true, there is an impressive sarcophagus; but invariably it is empty. In some cases the sarcophagi were discovered closed and sealed, untouched since they were deposited there in antiquity — but still empty.

The burial chamber of the Great Pyramid was apparently first located by Caliph Al Mamun in AD 820. After a number of false starts, Mamun's workmen discovered the famous Ascending Passage leading to the burial chamber. The passage was blocked by a number of granite plugs, each two meters long and wedged tightly into the positions they had been set by the builders many centuries before. The workmen could only proceed by tunnelling around these iron-hard barriers. When the Caliph's men reached the burial-chamber they found that the tightly-jointed blocks of granite comprising the walls, floor and roof were totally undisturbed. But the sarcophagus was empty and the lid was missing.

The sarcophagus itself was problematic, for it was too short to accommodate a man of average height. This, together with the testimony of al Mamun's men, makes it a virtual certainty that Cheops was never interred in the pyramid. The only possible way by which tomb robbers could have entered the so-called King's Chamber (with its undersize sarcophagus) is through a largely perpendicular passage cut between the lower end of the great Ascending Passage and the descending shaft which formed the main entrance to the monument. But this passage is extremely narrow and largely vertical, and would certainly have been too small for the conduit of the large treasure objects which surely must have accompanied Cheops to his tomb. These would need to have been cut in small pieces, an operation which would unquestionably have left traces of gold and silver throughout the pyramid. Yet though the monument has been examined in a

---

80 See e.g. L. Cottrell *The Mountains of Pharaoh* (London, 1956) pp.61-73

way that would do any forensic detective proud, no trace of any of these treasures has ever been detected.

In antiquity, Diodorus of Sicily left an interesting account of the Great Pyramid, accurately recording that Cheops was never buried there, and offering his own explanation as to why:

> Though the two kings [Cheops and Chephren] built the pyramids to serve as their tombs, in the event neither of them was buried in them; for the multitudes, because of the hardships which they had endured in the building of them and the many cruel and violent acts of these kings, were filled with anger against those who had caused their sufferings and openly threatened to tear their bodies asunder and cast them in despite out of their tombs. Consequently each ruler when dying enjoined upon his kinsmen to bury his body secretly in an unmarked place.[81]

This explanation is indeed a plausible one, and leaves open the fascinating possibility that Cheops's real tomb may still be awaiting discovery. It is perhaps of interest to note that in Herodotus's testimony Cheops was buried in a subterranean chamber underneath the pyramid. This chamber, partly filled with Nile water, had in its midst a small island; and on this island Cheops was said to lie.[82] Since the whole of the Great Pyramid and the rock beneath has been exhaustively searched and surveyed, it is unlikely that Cheops's resting place could be there. It is much more probable that "underneath" the pyramid refers to somewhere not too far distant from the foot of the structure. I would suggest, as a very rough guess, that Cheops's resting place be sought in a subterranean chamber somewhere in the vicinity of the monument — probably no more than a couple of hundred meters' distance.

Wherever he may lie, it is clear that Cheops was not interred in the so-called "burial chamber" of the pyramid, and we must look with renewed respect upon the testimony of Diodorus. However, Diodorus's suggestion fails to confront one problem: if the Great Pyramid had originally been intended as a tomb, why did Chephren not secure his father's (or brother's?) burial in it? And why did he too build an equally enormous and equally redundant "tomb", knowing full well that it would never be used?

The meaning and purpose of the pyramids has already been touched upon and will be further discussed as we proceed. For the moment however all we need stress is that the conventional explanation, offered in all the reputable textbooks, that these were simply the tombs, the "houses of eternity" of a few megalomaniac kings, simply does not stand up to scrutiny. The monumental effort and technological expertise that went into raising these structures was not simply to satisfy

---

81 Diodorus Siculus, i,64, 3-4

82 Herodotus, ii, 124

the inflated egos of a dynasty of men who thought they were gods. Some other explanation is called for.

Yet the question of how the pyramids were built remains almost as intractable as the why. The astonishing technological and scientific knowledge of the architects and masons has prompted the question, asked over the years again and again: How could craftsmen of the third millennium BC have accomplished such feats? How could architects of the third millennium employ a geometry hardly less advanced than that of Pythagoras; and how could artisans of the same period carve iron-hard granite with copper tools? Yet, though these questions are valid, there is nevertheless an element of rhetoric in them; an element of mystification for its own sake; for serious students of Egyptology have long been aware that the Egyptians of the Pyramid Age made extensive use of iron. An iron plate, for example, was found by the 19th century explorer Vyse deep in the masonry of the Great Pyramid.[83]

If indeed chronology were to be based solely on technological achievement, we would be forced to place the pyramid-building pharaohs firmly within the Iron Age, or at least the early part of it; say in the 9th or 8th century BC. The pyramid-builders were well-acquainted with iron and references to the material are common in the literature of the period. The Pyramid Texts, for example, credit the four children of Horus with having "fingers of iron", whilst the Duat (Heaven) had gates of iron, and in the Duat Osiris sat on a throne of iron. Yet there was much more than a literary acquaintance with the metal. A greater quantity of iron has been found associated with the pyramid-builders of the Fourth, Fifth and Sixth Dynasties than with almost any other period of Egyptian history! For example, several iron chisels and other tools dated to Dynasty 5 were discovered at Sakkara,[84] whilst from Dynasty 6 a pickaxe was discovered at Abusir,[85] as well as a collection of broken tools of the same period unearthed at Dahshur.[86] If these strange finds are considered at all (and usually they are not), they are generally dismissed as an historic anomaly: tools made of meteoric iron and not smelted from ore. However, whilst some of the above implements certainly did contain traces of nickel, and were therefore made of meteoric metal (which explains the religious associations), not all of them did. Thus there is no doubt that some at least were made of iron smelted from ore, and are true products of an Iron Age.[87]

---

83 R.W.H. Vyse, *Operations Carried on at the Pyramids of Gizeh in 1837* (London, 1840-1842) This plate contained "traces of nickel" and its metal was therefore probably meteoric in origin.

84 O. Olshausen, *Zeitschrift für Ethnologie* (1907) p.373

85 Discovered by Maspero. Cited from Velikovsky, *Ramses II and His Time* (1978) p.226

86 Ibid.

87 Ibid. p.227

Discoveries such as these so confused Egyptologists that two were moved to pronounce that in Egypt, "the Iron Age may yet be proved to have even preceded the Bronze Age."[88]

If it were only metallurgy we were dealing with, it would be serious enough; yet the evidence from a whole host of other technologies points in exactly the same direction. The pyramid-builders, for example, had knowledge of pottery and glassmaking techniques which they should not have possessed, knowledge which scholars would not have expected before the first millennium BC. Thus in his *Minerals, Metals, Glazing, and Man*, the mineralogist John Dayton remarked on the advanced glazing techniques employed by the pyramid-builders. Certain colors of glaze, for example, which could not have been known before the Late Bronze Age, were already being employed during the Pyramid Age. In the tomb of queen Hetepheres, the mother of Cheops, Dayton noted the occurrence of, "Tiny ring beads in blue, black, red and yellow" which are among the "mysteries of archaeology". According to Dayton, "If these [beads] were of faience, the tomb must date to the XVIIIth [18th] Dynasty."[89] Again, Dayton remarked on how certain colors of glaze found in Sixth Dynasty pottery could not have been developed much before the Eighteenth Dynasty.[90]

So it appears that not only were the pyramid-builders employing mathematics two thousand years ahead of their time, they also had a knowledge of metallurgy and glazing techniques in advance of their time by the same stretch. Indeed, the magnitude of the problem is only seen when we realize that during the two millennia which according to conventional ideas separate the Pyramid Age from the Iron Age, most or all of this impressive technological knowledge was lost — only to be rediscovered as Egypt moved towards the Iron Age.

PHOENICIA AND EGYPT DURING THE PYRAMID AGE

During the Pyramid Age the Egyptians performed numerous feats that could not have been performed in the third millennium BC, but certainly could have been performed in the first. They made long and frequent sea voyages, for example. An official of Dynasty 6 casually remarked that he had visited Punt and Byblos eleven times.[91] Similarly, Egyptian artifacts of the Pyramid Age are frequently discovered at immense distances from their place of origin. Thus for example two hoards of treasures, of Fifth Dynasty age (one of which mysteriously

88 H. Garland and C. O. Bannister, *Ancient Egyptian Metallurgy* (London, 1927) p.5

89 J. Dayton, *Minerals, Metals, Glazing, and Man* (London, 1978) p.84

90 Ibid. p.33

91 J.H. Breasted, *Ancient Records of Egypt* Vol.1

disappeared), are said to have originated in far-off Anatolia, whilst an inscribed cup with the name of the sun temple of Userkaf (Dynasty 5) was found on the island of Cythera, off the coast of the Peloponnese in Greece; "how this small object could have travelled so far poses a problem," says W.C. Hayes.[92]

Other evidence of contacts with the Aegean are even more problematic. For example, a scarab of King Cheops was discovered in a Greek Geometric (9th/8th century) context at Camirus in Rhodes. As with most of such discoveries, it was dismissed as a late copy.[93] The vase of the sun-temple of Userkaf was found along with Mycenaean-style artifacts; whilst in Egypt Mycenaean vases were discovered in a tomb dating from the time of Niuserre (also Dynasty 5).[94] Even more disturbing, Pyramid Age material was found along with Greek remains of the 7th century BC — a fact that astonished early Egyptologists.[95]

But that was not all. In later times the term *Haunebut* (or *Hanebu*) was used by the Egyptians when referring to the peoples of the Aegean — and was particularly applied — (as for example in Ptolemaic texts) to the Greeks. We can imagine scholars' astonishment then when they found the word in the Pyramid Texts and upon inscriptions of Cheops and Sahura.[96] In explanation it was suggested that during the third millennium BC the term Haunebut must have been used to denote peoples other than the Greeks and Cretans; this in spite of the discoveries mentioned above.

Not too many years ago archaeologists discovered the remains of a great ship in a rock-cut chamber just to the east of Cheops's pyramid. The fully-restored vessel now stands in its own mini-museum on the spot where it had lain for so many centuries. Cheops's magnificent Ship of the Sun, along with the subsequently-discovered Ship of the Moon, on the other side of the pyramid, brought scholars face to face, for the first time, with the seafaring prowess of the pyramid-builders. Both ships were fashioned with masterful skill from planks of Lebanese cedar, and it is clear that they were designed for voyages on the open sea.

---

92 W. Stevenson Smith, "The Old Kingdom in Egypt and the Beginning of the First Intermediate Period" in *CAH* Vol.1 part 2 (3rd ed.) p.180

93 See *Revue Archéologique* (1863) Vol.8 p.2

94 C.R. Lepsius, "Saqqarah" *Denkmäler aus Aegypten und Aethiopien* (Leipzig, 1897) pt.2 plates 60-64. The Greek connection is of great importance. The Mycenaean Age, as we shall demonstrate, was actually contemporary with the Geometric, which explains the fact that Old Kingdom material is found associated with both periods.

95 F. Petrie, *A History of Egypt* Vol.1 (1894) pp.62-3 "in the 26th Dynasty his name [Menkuhor's] is common on scarabs, cylinders and plaques, found — and probably made — at Naukratis, Marathus and elsewhere."

96 W. Stevenson Smith, "The Old Kingdom in Egypt and the Beginning of the First Intermediate Period" in *CAH* Vol.1 part 2 (3rd ed.) p.181

Thus Cheops's ships dramatically confirmed what historians had suspected for many years: that the Egyptians of the Pyramid Age were accomplished seamen who made frequent visits to the Phoenician coast. Throughout Syria, but particularly in the coastal cities of ancient Phoenicia, scarabs and other artifacts belonging to the pyramid-builders are found in some abundance. So close indeed were their ties to Phoenicia that the Egyptian term for a seagoing ship at the time was actually "Byblos-boat" (*kbnwt*).[97] To emphasize the point, a monument of Unas (Dynasty 5) on Elephantine Island shows bearded Asiatics on board large seagoing vessels;[98] whilst a monument of Sahura, from the same epoch, shows Egyptian and Asiatic sailors aboard the same ships.[99] Although not stated explicitly, it is generally admitted that these men hail from Phoenicia; and they in fact serve to confirm a number of inscriptions in which Sahura speaks of close relations with the Syrian and Palestinian states. The pharaoh speaks of frequently friendly trips to "God's Land" (*Ta Netjer*, recognized as located in Syria-Palestine), from where he obtained an abundance of fragrant gums and resins. But the contact was established right at the beginning of the Pyramid Age. The annals of King Sneferu record the bringing to Egypt of forty ship-loads of cedar from Lebanon.[100]

Yet the problems raised by these facts are enormous. It is generally recognized that the Phoenicians (if their own records and histories are anything to go by) did not become a great seafaring nation until the start of the first millennium BC. Phoenician seamen could not have sailed Egyptian ships in the third millennium; but they could have, and did, navigate Egyptian ships from the 9th century onwards.

At a later stage we shall see how evidence, even more damning to conventional chronology, suggests that by the Pyramid Age sailors from Egypt and the Phoenician coast were in apparently regular contact with the western Mediterranean and the British Isles, from which region, by the Sixth Dynasty at least, they were securing tin for the production of bronze.

RELIGION OF THE PYRAMID AGE

We know a great deal about the religion of the pyramid-builders, due primarily to the fact that they inscribed much of their sacred literature on the passageways and burial-chambers of the monuments. These Pyramid Texts have revealed an astonishingly high level of moral development. In many ways they

---

97 Margaret S. Drower "Syria Before 2200 BC." in *CAH* Vol.1 part 2 (3rd ed.) p.348

98 W.C. Hayes, loc. cit. p.198

99 J.H. Breasted, *A History of Egypt* (London, 1951) p.126

100 W. Stevenson Smith, loc. cit. p.167

mirror the thinking of the Old Testament Hebrew prophets, and at times they verge on monotheism. But the religion of the Pyramid Texts has much more in common with that great and ill-fated Egyptian experiment in monotheism, the Aton faith of Amenhotep IV (Akhnaton).

The Pyramid Texts show us that the kings of the age were great devotees of an apparently solar deity named Atum. In the Pyramid Texts Atum is the principal, even the supreme god: he is the "One Alone", who "brought himself into being." According to Breasted: "The supremacy of the Solar theology, even in the Memphite system, is ... discernible in the inevitable admission of the fact that Atum the sun-god was the actual immediate creator of the world."[101] In the Pyramid Texts there are hymns composed to Atum which remind us strongly of those composed by Akhnaton to the Aton, supposedly a thousand years later. One of these reads:

> Hail to thee, O Atum.
> Hail to thee, O Kheprer, who brought himself into being.
> Thou art high, in this thy name of High One.
> Thou comest into being, in this thy name of
> Kheprer, He-Who-Comes-Into-Being
> O Atum-Kheprer, thou didst spit out that what was
> Shu, thou didst spurt out that what was Tefnut.
> Thou didst put thine arms around them as the arms of a
> Divine Essence, that thy Divine Essence might be in them.
> O great Enneas which is in Ionu:
> Whom Atum begot, his heart is joyful in that which
> he has begotten, in your name of Nine Bows.[102]

Most of the surviving Pyramid Texts date from the Sixth Dynasty, so the majority of the literature is associated with these kings. One text of Teti, first pharaoh of Dynasty 6, reads: "King Teti is Shu who came forth from Atum." In another text Teti is identified with Atum limb by limb, or with Atum and the celestial gods, who are also identified with Atum (as seen above).[103] Throughout the Sixth Dynasty there was apparently no diminishing of devotion to the sun-god. From the time of Merenre I, for example, we read: "O Atum, put thou thy arms behind King Merenre, behind this building, and behind this pyramid, as a ka-arm, that the ka of King Merenre may be in it enduring for ever and ever. Ho Atum! Protect thou this king Merenre, this his pyramid and this building of king Merenre."[104] The mention of Atum's arms calls to mind an inscription from the time of Unas (Dynasty 5), which reads, "The arm of the sunbeams is lifted with

---

101 J.H. Breasted, *The Development of Religion and Thought in Ancient Egypt* (London, 1912) p.44

102 Ibid. Pyramid Text 603

103 Ibid. Pyramid Text 600

104 Ibid.

king Unas."[105] Scholars have repeatedly been drawn to compare this concept of arms emanating from the sun with Akhnaton's very similar ideas.

The above evidence, added to the other material already examined, would suggest that the Late Bronze Age, the epoch of the New Kingdom and the monotheist Akhnaton, should be placed very close to the Pyramid Age, and that the seven or eight centuries separating the two epochs in the textbooks are illusory. The cult of the sun-god Atum, it would seem, was closely related to the cult of Akhnaton's sun-disc, the Aton. Yet such an attempt to associate these two aspects of the solar god may draw objections. Surely, it will be said, the Aton cult, as practiced by Akhnaton, bore little relationship to the cult of Atum. It may also be protested that the names of these deities, which sound and look so similar in English, have entirely different spellings and meanings in the Egyptian. All of which, of course, is valid and partly correct; but the real strength of these objections lies in the chronology and they would collapse if the true timescale demanded no more than a century or so between the Pyramid Age and Akhnaton. Tutankhamun, who succeeded Akhnaton, devoted a number of inscriptions to Atum, as did Ay.[106] *The Great Hymn to Amon*, dated to the time of Tutankhamun or Horemheb, mentions both Amon and Ra-Atum, and "contains evident echoes of the Aton faith."[107] The prayer however also reminds us strongly of those of the Pyramid Texts, and names Atum as the creator of mankind.

As might be expected, the close similarities between Akhnaton's sun-worship and that of the Old Kingdom have not gone unnoticed by scholars, one of whom was moved to remark that "when Ikhnaton [Akhnaton], the world's first monotheist, came to the throne he emphasized the connections between his new sun worship and the old sun cult at Heliopolis. In fact he built his sun temples on the same lines as the 5th dynasty temples at Abu Sir. And the symbol of his god, the Aten, was reminiscent of the description of the Sun-god in the 5th dynasty Pyramid Texts: 'The arm of the sun beams.'"[108]

It would appear that Akhnaton, in rejecting the gods and culture of Imperial Egypt, was involved in a deliberate attempt to recreate the religion and cult of an epoch he regarded as morally superior to his own. Akhnaton ended the custom of human sacrifice and made real attempts, in some areas, to bring about a moral and spiritual rebirth. In this crusade, why, we might ask, should he look for inspiration to the pyramid-builders? The answer is no mystery: the Pyramid Age

105 Breasted, op. cit.

106 Christiane Desroches-Noblecourt, *Tutankhamun* (London, 1963) p.181

107 Breasted loc. cit.

108 Jill Kamil, *The Ancient Egyptians: How they Lived and Worked* (1976) p.9

was an epoch celebrated amongst later Egyptians for its high moral and ethical standards.

The first great pharaoh of the Pyramid Age, Sneferu, was regarded by later generations as a paragon of virtue and his reign a veritable Golden Age. His son Cheops, however, was accused of closing the nation's temples, an act which, we shall demonstrate, signifies the launch in his epoch of a cultural and religious revolution, a revolution which involved the definitive end to the custom of blood and (more particularly) human sacrifice. Temples, in ancient times, were essentially little more than sacred slaughter-houses, where victims were immolated on a high-place (altar), and their lives offered to the sky-gods in expiation of the community's misdeeds. Even the use of incense (to disguise the stench of putrefaction) dates from this far-off epoch. The Pyramid Age in Egypt saw a dramatic movement away from these barbarous ideas. According to Breasted, the period saw the first "emergence of the moral sense." The Pyramid Texts of Dynasties 5 and 6 display a "keen moral discernment."[109] Seers, sages and philosopher kings were active throughout the period. For example the wisdom of Ptahotep, the vizier of Isesi, was celebrated in later ages. Books on the wisdom of Ptahotep were read by commoners and kings. A "respect for moral ideas in high places" is recognized in the Horus-name of Userkaf (Dynasty 5), who called himself Doer-of-Righteousness."[110] A Nomarch of the period wrote:

> I gave bread to all the hungry of the Cerastes-Mountain (his domain); I clothed him who was naked therein.... I filled its shores with large cattle and its [lowlands] with small cattle. I satisfied the wolves of the mountain and the fowl of the sky with the [flesh] of small cattle. I never oppressed one on possession of his property so that he complained of me because of it to the god of my city; [but] I spake and told that which was good. I was a benefactor to it (his domain) in the folds of the cattle, in the settlements of the fowlers.... I speak no lie, for I was one beloved of his father, praised by his mother, excellent in character to his brother, and amiable to his sister.[111]

Such talk is all very reminiscent of the better-known utterances of the Hebrew prophets. But even commoners of the Pyramid Age expressed themselves in moral terms: "Never did I do anything evil towards any person," says the chief physician of king Sahura.[112] Breasted spoke in glowing terms of the general spiritual and intellectual achievements of the epoch: "The development of moral discernment,"

---

109 Breasted loc. cit. p.166
110 Ibid. p.167
111 Ibid. p.168
112 Ibid.

he said, "had indeed gone so far in the Pyramid Age that the thought of the age was dealing with the origin of good and evil, the source of human traits."[113]

One of the most striking features of the Pyramid Age is the fact that the concept of reward and punishment in the afterlife was already fully developed. "Throughout his life ... he [the Egyptian] looked forward to standing in that dread presence to answer for the ethical quality of his conduct. As the earliest evidence of moral responsibility beyond the tomb, such utterances in the cemeteries of the Pyramid Age, nearly five thousand years ago, are not a little impressive. In other lands, for over two thousand years after this, good and bad alike were consigned to the same realm of the dead, and no distinction whatever was made between them."[114] Now the idea of reward and punishment in the afterlife is the mark of all the higher religions, and even the Hebrews possessed no such concept until they received it from the Zoroastrians of Persia in the 5th century BC. Even in the time of Christ the theory had by no means triumphed, and those who held by it were termed Pharisees, a name which may simply mean "Persians". Breasted marvelled that the Egyptians should have come up with such an idea at so early a stage. "It is," he said, "as it were, an isolated moral vista down which we look, penetrating the early gloom as a shaft of sunshine penetrates the darkness."[115]

But the moral achievement of the Egyptians, whilst still impressive, is at least understandable, if the Pyramid Age — along with its seers and prophets — belongs to the early first millennium BC and not the third.

BIBLICAL PARALLELS

When in the year 1821 news of Champollion's success in reading the hieroglyphs first broke, there was widespread hope and expectation that dramatic new light was about to be shed on the Bible. It was believed that many of the questions long perplexing biblical scholars were soon to be answered. Perhaps we might find Egyptian corroboration of Old Testament history. The name of the pharaoh of Abraham, as well as that of Joseph and the Oppressor of Moses, would perchance shortly be revealed.

But alas, nothing of the sort happened. Search as they might for even a passing mention of these great figures, scholars drew only a blank. Not, apparently, a single reference. Yet in the hieroglyphic documents the Egyptologists did indeed find allusions to events that seemed to concur remarkably well with many of those described in the Bible. In particular, a whole body of documents, soon to

---

113 Ibid. p.166
114 Ibid. p.170
115 Ibid.

be termed the "Pessimistic Literature", recorded events that apparently echoed in a remarkable way the disastrous happenings of the Exodus, when the Bible said that Egypt had been struck by ten devastating plagues. But there was a problem; the events described in the Pessimistic treatises (e.g. in the Lamentations of Ipuwer and the Prophecy of Neferty), it was said, could not possibly refer to those described in the Book of Exodus because the experts on chronology had already decreed that the Pessimistic works were written centuries before the departure of the Israelites from Egypt.

So even this possible link between the two histories had to be abandoned.

We hope to demonstrate here that once again a faulty chronology is to blame. As with other mysteries and puzzles in Egyptian history, so it is with Egypt's relationship with the land and people of Israel. There are in fact abundant meeting points between the two histories, but they have been missed because of the erroneous chronology. Historians, essentially, have been looking in the wrong places. The disasters described in the Pessimistic Texts really do describe the disasters of the Exodus, and the centuries believed to separate the two are illusory.

Even though they failed to identify the events and characters of the Bible in the hieroglyphs, scholars were nevertheless astonished to find remarkable parallels between the literature of the Old Testament and that of the Egyptians. Their astonishment was increased by the fact that many centuries were believed to separate the two. Prayers, prophecies, instructions and decrees from Egypt, said by their translators to date from the middle of the third to the middle of the second millennia BC, nevertheless showed striking similarities with the works of the Hebrew prophets and chroniclers of the 8th, 7th and 6th centuries BC. Often idioms, metaphors, words and phrases provided identical matches in the two sets of literatures, supposedly separated from each other by over a thousand years.

Even the hope of a coming messiah or savior, it appears, was not unique to the Jews, but had its parallel or possibly origin amongst the Egyptians of the early second millennium BC. As we have seen, the famous prophecy of the Egyptian priest Neferty, generally dated to the end of the Old Kingdom, around 2000 BC, looks forward to a coming royal savior named Ameny, who would overcome Egypt's enemies and establish justice and peace. Scholars have long been astonished by the way Neferty's Messianic utterings are almost structurally identical to the Messianic prophecies of 7th and 6th century Hebrew writers. The parallels are closest perhaps with the work of Amos. Neferty for example begins:

> What was spoken by the Lector Neferty, that wise man
> of the East, who belongs to Ubast in her rising ... as he was
> brooding over what should come to pass in the land ...
> Compare this with the open words of Amos,

> The words of Amos, who was among the herdsmen of Thecua ... which
> he saw concerning Israel in the days of Uzziah king of Judah ...

From his opening preamble, Neferty proceeds to warn of coming danger from Egypt's enemies; "when the Asiatics," he says, "approach in their might and their hearts rage against those who are bringing in the harvest." In the same way, after the opening, Amos warns of the coming danger from Israel's enemies: "The Lord sent word to Jacob, and it hath lighted upon Israel.... The bricks are fallen down.... And the Lord shall set up the enemies of Rasin over him, and he shall bring on his enemies in a crowd, the Syrians from the east, and the Philistines from the west: and they shall devour Israel with open mouth."

Not only would Egypt, according to Neferty, and Israel, according to Amos, be oppressed by foreign enemies, but the land would also be devastated by the forces of nature. Neferty refers to how "Ra, the sun, removes himself from men.... None knoweth that midday is there; his shadow is not discerned," whilst Amos predicts that "it shall come to pass in that day, saith the Lord God, that the sun shall go down at midday, and I will make the earth dark in the day of light."

From this point both writers proceed to explain how, at the country's darkest hour, a royal savior, born of the noblest family in the land, will arise to oust the invaders and deliver the people.

Such striking agreement between the two literatures has caused no end of debate, and whole volumes have been devoted to the topic. Yet because the Egyptian material is still believed to have been composed over a thousand years before the Hebrew, the full significance of these parallels is not understood. Thus for example T. Eric Peet commented:

> Though the original utterances of the Hebrew prophets must have been fundamentally different in form and purpose from the complaints of Ipuwer and Neferrohu [Neferty], yet the Biblical books in which these utterances are preserved have much in common with the Egyptian compositions.[116]

In the *Instruction for Merikare*, which, like Ipuwer and Neferty is supposed to date from sometime near the fall of the Old Kingdom, Peet found other precise parallels with Hebrew prophetic work. "In reading this combination of political advice and exhortations to righteousness it is impossible not to be reminded of the Hebrew prophets, whose writings form such an important part of the Old Testament."[117] Though in Peet's opinion the writer of the Instruction could not have been a "true" prophet, nevertheless, "the superficial resemblance between the Instruction for Merikere and the Book of Amos, for instance, is one which

116 T. Eric Peet, *A Comparative Study of the Literatures of Egypt, Palestine and Mesopotamia* (London, 1931) p.122
117 Ibid. pp.108-9

cannot fail to strike the reader, and there is an astonishing parallel between the incomplete monotheism of Amos and that of the Instruction."[118]

An entire volume could be devoted to enumerating the various links between the two bodies of literature, but the sample presented above should serve to illustrate the point. It seems fairly clear therefore that the apocalyptic/messianic literature of 8th/7th century Israel and Judah was merely part of a *genre* common throughout the Near East and perhaps even further afield, between the 8th and 6th centuries BC. The prophets named above — Amos, Isaiah and Hosea — actually belong not to the 8th but to the 6th century BC. Nevertheless, their messianic and apocalyptic utterances are in direct line of descent from those of Moses, a prophet normally placed in the 15th or 14th century BC, but actually belonging to the 9th/8th century. The previous chapter has already touched on some evidence linking the Israelite Exodus with the cosmic events described in the Pyramid Texts and the Pessimistic treatises; and this theme shall be illuminated further at a later stage. Suffice for the moment to say that it was Moses, with his talk of a Promised Land, a land flowing with milk and honey, who set the tone for the messianic writings of the later prophets. These men however were not removed from Moses by six or seven centuries, as is supposed, but by one or two. They were removed from the Pessimistic writers of Egypt by the same margin.

As we proceed through our investigation we shall find ourselves being drawn again and again to compare the culture of 8th–6th century Israel with that of Pyramid Age Egypt. Again and again the names of the prophets, from Moses down to Isaiah and Amos, will figure in our deliberations.

ECHOES OF THE OLD KINGDOM

From what has been said in the present chapter, it should be clear that the art, architecture, religion and culture in general of the Pyramid Age, the Egyptian Old Kingdom, did not differ radically from that of the New and, as we saw, many strange echoes of Old Kingdom custom and usage persisted into the New Kingdom and Late Period. Indeed, cultural features of the Old Kingdom which were supposedly dead and buried for almost two millennia make startling and altogether incomprehensible reappearances in the epochs of the New and Late Kingdoms.

Thus it was with the custom of pyramid-building itself.

It is generally believed, and so it is stated in publication after publication, that the art of pyramid-building declined at the end of the Sixth Dynasty, and came to a complete halt at the end of the Twelfth Dynasty — generally dated to

---

118 Ibid. p.109

around 1800 BC. Yet nothing could be further from the truth. Pharaoh Ahmose, who expelled the Hyksos and founded the New Kingdom, left a fairly impressive pyramid at Abydos, the ruins of which can be seen to this day:[119] Nor did the fashion for pyramid-erection end with the Eighteenth Dynasty. A series of smallish pyramids at Memphis were erected as part of the mortuary temples of Nineteenth Dynasty court dignitaries,[120] whilst to the south of Egypt, in Nubia and the Sudan, pyramids continued to be erected as late as the 4th century AD!

Indeed, a whole host of evidence combines to suggest that the New Kingdom was separated from the Old by no great stretch of time, and that little more than a few decades, at most, come between them. In many respects the art and architecture of the Old Kingdom anticipates, and shows striking parallels with that of the New. As a matter of fact, the most striking parallels are to be found between the work of the last Old Kingdom Dynasty, the Sixth, and the first dynasty of the New Kingdom, the Eighteenth; parallels so precise as to make us wonder whether these two should be placed together, with the Eighteenth Dynasty immediately following the Sixth. In this regard we may cite a kneeling statue of Pepi I (Dynasty 6), whose posture and appearance are very reminiscent of Eighteenth Dynasty works — most famously perhaps that of Hatshepsut and Thutmose III.

The burial customs of the Sixth Dynasty, it would appear, were also strikingly similar to those of the Eighteenth, a fact noted by the great anatomist Elliott Smith,[121] whilst cult practices and religion in general tells a similar tale.

We shall have more to say about these Sixth/Eighteenth Dynasty parallels at a later stage, when we come to establish an exact chronology for the epoch.

Whilst the art and architecture of the New Kingdom contains strange echoes of the Old, so the work of the Old Kingdom prefigured that of the New. As mentioned above, features such as the arch and Pythagorean geometry make a lot of Old Kingdom architecture look very modern. Such "modernity" also extends to art styles. Most spectacular in this category is the well-known stele of Menkuhor (Dynasty 5) from Sakkara. Maspero and others were alarmed by this piece, which was apparently executed in an advanced New Kingdom style. Accordingly it was dismissed as yet another anomaly; yet another New Kingdom reworking of an Old Kingdom original.

The evidence would therefore place the Old and New Kingdoms extremely close to each other, and not separated by the so-called Middle Kingdom which, according to the prevailing dogma, separates these two and endured for some six

119 Margaret A. Murray, *Egyptian Temples* (Sampson Low, Maston and Co.) p.4; also I.E.S Edwards *The Pyramids of Egypt* p.244

120 Geoffrey T. Martin, *The Hidden Tombs of Memphis* (London, 1991) pp.112-3

121 J. Elliott Smith, *American Journal of Archaeology* Vol.1 p.193

centuries. There are actually good grounds for believing what we call the Middle Kingdom ran simultaneously with the last of the Pyramid Age dynasties, the Sixth, and the first of the New Kingdom dynasties, the Eighteenth. Again, this is demonstrated by strange artistic echoes over what is generally supposed to be many centuries.

The great temple of Queen Hatshepsut (Eighteenth Dynasty) at Deir El Bahri is one of the most celebrated of Egyptian monuments. Its pleasing design and layout makes it a recognized architectural masterpiece. But Hatshepsut's temple closely resembles the adjacent monument of the Middle Kingdom pharaoh Nebhepetre Mentuhotep — supposedly six centuries older. Nebhepetre's temple itself is an architectural enigma. The central feature of the building was originally a substantial pyramid, whilst many other features of the monument closely mimic the work of the Pyramid Age — particularly the early Pyramid Age. Thus for example Nebhepetre's temple included a series of colonnades whose rectilinear shape and lack of decoration find their strongest parallels in the "megalithic" columns of Chephren's funerary temple at Giza. Columns of exactly the same design are also found in the temple of Hatshepsut.

But just as pyramid-erection did not die out in the Eighteenth Dynasty, neither did the fashion for raising these "megalithic" columns. The style was revived yet again during the Nineteenth Dynasty, where the so-called "Osireion" of Seti I at Abydos displays the same feature.[122]

What the evidence clearly tells us then is that the entire sequence of dynasties and "Kingdoms" outlined in countless textbooks and learned journals, together with the chronology within which these are placed, is deeply suspect. Above all, it begins to look very likely that the so-called Old Kingdom was not separated by a six-centuries long Middle Kingdom from the later New Kingdom; and that in all probability the New Kingdom followed on directly from the Old. Yet even the New Kingdom (supposedly commencing in the 16th century BC) is apparently placed far too early in the textbooks; and it would appear that both Old and New Kingdoms belong in the first millennium BC, with the Old Kingdom seemingly ending sometime in the 8th century BC, and the New Kingdom (Eighteenth Dynasty) commencing immediately thereafter.

---

122 I. Woldering, *Egypt: The Art of the Pharaohs* (Baden-Baden, 1963) pp.169-171

Chapter 4. Ancient History in Chaos

How Egyptian Chronology was formulated

The average member of the public with an interest in these things will imagine that the chronology of Egypt provided in all the textbooks must have some firm scientific foundation. That impression is reinforced by the confidence with which the historians quote exact dates for specific pharaohs and their reigns. Yet the fact is that Egyptian chronology has no scientific basis whatsoever; and that the dates provided in modern textbooks and journals are essentially (with only minor alterations) those provided by early Christian scholiasts, who made their calculations via a fundamentalist interpretation of the Old Testament.

Even before the Christian age there were repeated attempts to "tie-in" the history of Egypt with that of the Jews. These two nations were, after all, close neighbors, and, according to the Bible, had interacted in a most intimate way over the centuries. Thus even the Egyptian chronicler Manetho, writing in the 3rd century BC, seemingly felt compelled to establish synchronisms between Egyptian and Jewish histories. It was this endeavor that produced the controversial equation of the Jews with the brutal Hyksos (exploited by Apion), and which led, in turn, to the polemical response from Josephus, in the first century AD. But even in Manetho's own time Jewish scholars used his work to verify the early parts of the Bible. This was a fact noted by Eduard Meyer:

> Unlike his writings on Egyptian religion, the influence of which can be shown in many places in later literature, this historical work [of Manetho] was paid no attention by the Greeks. However, it found all the more response among the Jews, since it was here, in the authentic Egyptian traditions, that they hoped to find evidence of the origins and age of their people.[123]

The Ptolemaic Age saw the triumph of Greek culture and civilization, which in turn produced attempts by Egyptians and Jews to establish the antiquity and venerability of their own civilizations. Thus the Jewish scholars of Alexandria, in the third century BC, were at pains to prove the reliability of their own history, as recorded in the Torah. This was all the more urgent in view of the anti-Jewish prejudice which had arisen, even then, in parts of Egypt. They therefore utilized Manetho to prove their own past. One result of these endeavors was the equation of Menes, the first pharaoh, with Adam, the first man; thus making Egyptian history commence, supposedly, around 3750 BC, the date calculated by the Jewish authorities as the year of creation.[124] The rest of Egyptian history was made to fall in behind this date, with important events from Genesis and Exodus forming key anchor-points. Thus for example the second Ramses, who reigned over sixty years, was identified as the pharaoh of the Exodus, since the biblical story named "Ramesses" as one of the store-cities built by the enslaved Israelites. Ramses II was thus placed roughly between 1400 and 1350 BC.

Biblical-Egyptian tie-ins took on a new significance with the advent of Christianity. Now Egyptian history was to be called upon to support the literal truth of the Old Testament, particularly the Book of Genesis, against the non-Christian Greek and Roman skeptics who viewed Genesis as a fable, little more than the Jewish creation myth. It was with this task in mind that Eusebius (4th century AD) made his extensive commentaries on Manetho's *Aegyptiaca*. Right at the beginning, Eusebius states plainly his belief that Egyptian history offers powerful confirmation for the Sacred Scriptures. Without openly following those Jewish writers who had made Adam and Menes one and the same, it is quite evident that he was following a line of reasoning that would more or less produce the same result: namely, that Egyptian history commenced around 3750 BC.

Incredible as it might seem, this date was still accepted by most Egyptologists until near the start of the 20th century! And even the fact that the figure given in modern textbooks is reduced by a few centuries has little to do with the adoption of any new or alternative system. In fact, the thousand years was

---

123 E. Meyer, *Geschichte des Altertums* Vol.1 (9th ed. Stuttgart, 1952-59)

124 Wolfgang Helck, "Manetho" in *Der kleine Pauly* Vol.3 (Munich, 1979) col 952 In the words of Helck, Jewish scholars before Josephus, "had already amended the early dynasties [of Egypt] in particular, so as to be able to equate Menes with Adam."

subtracted from the date given by the early Jewish and Christian writers largely on the insistence of Flinders Petrie, who argued (and this reveals how haphazard the entire process was) that Egyptian history simply could not provide another half-millennium of dynasties and kings to justify such a date.

The application of biblical chronology to the history of Mesopotamia had an equally unhelpful influence on that region, and added a further major element of confusion.

The problem for the early Egyptologists, and the reason why biblical dates stood unchallenged for so long, was that the Egyptians themselves provided no real help. On the contrary, they, in common with most ancient peoples, were involved in a program of deliberately exaggerating their own antiquity. They encouraged, and probably believed themselves, the view that they were the first of nations, a people with origins lost in the mists of time. In Herodotus's testimony they claimed to count three hundred and forty-five generations of pharaohs since the foundation of the kingdom. According twenty-five years to a generation, this would amount to a history going back 8,625 years before Herodotus — i.e. to around 9000 BC!

The Greeks, it seems, had little reason to doubt these computations, and they were given further authority by Manetho. Manetho's work was lost in antiquity, though from the summaries and fragments preserved in Julius Africanus, Eusebius and Josephus, it is evident that he too claimed an enormous span for the length of his country's history.

Manetho's system of thirty dynasties, which in a garbled and contradictory form has survived through Eusebius and Africanus, is still retained by scholarship, though it is freely admitted that in almost every detail of his history Manetho was wrong. Nevertheless, for almost two thousand years, Manetho's was the only native history of Egypt available to scholarship, and this, combined with the biblical dates supplied by Eusebius and others, produced a chronology whose authority went virtually unchallenged in Christian Europe. The Eusebius-Manetho system became the accepted "traditional" timescale for Egypt, with minor changes and refinements being calculated by such people as the sixteenth century chronographer Joseph Scaliger, and various other Renaissance scholars like Calvisius. So weighty was the authority of Eusebius/Manetho that even after the translation of the hieroglyphs during the 19th century, his basic system of dynasties, as well as the (Bible-based) framework in which they were placed, was retained with only very minor amendments. Thus for example, in a book by a Scottish psychiatrist, J.C. Prichard, published in 1819, two years before Young and Champollion had found the key to unlocking the secrets of the hieroglyphs, the date of 1147 BC is given for the start of the reign of Ramses III. Prichard provides no source for this figure, though it is evidently derived one way or another from Eusebius's commentaries on Manetho, and therefore ultimately from the Bible.

This date, again, is very close to that still provided for Ramses III in modern textbooks!

More famously, or perhaps infamously, just before the Battle of the Pyramids, in 1798, Napoleon pointed to the Great Pyramid and reminded his men that "forty centuries look down on you". The French commander thus placed the construction of the monument around 2200 BC — within little more than a century of the date still accepted in academic publications. Yet this was over twenty years before Champollion made his breakthrough and thereby established the science of Egyptology. In addition, as we have seen, Ramses II (because of the supposed Exodus connection) was placed around 1350 BC by the early chroniclers — still the date found in the textbooks!

Yet modern Egyptologists confidently assert that their chronology is firmly based on that most exact of sciences, astronomy; and they point to the Sothic Calendar as the solid foundation of their system. The question of the Sothic Calendar has been dealt with over the past few years by various writers, and the critique they have presented has been devastating; here however I shall be content to give a very brief outline of the system, and to demonstrate just how spurious were the concepts it was based upon. Before I do that, however, the reader will no doubt draw his own conclusions about the validity of a "scientific" dating-system which nevertheless managed to come up with almost precisely the same dates as did the early Jewish and Christian writers using the Book of Genesis.

The idea that Egyptian history might be astronomically dated was first mooted in the early 19th century by Biot and others, even before the hieroglyphs had been translated. Throughout that century the goal of an astronomically calculated chronology was pursued by various scholars, most notably by Eduard Meyer and somewhat later by Ludwig Borchardt. It was suggested that certain references to a "Great Year" and to a "Sothic" calendar in a number of Roman and early Christian writers might provide the basis for a definitive Egyptian chronological system. What then was this Great Year and Sothic calendar?

The Egyptians, in common with other ancient peoples, are well-known to have employed a calendar of 365 days. This of course is not the true length of the year, which is just short of 365.25 days. Insistence on a calendar of 365 days meant that the festivals and important days of the Egyptian calendar did not match the true or sidereal year, and gradually moved throughout it. The problem is solved by adding an extra day every four years, the so-called leap year. In Rome, the leap year was only adopted officially in the reign of Augustus, whilst a few years later, in 26 BC, it was adopted in Alexandria.

A very simple calculation reveals that a quarter of a day each year accumulates to a full year in 1461 years of 365 days. This was a computation that the Roman authors, many of whom delighted in such number games, were familiar with.

Censorinus, a Roman author of lesser stature, wrote in his *Liber de Die Natali* that the Egyptians, who had earlier resisted an attempt by Ptolemy III (the famous Canopus Decree) to reform the calendar, specially marked the one thousand four hundred and sixty-first year of the great year, which they called "the year of the God," because it was then that harmony was restored between their calendar and the solar calendar.[125] Censorinus explained that the Egyptians marked the commencement of a "great year" with the heliacal rising (i.e. appearing in the east just before the sun) of the star Sothis over Egypt. He further explained that Sothis was the Egyptian name for Sirius, and that in the one hundredth year before he wrote his work (*Liber de Die Natali*) a new Sothic period had begun. Since the latter book was written in the year AD 238, this meant that the new Sothic period had begun in the year AD 139: thus the previous Sothic age must have started in 1322 BC. This date then was seized upon by Borchardt and Meyer as the foundation stone of Egyptian chronology.

On a manuscript of Theon of Alexandria, an author of the fourth century AD, an annotation remarked that "since Menophres and till the end of the era of Augustus, or the beginning of the era of Diocletian, there were 1605 years."[126] The last year of the era of Augustus was in AD 283 or 284. Subtracting 1605 years from this, we arrive at 1321 BC — almost exactly the same year indicated by Censorinus as marking the beginning of a Sothic period.

The coincidence seemed too great to be the result of chance, and it was assumed (though Theon himself made no such claim) that the reign of Menophres must have marked the beginning of the previous Sothic period.

Borchardt and Meyer, along with other scholars of the age, concentrated their efforts in identifying Menophres from the hieroglyphic records. The immediate consensus was that he represented Ramses I (Men-nefer-re), founder of the Nineteenth Dynasty. Thus the year 1321 BC was fixed as the year that Ramses I mounted the throne. However, a number of other possibilities were suggested for Menophres, and one scholar at least suggested that the name represented not a king at all, but the city of Memphis (Men-nefer).[127] Since the heliacal rising of Sothis (supposedly Sirius) is of central importance in marking the inauguration of a

125 Censorinus, *Liber de Die Natali* xviii

126 T.H. Martin, "Mémoire sur la date historique d'un rénouvellement de la période sothiaque" in *Mémoires presentes par divers savants a l'Academie des Subscriptions et Belles-Lettres*. Serie 1 Vol.8 part 1 (Paris, 1869)

127 J.B. Biot, *Études sur l'astronomie indienne et sur l'astronomie chinoise* (Paris, 1862) pp. xxxvi-xxxix

Sothic period, and since Sirius rises at different dates in Egypt depending on the latitude (one degree north adds roughly a day), scholars have always wondered at precisely which point in its appearance over Egypt a Sothic period began. Did it begin when the star appeared in the far north of the country, or did it begin a few days earlier, when it arose first in the south of the country? A comment from one Olympiodorus, a Greek writer of the fifth century AD, may throw some light on the subject; for he states that the date of the rising of the star at Memphis was accepted in Alexandria.[128]

From this, it begins to look that the Sothic period associated with the name Menophres does not refer to a king at all, but to the city of Memphis. As such, the reference is utterly useless from a chronological point of view.

But there are even more serious objections to the entire system. To begin with, as numerous writers have stated over the past few years, the extremely ambiguous comments of two obscure early Christian authors seem to be tenuous grounds on which to base the entire chronology of the ancient world. Roman writers of much greater repute than either Censorinus or Theon were given to expounding what to us are clearly outrageous statements about Egypt and her history as a matter of course. Take for example a comment by Tacitus, one of the most renowned and respected of the Roman historians.

> In the consulate of Paulus Fabius and Lucius Vitellius [in the reign of Tiberius], after a long period of ages, the bird known as the phoenix visited Egypt, and supplied the learned of that country and of Greece with the material for long disquisitions on the miracle.... As to the term of years [between two visits of the bird], the tradition varies. The generally received number is five hundred; but there are some who assert that its visits fall at intervals of 1,461 years, and that it was in the reigns, first of Sesostris, then of Amasis, and finally of Ptolemy, that the three earlier phoenixes flew to the city called Heliopolis with a great escort of common birds...[129]

Pliny, another of the greats in Roman literature, wrote in a similar vein: "...the period of the Great Year coincides with the life of the bird [the phoenix], and the same indications of the seasons and the stars return again."[130]

Commenting upon these statements of great Roman writers, Velikovsky noted how "Censorinus and Theon are among those writers of late antiquity who seem to consider it legitimate to retroject a 1,460-year period into the Egyptian past. But no such Sothic period is ever mentioned by the Egyptians themselves."[131]

---

128 See Velikovsky, *Peoples of the Sea* (London, 1977) pp.226-7

129 Tacitus, *Annals of Imperial Rome* vi,28

130 Pliny, *Natural History* x,2

131 Velikovsky, loc. cit. p.225

This latter statement of Velikovsky is of crucial importance. Try as they might, Egyptologists could find no mention of a Great Year or even of a Sothic period in the whole of Egyptian literature. Even the identity of Sothis is uncertain, for it too makes no appearance in the hieroglyphic literature. Thus the entire chronology of pharaonic Egypt is based on two highly contentious and almost certainly fictitious statements by two Christian writers of late antiquity regarding a 1,461-year period, which the Egyptians of pharaonic times knew nothing about, or at least failed to mention in the copious hieroglyphic literature that has survived!

Such then is the "scientific" basis for Egyptian chronology, a chronology which as early as 1961 was described as little more than a "collection of rags and tatters."[132] Since that time the entire Sothic system has been formally abandoned, as least in some quarters. Thus in 1985 Wolfgang Helck, the editor of the *Lexikon der Ägyptologie*, announced that, "Work on chronology has clearly arrived at a crisis. The reason for this is in part the adoption of dogmatic scientific facts without testing their applicability to Egyptian material and the serviceability of this material."[133] Whilst a rearguard attempt has since been made to save Sothic chronology, it is apparent that the credibility of the entire system, even amongst top-ranking members of the Egyptology establishment, is now in question.

It is evident then, from this cursory examination of the facts, that in piecing together pharaonic history we must begin again from the beginning, and that all received wisdom relating to either dates or the length of Egypt's past need to be set aside. It is just this task that the present volume shall attempt.

Before proceeding however we must first look at the chronology of ancient Mesopotamia; for it too is grossly distorted, though for a different reason.

STRATIGRAPHY AND CHRONOLOGY

Even as scholars sought to unveil the ancient history of Egypt, other men worked to cast new light on the story of that other biblical land, the land of the Two Rivers and original home of the Hebrews, Mesopotamia. As was the case with Egypt, the Book of Genesis figured largely in the considerations of the historians. Here too, in antiquity, Eusebius had sought a synthesis of biblical and classical tradition. Using the Babylonian historian Berossus, along with the various classical authors, he had equated the semi-legendary Assyrian king Ninos with the biblical Nimrod, and then placed Abraham, the father of the Jews, roughly ten

---

132 A. Gardiner *Egypt of the Pharaohs* (1961) p.53 "What is proudly advertised as Egyptian history is merely a collection of rags and tatters."

133 W. Helck, "Zur Lage der aegyptischen Geschichtsschreibung" (résumé) in S. Schoske, ed. *4 Internationaler Aegyptologenkongress, 26/8 — 1/9/1985, München, Resümees der Referate* (Munich, 1985) p.95

generations after the founding of the Assyrian Empire. Since biblical chronology placed Abraham just before 2000 BC, this meant that the Assyrian Empire must have been established around 2250 BC.

In this way, the existence of a Mesopotamian civilization dating from the third millennium BC became part of accepted wisdom; and, as was the case with Egypt, this chronology remained essentially unchallenged even after the decipherment of the cuneiform script.

Yet it is little wonder that the Mesopotamian archaeologists clung for dear life onto the Bible-based chronology. For here, archaeologists were faced with problems that dwarfed those of their colleagues working in Egypt. The cuneiform literature of the region revealed the existence of monarchs, nations, and civilizations previously unknown to history. Thus for example in Lower Mesopotamia, which classical authors designated as the home of the Chaldaeans, a new and mysterious nation, whose language bore no relationship to any other known, was discovered. Scholars labelled these people "Sumerians", after the ancient name of the region. Of the Chaldaeans, whom they had expected to find, there was hardly a trace.

The Sumerians, it was found, were actually the oldest literate nation; for in the deepest strata of the Lower Mesopotamian sites, archaeologists discovered mankind's first transitional pictographic/syllabic script, written in the Sumerian tongue.

In the strata above the Early Dynastic Sumerians, as they came to be called, scholars found evidence of yet another previously unknown race; the Akkadians. This nation, which used a Semitic language, was found to have built a great empire that eventually encompassed the whole of Mesopotamia. Indeed Akkadian kings claimed to have subdued lands outside Mesopotamia, and it soon became clear that archaeology had stumbled upon the world's first great military power. The Akkadian kings claimed to have conquered the ancient land of Assyria, and one of them, Sharrukin, bore a name strangely reminiscent of the Assyrian king Sargon, well known from the Hebrew Scriptures.

After a few generations, the Akkadian empire crumbled, and the non-Semitic Sumerians regained their independence. In the cities of Lower Mesopotamia, scholars found eloquent testimony to the high level of civilization now attained by these "Neo-Sumerians". There was clear proof of an accurate and standardized system of weights and measures, as well as an established form of currency. This was astounding, because scholars had expected no such thing until the 7th century BC, whilst the Neo-Sumerians, for reasons we shall touch on presently, had already been placed much earlier. But then everything about the Neo-Sumerians looked incredibly advanced. Their buildings, for example, were found to have employed the arch,[134] an architectural feature supposedly unknown till the 7th century; indeed until the time of the Chaldaean Neo-Babylonians.

Now there were one or two voices who initially did try to link the Sumerians with the Chaldaeans,[135] and the Akkadians with the Assyrians, for the sequence of Early Sumerians, followed by Semitic Akkadians, followed by Neo-Sumerians, seemed to correspond with the sequence of Mesopotamian history as described by the Classical authors, which went from Early Chaldaeans, to Semitic Assyrians, to Neo-Chaldaeans. This was further suggested by the fact that the only ancient people discovered in Lower Mesopotamia, which the ancients described as the home of the Chaldaeans, were the Sumerians.

Archaeology steadfastly refused to reveal the existence of any other people who could be identified with the Chaldaeans.

But attempts to link the Sumerians and Chaldaeans were quickly discarded, because such an identification also implied the equation of the Akkadians with the Assyrians, and this could not be correct since archaeologists were already excavating material from the Assyrian period far above the levels of Akkadian and Sumerian occupation. The remains of this Assyrian culture, later to be designated Neo-Assyrian, left no doubt that this was the epoch of the mighty Assyrian Empire known through the classical and biblical authors. Amongst the records of the Neo-Assyrian kings were found the cuneiform versions of well-known names such as Sargon, Sennacherib, and Esarhaddon. Scholars were jubilant at the discovery of these men, and the Hebrew Scriptures, which were our main source of information about them, seemed to be completely vindicated. Thus it was agreed that the Akkadians and Sumerians, both of whom came stratigraphically long before the Neo-Assyrians, were indeed races unknown to classical antiquity. The discovery of these peoples was hailed as one of the great triumphs of modern scholarship.

However, alongside such triumphs, there were major disappointments to be faced. The non-appearance of the Chaldaeans in the very place they should by all accounts have occupied, was bad enough; but it soon emerged that an even greater disappointment was in store. The Persians, who were known to have occupied Mesopotamia for two centuries, appeared to have left virtually no evi-

---

134 See e.g. Sir Leonard Woolley, *Ur of the Chaldees* (2nd ed. 1983) p.102 "Not the least surprising aspect of the civilization which the tombs [of Ur] illustrate is the advance it had made in architecture. The doorway of Rt789 was capped with a properly constructed brick arch."

135 Loftus for example labelled all the Sumerian epochs as Early Chaldaean, and basically adhered to the general outline of Mesopotamian history provided by the classical authors.

dence of their stay in the region at all.[136] This was incredible. The Persians rule in the region marked one of the most vibrant periods of Mesopotamian history; how could they not appear in the archaeological record?

Asking themselves this question, scholars desperately sought for Achaemenid material in site after site. But to no avail. With the exception of a few paltry remains, some small artifacts and a handful of smallish buildings, the expected Persian material could not be located. Neither Lower nor Upper Mesopotamia could produce a single major Persian Age monument, and the minor remains that were found were quite insufficient to account for two of the wealthiest centuries of Mesopotamian history. The stratigraphies of Lower and Upper Mesopotamia generally contain significant differences; but in this they consistently agreed. A typical Assyrian stratigraphy (as for example at Tell Hamadiyah, Munbaqa, Barak, Balawat, Nimrud and Tell Beydar)[137] looks thus:

Hellenists (after 330 BC)

———————

Neo-Assyrians (850-610 BC)

———————

Mitanni (1550-1350 BC)

———————

Akkadians (2300-2200 BC)

———————

Early Dynastic Sumerians (till c. 2300 BC)

It will be observed that aside from the strange absence of the Persians, these stratigraphies also reveal two other hiatuses, or periods of non-occupation; namely a gap of roughly 650-700 years between the Akkadians and the Mitanni, and a gap of 500 years between the Mitanni and Neo-Assyrians. When discussing the archaeology of any north Mesopotamian site, these gaps are usually described as periods of abandonment, and no real attempt is made to explain them.

---

136 See e.g. A.L. Oppenheim's, "The Babylonian Evidence of the Achaemenian Rule in Mesopotamia" in *The Cambridge History of Iran* Vol.1 (Cambridge, 1985) p.530 "The encounter between the Achaemenian Empire and Babylonia [Mesopotamia] seems to have left surprisingly little impact on the latter."

137 The most recently excavated of these is Tell Beydar, ancient Nabada, a site very close to the Khabur River, in what is now northern Syria. A report by Joachim Bretschneider, entitled "Nabada: The Buried City", appeared in *Scientific American* in October 2000. The site was explored by a multinational team during the 1990s and fully confirmed a 700 year hiatus between Akkadians and Mitanni, as well as a 500 year gap between Mitanni and Neo-Assyrians, and, as usual, a complete absence of the Persians.

As an example, consider the following account of Tell Brak's archaeology from the prestigious *Dictionary of the Ancient Near East*; "Following the collapse of Ak-kadian rule in north Mesopotamia, much of the site was abandoned. During the middle of the second millennium the site revived with the construction of a Mi-tannian palace on the summit of the mound, but by 1200 BC the settlement was completely abandoned."[138] Or consider the archaeology of Tell Beydar, ancient Nabada, a settlement very close to the Khabur River, in what is now northern Syria. "After 500 years of prosperity [in the Early Bronze Age], Nabada was aban-doned around 2350 BC. Why, we do not know; the other cities of northern Meso-potamia declined at the same time.... Around 1600 BC a Hurrian empire called the kingdom of Mitanni developed in the Khabur area.... The Hurrians [Mitannians] settled amid the ruins of Nabada, 1000 years after the fall of the early Bronze Age metropolis.... The empire of Mitanni perished in its turn, and in the eighth cen-tury BC Assyrians conquered the Khabur region.... The invaders settled on top of the earlier Hurrian [Mitannian] occupation in the lower regions of Tell Beydar.... With the fall of the Assyrian empire, Tell Beydar once again returned to dust and silence."[139]

As with all the other sites of the region, there was not a trace of the Persians.

It will presently be shown that these hiatuses do not represent actual peri-ods of abandonment, but are rather textbook constructs resulting from a faulty chronology. Rather than abandonment, there was a pronounced cultural conti-nuity from Akkadians to Mitannians and from Mitannians to Neo-Assyrians, a fact demonstrated in great detail by a German expedition less than twenty years ago.[140] The stratigraphic gaps therefore do not represent empty periods or "dark

---

138 Bienkowski, P. and A. Millard *Dictionary of the Ancient Near East* (British Museum Press, London, 2000) p.59

139 Joachim Bretschneider, "Nabada: The Buried City", *Scientific American* (October, 2000) pp. 67-9. Nabada was explored by a multinational team during the 1990s.

140 The non-existence of the "occupation gap" between the Akkadian Age and the Mitannian was in fact demonstrated by a team from the University of Hamburg-Harburg in the late 1980s. The team focussed their attention on Munbaqa, one of the major Assyrian sites. In Gunnar Heinsohn's words, "Like ... Tell Hamadiyah, Munbaqa was known for a hiatus between the Old-Akkadian "Early bronze Age" and the Mitanni "Late Bronze Age" strata. In 1988, W. Pape devoted the first special sounding to refute the claim of the Akkad-Mitanni-gap's non-existence. It focussed on the sequence of building foundations. To his surprise the archaeologist could not confirm the gap between ca. −2250 and ca. −1475 but found clear cut architectural continuity ... Instantly understanding the far-reaching impact of its discovery, the team went back to Munbaqa in 1989 and, this time, devoted three spe-cial soundings to the Akkad-Mitanni-gap. To go beyond the limits of their own expertise (architecture, pottery, crafts and arts), they asked a geologist (Dr Rösner, University of Erlangen) to join the team. She specialized in sediments and aeolic layers. Her preliminary draft with the results of her research dates from August 23, 1990. Her findings confirmed the archaeologists'. There is no gap between the Akkadian stratum and the Mitanni stra-tum in Munbaqa (Rösner, 1990)." (Heinsohn, "Old-Akkadians and Hyksos: Stratigraphic

ages", but are gaps that exist only on paper, forced on the historians by the tyranny of accepted chronology. The three "gaps" actually correspond precisely to a triplication of history originating in three quite separate dating systems which were used by scholars to construct the region's history.

Our main concern however at present is the most recent of these gaps — that between the Neo-Assyrians and Hellenic Seleucids. Try as they might, archaeologists could find no clearly defined Persian stratum in any Assyrian site. In face of such difficulty, it was eventually suggested that the destruction of Assyria by the Medes and Chaldaeans in the years following 610 BC had been so total that the area was not reoccupied. Assyria, it was conjectured, must have been a wasteland during the Persian epoch. However, it had to be admitted that such a solution seemed to be contradicted by Herodotus, who informed us that the satrapy of Assyria was the wealthiest in the empire, contributing more in taxes than any other region.[141] Furthermore, Babylonia and southern Mesopotamia were very definitely not wastelands during the Persian epoch; and, if the classical authors are to be believed, for a while Babylon became the second capital of the Empire. Yet the Persians were as absent from Babylonia as they were from Assyria. How was this to be explained? Quite simply, it was not. The problem was declared "intractable" and left at that.

Thus the archaeologists, whose histories of the ancient world are housed in the great libraries of the world, disclosed to us the existence in Mesopotamia of peoples and kingdoms unknown to the classical authors, but failed completely to elucidate the histories of the ancient peoples mentioned by those same authors. Only the Assyrians, it is held, are equally well represented in the archaeological and classical sources. Thus our knowledge of the previously unknown Sumerians and Akkadians comes *entirely* from the materials excavated by the archaeologists, whilst our knowledge of the Chaldaean and Persian epochs comes *entirely* from the classical authors.

For almost a century now, scholarship has by and large been content with the state of affairs. Over the past few years, however, this and related problems have been highlighted by Professor Gunnar Heinsohn of Bremen who has advocated some radical solutions involving what can only be described as major surgery to our whole Mesopotamian historiography. According to Heinsohn, the Sumerians and Akkadians were indeed the Chaldaeans and Assyrians of the ancient authors; and it is no coincidence that the sequence of Early Sumerians — Akkadians — Neo-Sumerians matched so well the sequence known to us from the

---

room-mates only or identical nations also?" (Paper presented at SIS Ancient History Study Group Meeting, Nottingham, November, 1990)).

141 Herodotus, i,192

classical sources; Early Chaldaeans — Assyrians — Neo-Chaldaeans.[142] However, having made these equations, Heinsohn was still presented with the problem of the Neo-Assyrians who, after all, come well after the Akkadians stratigraphically. Observation of the Assyrian sites revealed the presence of Neo-Assyrian remains in the last pre-Hellenic layers — in other words in just the place we should have expected to find the Persians. Thus Dr. Heinsohn was compelled to identify these Neo-Assyrians with the Achaemenids, who otherwise were completely unrepresented.[143] This conclusion was further strengthened by the fact that the Mitanni, whom Dr. Heinsohn had already equated with the Medes, always appeared in the stratum directly preceding the Neo-(or sometimes Middle) Assyrians.

Such a conclusion of course has far-reaching consequences. Most immediately, it means that the Neo-Assyrians mentioned in biblical sources, such as Tiglath-Pileser, Sargon, Sennacherib, and Esarhaddon, were not Assyrians but Persians, and therefore could not possibly be the same as the Assyrian kings overthrown by the Medes and Chaldaeans, known from classical literature. By assuming that the biblical Neo-Assyrians were the same as the classical Empire Assyrians, scholars had unwittingly unhinged the whole of ancient Mesopotamian history. Biblical chronology was unnaturally lengthened, as was that of Mesopotamia, with the distortion reaching far beyond the Land of the Two Rivers.

THE TRIPLICATION OF ANCIENT HISTORY

It is evident from the above that scholarship entered the age of scientific archaeology with a hopelessly confused image of ancient Near Eastern history. This confusion was based on an already entrenched reliance upon certain Hellenistic and early Christian authors, and most especially upon the Bible. As we have seen, scholars working in Mesopotamia were doubly confused by accepting on the one hand the biblical date of Abraham, and attempting to reconstruct early Mesopotamian chronology around that, and on the other hand by accepting the Neo-Assyrian monarchs such as Sennacherib and Esarhaddon as identical to the Assyrian monarchy referred to by the classical historians — and then attempting to reconstruct later Mesopotamian history around these. The Egyptologists imagined that they had formulated their chronology independently of the Bible; though ultimately, no matter how much they tinkered round the edges with the "Sothic Calendar", their system was also based on the Book of Genesis, this time via the date of Adam, whom early Jewish and Christian writers imagined to be one and the same as Menes. The Sothic system of Meyer and the others did not

---

142 See e.g. Heinsohn's *Die Sumerer gab es nicht* (Frankfurt, 1988)

143 e.g. Heinsohn's *Perserherrscher gleich Assyrerkönige?* (Frankfurt, 1992)

break away from this chronology, but was unwittingly used to support it. Yet even if scholars had completely abandoned Eusebius and the Bible, they would have gone nowhere with Sothic dating, for as a method it was every bit as spurious as that employed by Eusebius.

Thus two entirely separate dating-systems, both equally fictitious, were now employed in the reconstruction of the history of mankind's earliest civilizations: And in this way was produced what can only be described as a massive distortion of ancient history: Not only was world history duplicated in the second millennium, as Velikovsky believed, but also triplicated in the third millennium. Yet this veritable comedy of errors had a rationale, and followed its own internal logic. Indeed it was constructed upon three quite separate dating blueprints. Thus the history of the first millennium, which is in fact the true history of the region, is known solely through the classical and Hellenistic sources, and is dated according to these sources. A "history" of the second millennium however is supplied by cross-referencing with Egyptian material, and this chronology is based solely on these sources, which are dated according to the Sothic Calendar combined with the biblical date of Adam. The final part of the triplication, the ghost kingdoms of the third millennium, is supplied by cross-referencing with Mesopotamian cuneiform documents, and this chronology is based solely on these sources, which are ultimately dated on the basis of biblical history.

Thus the Imperial Assyrians of the 8th century BC, whom we know from the classical writers, are identical to the Hyksos of the 16th century, whom we know from the Egyptian sources, and are also identical to the Akkadians of the 24th century, whom we know from the Mesopotamian sources.

These identifications, as Professor Heinsohn has demonstrated, can be supported not only with a wealth of textual and historiographic evidence, but also with the much more powerful evidence of stratigraphy. When for example a complete stratigraphy of Syria/Palestine (dated according to Egyptian chronology) is compared with a complete stratigraphy from Mesopotamia (dated according to the Mesopotamian/biblical chronology), a very strange anomaly is observed. What the archaeologists working in Syria/Palestine call the Early and Middle Bronze Ages is *not* what archaeologists working in Mesopotamia mean by the same terms. Thus in the Syrian port of Ugarit a settlement deemed Early Bronze 2, and dated around 2400 BC (and destroyed in a vast upheaval of nature), used 'Ubaid pottery typical of Mesopotamia. But in Mesopotamia (as for example at Ur) the 'Ubaid period is deemed to have been terminated — again by a natural cataclysm — a thousand years earlier, around 3400 BC. In fact, the thousand year gap between these two catastrophes is fictitious, a textbook construct. Not only is Early Bronze 2 Ugarit comparable to Chalcolithic Ur, but all the above cultural levels, separated in the textbooks by a thousand years, are also more or less iden-tical. Thus Early Bronze 3 Ugarit (so-called Khirbet-Kerak) is culturally identical to Early Bronze 1 Ur (Jamdat Nasr), whilst Ugarit Middle Bronze 1 and 2 display precise parallels with Ur Early Bronze 2 and 3.

But this situation, absurd though it may be, is precisely what we should ex-pect if Heinsohn's thesis is correct. The archaeologists working in Syria/Palestine had to designate the Hyksos strata as Middle Bronze 2 because they had already *a priori* placed the Hyksos almost a thousand years after the Akkadians, whose strata in Mesopotamia was defined as Early Bronze 3.

Yet in case the admittedly straightforward evidence of stratigraphy should not fully convince, Heinsohn has brought forward a veritable plethora of other material to illustrate this most pivotal of identifications. Tin Bronze, for example, is associated with both Hyksos and Akkadians; the scimitar-sword is likewise associated with both peoples; the two-wheeled chariot gave both peoples mas-tery of the Near East; both peoples were Semitic; both peoples used the Akkadian language; both peoples conquered Egypt.

Of course, once we accept the equation of Akkadians and Hyksos, of which more will be said at a later stage in the present study, we have already dealt with half the problem, half the triplication. All that then remains is to prove the latter two nations also identical with the Assyrians of the first millennium. This second part of the triplication is clearly exposed by the stratigraphies examined in the previous section, where we see the Hyksos lying directly underneath the Mitanni, the recognized conquerors of the "Old Assyrian" Empire, who are one and the same as the Medes, recognized conquerors of the 8th century Assyrian Empire. The following identifications are therefore indicated.

MESOPOTAMIAN SOURCES	EGYPTIAN SOURCES	CLASSICAL SOURCES
Sumerians	Early Dynastic Pharaohs	Early Chaldaeans
Akkadians (Old Assyrians)	Hyksos	Imperial Assyrians
Mitanni(Middle Assyrians)	Mitanni	Medes
Neo-Assyrians	Neo-Assyrians	Persians
Hellenists	Hellenists	Hellenists

The stratigraphic anomaly, which we have already observed in the earliest epochs of Mesopotamia and Syria/Palestine, is equally in evidence in these later phases. Thus Heinsohn has observed that whilst Mitanni remains are always, in Mesopotamia, found directly above those of the Akkadians, just a few miles away, in Syria, they are always found directly above those of the Hyksos.

It is evident then that the three hiatuses observed in the Assyrian stratigraphies are the natural consequence of applying these three dating systems. The Mitanni are separated from the Akkadians by 650 years because the former are dated according to the Egyptian chronology and the latter according to the Mesopotamian. The Neo-Assyrians in turn are separated from the Mitanni by a further 500 years because the former are again dated according to the Mesopotamian scheme; whilst the Neo-Assyrians are separated from the Hellenists by almost three centuries because the latter are dated according to the classical scheme. Removing therefore the three hiatuses, the actual order of the Assyrian strata conforms precisely to the sequence given by the classical historians. The Akkadians are the Assyrians; the Mitanni, who conquer them, are the Medes; and the Neo-Assyrians, who come after the Mitanni, are the Persians.

The remainder of the present work will show that the pyramid-builders of Egypt, contemporary with the Akkadian kings of Mesopotamia (who are of course the Assyrians of the 8th century), belong with their Semitic contemporaries in the same century.

RADIOCARBON DATING

At this point the reader may well be tempted to criticize the author's basic thesis; namely that the pre-Christian chronologies of Egypt and Mesopotamia have no scientific basis, but are dependent entirely upon scholastic interpretations of the Old Testament. Even if Sothic dating has now been abandoned by the Egyptologists, surely, it might be protested, there are other supports. What about the new dating methods devised over the past half century — particularly radiocarbon and dendrochronology? Is it not true that these processes are thoroughly objective, and they have vindicated traditional chronology? New textbooks are published every year supplying radiocarbon dates for pharaohs and kings of Mesopotamia that are very much in line with accepted norms. Have not these results proved the traditional chronology correct? Irrespective of how that chronology was originally formulated, its basic accuracy has surely now been demonstrated beyond reasonable doubt!

In answer to the above, I have to agree that this is certainly the impression given by the textbooks and journals. But before even going on to question the validity of the radiocarbon and dendrochronology methods, I would call the reader's attention to one point. We recall how the first of these "scientific" systems, the Sothic Calendar, managed somehow to confirm the dates already established by Eusebius and the medieval scholiasts. At the time, academics said precisely the same thing; irrespective of how Eusebius came about his figures, he must somehow have got them more or less right. Yet we now see that Sothic dating was no more scientific than the methods employed by Eusebius. That the Sothic chronology showed such dramatic agreement with the scholastic merely reflects on the psychology of the academics who devised it. Human nature abhors chaos. We all like things neatly packaged; facts and figures that we can rely upon. Without being fully aware of what they were doing, the Sothic proponents worked towards making their calendar as agreeable to the accepted system as possible: and sure enough, lo and behold, the two agreed almost down to the year.

Exactly the same process was at work when radiocarbon dating was applied.

The great irony in all of this was that radiocarbon was used to bolster the traditional chronology even as many 20th century scholars began to find an increasing number of reasons to question the validity of that chronology, and were arguably on the verge of taking the courageous step of abandoning it.

The discovery by Libby in 1946 that living organisms absorb a radioactive carbon isotope (Carbon 14) from the atmosphere was quickly recognized as a potentially valuable new tool in the archaeologist's repertoire. As soon as a living organism dies, it ceases to absorb Carbon 14; from then on the proportion of radioactive carbon in the organism's body begins to decline. Since this decline or "decay" occurs at a fixed rate, it is held that we can determine with great accuracy the age of any artifact containing once-living organic material. Archaeologists were quick to avail themselves of the revolutionary new technique, and samples from ancient sites throughout Egypt and the Near East were soon being subjected to analysis. Whilst the results obtained were not always consistent — indeed some were wildly inconsistent — enough information was apparently gathered to convince scholars that the accepted dates for Egyptian and Mesopotamian civilization were broadly correct. Any doubt about the great age of pharaonic history was finally put to rest. One after another, it was claimed, samples from the Fourth, Fifth and Sixth Dynasties yielded dates in the third millennium BC.

So great is the prestige of "hard science" in our culture that few people have dared to even question these results. Nevertheless, in many other fields, scientific conclusions are regularly questioned, and frequently overturned. This is particularly the case with regard to medical and dietary science, as well as forensic science applied to criminal investigation.

As a matter of fact, the radiocarbon system of dating is well-known by those in the field to have a number of major drawbacks.[144] For one thing, samples can be contaminated, and it is virtually impossible to know that they have been. Con-

---

144 See for example *New Scientist* (September, 1989) p.26, where it is noted that the margin of error quoted by some laboratories in their dating techniques may be two or three times greater than admitted. Whilst some laboratories, it is claimed, are consistently correct, others have been shown to produce dates that are up to 250 years out. Unforeseen errors,

tamination comes in many forms, and can either increase or decrease the readings, making the sample under investigation appear either much younger or much older than it is. The most simple, yet possibly most pervasive form of contamination is that of water. Water can literally wash the radioactivity out of a sample, making it look older. There is absolutely no way of knowing whether a control sample has been exposed to water. Now even in Egypt and Mesopotamia few artifacts have never been exposed to water, either from the flooding great rivers of these lands, or from flash-floods caused by admittedly fairly infrequent rainfalls. Just how much water contamination can affect radiocarbon results was dramatically illustrated in a recent *Horizon* documentary screened by the BBC.[145] An Englishman who, in a fit of remorse, had confessed to murdering and dismembering his wife brought police to the spot where he had buried her head. Sure enough, the detectives uncovered the partial skull of a woman, complete with some still surviving fleshy tissue. They were astonished however when scientists from the British Museum, who had not been informed of the skull's provenance, radiocarbon dated it and declared it to be 1,500 years old. Other forensic scientists however, who reconstructed the woman's features, declared that in their opinion the body was indeed that of the vanished wife. The documentary concluded by offering the opinion that bodies found in boggy conditions take on the date of the sodden earth wherein they are interred. In short, the water had leeched much of the carbon isotope from the remains, making it appear vastly older than it was. A major plank in the radiocarbon edifice, the constancy of rates of day, is therefore demolished.

Given this remarkable fact, which in any case has always been well understood by the scholarly community, we may well wonder how esteemed academics can then propose to use radiocarbon readings of samples of wood, leather and bone recovered from the ground that have endured millennia of rainfalls and river floods? Yet such readings are still regularly published, without comment.

With wood there is an added complication. A tree can live for hundreds of years, but at any given time only absorbs radioactive carbon into its outermost layer. Thus it is necessary to know the age of the tree when it was cut down, as well as the part of the tree from which the timber was derived, before we can even begin to talk about an accurate reading. Yet once again, timber is indiscriminately dated by scientists and the results published without comment.

A third — and major — problem is the tendency of scientists to dismiss anomalous results that do not conform to preconceived ideas. Thus a very sub-

---

it is said, can arise in the chemical pre-treatment of small amounts of material, and dates can be way out on samples only 200 years old.

145 BBC 2 *Horizon*, 4th March 1999

stantial number of results obtained from Egypt and Mesopotamia have produced startlingly recent figures; yet these have not been published, or have at best been reduced to footnotes, because, ironically enough, the researchers have deemed them to be "contaminated". In the words of one eminent scholar:

> Some archaeologists refused to accept radiocarbon dates. The attitude probably, in the early days of the new technique, was summed up by Professor Jo Brew, Director of the Peabody Museum at Harvard, "If a C14 date supports our theories, we put it in the main text. If it does not entirely contradict them, we put it in the footnote. And if it is completely 'out of date', we just drop it."[146]

Perhaps the greatest problem with regard to radiocarbon dating is the question of environment. All researchers in the field assume that environmental conditions have more or less always been as they now are; at least as far back as humanity's first appearance on the planet. Yet if what we have proposed in the present paper is correct, if the earth has been subjected to repeated and devastating interaction with extraterrestrial bodies such as comets, then we must assume that atmospheric conditions were not always the same. During these episodes our planet's atmosphere would have suffered major disruption, and this would undoubtedly have had an effect upon the radiocarbon levels. Given a period of cosmic disturbances, with attendant massive volcanism as well as conflagrations, much "old" carbon (i.e. carbon with a depleted proportion of carbon 14) would be released into the atmosphere — to then be absorbed by living organisms. In such circumstances plants and animals would have a much lower percentage of radioactive carbon in their systems than present day organisms.

This is a well-documented problem, and is termed the "Suess effect" in honor of the scientist who first identified it. Its impact is not theoretical, but proven. In this way it was demonstrated, for example, how the massive use of fossil fuels in the 20th century (with their attendant release of great amounts of "old" carbon) led to some startlingly anomalous results:

> We are told that plants in a rich old carbon environment were radiocarbon dated several thousand years older than they actually were, and a tree by an airport was actually dated to be 10,000 years old.[147]

---

146 David Wilson, *The New Archaeology* (New York, 1974) p. 97 An example of this pernicious practice is seen in the fate of samples from the tomb of pharaoh Tutankhamun subjected by the British Museum to the radio-carbon method. The samples, consisting of fibers of a reed mat and a palm kernel, produced dates of 844 BC and 899 BC respectively. These were broadly in line with the date for Tutankhamun predicted by Velikovsky, but were roughly 500 years too recent for textbook chronology. In spite of assurances given to Velikovsky, the dates were never formally published. See Velikovsky's *Peoples of the Sea* (1977) p.xvi

147 Charles Ginenthal, "The Extinction of the Mammoth" *The Velikovskian* (special edition) Vol.III 2 and 3 (1999) p.184

Thus another major plank of the radiocarbon edifice, the constancy of initial conditions (as well as rates of decay), collapses.

The list of problems mentioned above merely scratches the surface. The whole question of how we date the ancient past will need to be reconsidered in a fundamental way. Other "scientific" systems, such as dendrochronology (to be discussed presently), have entered the fray over the past couple of decades, only to confuse the picture even further. Ultimately, they are all used very much as statistics (unfortunately) are: to prove whatever the researcher wishes to prove.[148]

In the final analysis, to repeat, the idea that human beings evolved high civilizations up to three thousand years before the dawn of the Christian era goes back to the Old Testament. Well before the appearance of the science of archaeology these dates were accepted by the scholastic intelligentsia of Europe; and so venerated and entrenched were they that science could not uproot them. They are still there, these dates based on venerated tradition, in the textbooks of the world's libraries.

Dendrochronology

Although dendrochronology, or tree-ring dating, has not been widely used in Egyptology, it has been used extensively to support the established chronology of megalithic and Bronze Age Europe. Since European Bronze Age cultures are recognizably contemporary with those of the Near East, dendrochronology can thus been employed, indirectly, to support the existing timescales of Egypt and Babylonia. For this reason, it is necessary to take a brief look at it.

The idea that tree-rings could supply an accurate record of the climate dating back many centuries has been around for some time. The rings of any felled tree tell, at a glance, which years were cold and which were warm. Warm summers of course produce more growth and therefore a thicker ring. Whilst an individual tree, such as an oak, may live many centuries, its lifespan is still limited. However, in the middle of the 20th century it was suggested that since the patterns of rings were quite specific to the climate of a particular locality (e.g. the rings may show that in the first decade of the 18th century in Ireland two warm years were followed by four cold years which were followed by five warm years etc), it might be possible to construct a tabular record of the climate far beyond the lifespan of any individual tree. And so, for example, the central rings of a 500-year-old oak would have a specific pattern of warm and cold summers which could be compared with patterns on old artifacts made of oak trees which had been felled just

---

148 Gwen Schultz, a prominent scientist, has stated her belief that "The possibility that all methods [of dating] used today are wrong must be acknowledged." *Ice Age Lost* (New York, 1974) p.28

short of 500 years ago. In this way, the ring-pattern at the core of the newly-felled oak should match the ring-pattern at the outside of the tree felled 500 years ago.

Over the past forty years great efforts have been made, particularly in a number of European universities, to thus construct a climate-record going back many centuries. If such a climate-record could be made, it would be possible also to verify whether existing chronologies are accurate. Thus an artifact made of wood, from an archaeological find of known date, could have that date either verified or refuted by the tree-ring pattern in the wood. And sure enough, a number of such comparisons have been made; and they all, surprise, surprise, confirm existing chronologies.

As I have said, I do not want to go into the dendrochronology debate in detail. But, once again, the reader must bear in mind how strange it is that a supposedly scientific system should nevertheless confirm a chronology which is ultimately based on nothing other than a fundamentalist interpretation of the Old Testament. For this is just the case: the timescales of ancient Bronze Age and Iron Age Europe are derived from those of Egypt — as anyone who has examined the debate surrounding the dating of the Mycenaean Age of Greece will know. So, we may thank the Book of Genesis for the belief that the European Bronze Age began around 2500 BC, just as the same book was responsible for placing Egypt's pyramids at this time.

In fact, it is virtually impossible to describe dendrochronology as an exact science: there are far too many unknowns involved. So, for example, we must be sure that all the trees are from the same climate area. This in itself is almost impossible to prove. Secondly: how do we define a climate area? Even regions fairly close can have very differing climates; and in the past may have differed even more — or less. The point is, no one really knows. In addition, although the climate record in any given area might be unique over a long period, it is almost certainly not unique over a short period. Thus, many regions of the world could have three warm summers followed by four cold ones followed by two warm ones. For a pattern to be really significant, we need a much longer unbroken record. Yet many historical artifacts made of wood provide us with a record of only ten or twenty years or even less. And one other problem cannot be ignored. As we go further back into the past, artifacts of all kinds, but especially those made of wood and other perishable materials, become much scarcer. From really ancient times, we are lucky to get enough wood to establish a pattern of more than five or six years. Such a scanty record cannot be used with confidence.

In short, dendrochronology is very much an inexact science, and its findings very much open to interpretation. It cannot, and should not, be regarded as providing a definitive judgment on the chronology of the ancient world.

STONE, BRONZE AND IRON

A major premise of the present work has been to establish that the pyramids of Egypt were erected within the historical period now assigned to what is called the Iron Age, an epoch generally reckoned to have commenced sometime between the 10th and 8th centuries BC. However, not even this writer would suggest placing the pyramid-builders alongside the rulers normally identified with the "Iron Age", kings such as the "Libyans" of the Twenty-Second Dynasty and the "Ethiopians" of the Twenty-Fifth. Clearly the pyramid-builders belong to an epoch that is archaeologically and stratigraphically identified as "Early Bronze" In short, the Early Bronze Age, the period during which copper is the most frequently encountered metal, is the true location of the Pyramid Age — the only difference being that I would move this epoch down into the 9th and 8th centuries. The other rulers normally associated with the Iron Age and the 9th/8th centuries — the Ethiopians and the Libyans — I would move down into the 6th and 5th centuries.

So, moving the pyramid-builders into the 9th and 8th centuries still leaves us with the problem of explaining how a predominantly copper-using culture could carve monuments of granite, basalt and diorite; stones so hard that modern artisans laugh at the idea of using anything other than good-quality steel to work them.

Conventional scholarship, as found in countless learned textbooks, insists that the great monuments of the Pyramid Age were erected using tools of stone and copper. It is furthermore held that the epochs of Stone, Bronze and Iron represent clearly defined historical periods, and that the beginning of the Bronze Age (or Early Bronze Age) marks the commencement of the age of history and civilization. The Early Bronze Age is of course dated very precisely in Egypt and Mesopotamia to circa 3000 BC, with the Middle Bronze Age beginning around 2200 BC, and the latter giving way to the Late Bronze Age around 1550 BC. It is agreed that the Iron Age began, very roughly, around 1000 BC.

Yet before going a step further, it needs to be emphasized again that this system was not devised independently of Egyptian and Mesopotamian chronology. Rather it was constructed around these already existing frameworks. Therefore, even if we find the concept of Stone, Bronze and Iron Ages valid, that does not mean we must be constrained by the timescales within which they are placed in the textbooks.

But even the validity of the terminology must be called into question; and it has to be stated plainly that the idea of a Stone Age, followed neatly by a Bronze Age, which was in turn followed by an Iron Age is a gross and misleading simplification. The discovery of widespread use of iron during the Pyramid Age suggests very strongly that Stone, Bronze and Iron Ages actually overlap, and that all three materials were used concurrently for many centuries. Indeed there is evidence to suggest that stone implements were widely used by the peasantry throughout the Near East and Europe well into the Christian era.[149]

During his famous excavations of Mycenaean sites in Greece, Heinrich Schliemann uncovered fairly large quantities of stone tools, including knives and arrowheads of flint and obsidian, fashioned in typically Neolithic style, together with tools and weapons of metal, in obviously Late Bronze Age contexts. Describing his findings at Tiryns, Schliemann remarks, "As in Troy and Mycenae, so in Tiryns, stone implements were in use at the same time as tools of bronze."[150] But obviously aware of the potentially controversial nature of what he had just said, he hastily adds, "I wish to mention on this occasion, that, according to Professor Heinrich Brugsch, battle-axes with stone hammers were among the spoils which Thutmes [sic] III brought back from the highly-civilized states of Western Asia, together with weapons and armor of bronze, and gold and silver works of art."[151]

But alongside the stone and bronze implements Schliemann also uncovered numerous artifacts of iron, and there is much evidence to suggest that iron was widely employed throughout the Near East at this time.[152] Homer, whose epic *Iliad* deals with the period studied by Schliemann, speaks frequently of iron, which has a very clearly defined place in this otherwise Bronze Age culture.

As noted earlier, both the Mycenaean epoch of Greece and the Eighteenth Dynasty of Egypt properly belong in the 8th and 7th centuries BC, and represent the beginnings of the Iron Age. But the Bronze Age too can only have begun in the 8th or 9th century (at which time the Phoenicians opened up the sea-routes to the tin-bearing regions of Western Europe, namely Spain and Britain). This means, essentially, that the Bronze and Iron Ages begin more or less simultaneously. This, I shall argue, is correct, though for two or three centuries iron played a secondary role to bronze, for reasons that will become apparent.

149 The layman (as well as many academics) may be astonished to discover that in parts of the Near East, but especially in Egypt, stone implements were used even into the 19th century AD. Noting this, Gaston Maspero commented upon the difficulty of assigning Egyptian flint implements to any particular epoch; "Until quite recently ... the flint implements which had been found in various places [in Egypt] could not be ascribed to them [the earliest Egyptians] with any degree of certainty, for the Egyptians continued to use stone long after metal was known to them. They made stone arrowheads, hammers, and knives, not only in the time of the Pharaohs, but under the Romans, and during the whole period of the Middle Ages, and the manufacture of them has not yet entirely died out." *A History of Egypt, Chaldaea, Syria, Babylonia, and Assyria* Vol.1 (1906) pp.61-2

150 H. Schliemann, *Tiryns* (London,1886) p.173

151 Ibid.

152 As demonstrated in the previous chapter, iron was widely employed in the pyramid-building epoch.

It is an accepted principle that any culture which can produce bronze already possesses the technology to produce iron. This is due to the fact that charcoal-burning furnaces are needed to melt copper (at 1,083°). But once the technology of charcoal-burning is understood, it is relatively easy to achieve the temperature necessary to smelt iron (1,535°). And this is exactly what we find. Iron-working, including the smelting of iron from ore, is found right at the beginning of the Bronze Age in all of the Near Eastern cultures. As well as the examples cited above, and those alluded to in Chapter 1, we may note the discovery of iron artifacts from the Early and Middle Bronze Ages in various parts of Mesopotamia and Syria/Palestine. According to E. Herzfeld, "the excavations of Alaja Oyük [south-eastern Turkey] have brought to light a necklace of gold and iron and an astonishing iron dagger with gold handle of a pure Sargonic style from one of the tombs which may even go back to the pre-Sargonic period of the Royal Tombs of Ur."[153] Almost certainly, the dagger was not "iron" but carbon steel. In addition to this, Mesopotamia itself has produced numerous iron objects from the Old Babylonian period — as well as fairly numerous literary references to iron from the same epoch.[154]

Attempts to suggest that these early occurrences of iron can be attributed to the occasional use of meteoric iron, founder on the science. Meteoric iron is full of impurities and cannot in general be used for anything, without first subjecting it to a process of smelting and purification. In short, to make meteoric iron usable, you still need an iron-producing technology. This and the related question of accidental and isolated early discovery of iron is examined at length by Thomas Arthur Rickard in his two-volume work, *Man and Metals*. The idea has often been advanced that somehow an accidental,

> ... smelting operation yielded little lumps of iron that were fabricated into small objects. It is assumed that long before the art of smelting iron was discovered and developed, there were accidental and sporadic productions of the metal, and that these explain such finds of iron as those of the Great Pyramid, of the Abydos grave ... [etc.]
>
> [It is possible that these accidents occurred.] This is not disputed. It is accepted as a likely contingency; but what is questioned is that such fortuitous smelting of iron could happen frequently in many places [in Egypt] and go unregarded or unappreciated. The production of iron of usable quantity was too great an event to be ignored; it would call for attempts to repeat the act, and presumably would lead eventually to the discovery, after many trials, of a method of reduction; in other words, it is extremely improbable that several accidental reductions of iron from its ores, even at intervals apart, would not provoke

153 E. Herzfeld, *The Persian Empire; Studies in Geography and Ethnography of the Ancient Near East,* edited from the posthumous papers of Gerald Walser (Wiesbaden, 1968) p.122
154 Ibid.

purposeful repetitions of the performance, and the consequent discovery of a rudimentary smelting process. We cannot suppose that more than a millennium would elapse before such accidental smeltings would become rationalized. . . .

The discrepancies of chronology are enormous — no less than three millenniums. A knowledge of any method of producing iron from ore argues the desire and ability to make use of this serviceable metal; it is most improbable that each of the few known iron relics of remote antiquity was merely the result of an accidental smelting operation, for the quality of the iron found in the Pyramid and the tomb of Tut-ankh-Amen appears to be excellent. We are justified, on the contrary, in presuming that if and when the Egyptians, or any other people, discovered how to make a pound of metallic iron out of ore [as found, according to G.A. Wainwright, "The Coming of Iron," *Antiquity*, vol. X (1939) p. 9-10, in a tomb from the 12th Dynasty which supposedly ruled 1991-1782 BC or almost 1000 years before iron was smelted in Egypt] they would make more of it, because many deposits of iron ore, in large quantity, were available in Egypt, as elsewhere. . . . The discovery of a process for smelting the metal would be of tremendous importance to the Egyptians, or to any other people, in their commerce and in their warfare with their neighbors.[155]

In short, the iron tools of the Pyramid Age were products of a true Iron Age, an age that knew how to smelt iron from its ore.

Yet there is no doubt that during what we call the Bronze Age iron plays a role subservient to that of bronze. Thus in the *Iliad* Homer describes a classic Bronze Age civilization, where bronze is the metal used for weapons, including swords, knives, spearheads and arrowheads. Iron however does occur, and is described in such a way as to indicate familiarity. Yet it is never used to make weapons. It is the metal of tools. Why should this be so?

A rudimentary understanding of the properties of metals reveals bronze to be a harder, though more brittle material than pure (or wrought) iron. Thus bronze is capable of taking a much sharper edge than iron — which explains why bronze was used for many centuries for weapons and razors. On the other hand wrought iron is not as brittle as bronze. A plough made of iron would not snap upon hitting a rock, as one of bronze certainly would. Thus in the *Iliad* iron is used for agricultural tools, with ploughs specially mentioned.

Yet agricultural implements, which generally require soft, wrought iron, were not the only kinds of tools fashioned from iron. Stone-cutting tools too were made from this material; though the iron from which they were manufactured was not the pure, wrought iron, but hardened iron, or steel. As the Appendix illustrates, steel (and not just iron) was well-known to the Egyptians of the Pyramid Age. Only good quality steel tools could have carved the immensely hard stones, such as granite and diorite, worked by the craftsmen of the Fourth, Fifth, and Sixth

---

155 Thomas Arthur Rickards, *Man and Metals*, vol. II (NY 1932), pp. 837-839. Cited from Charles Ginenthal, *Pillars of the Past* (New York, 2004)

Dynasties. The difficulty was not in the forging of carbon steel — a relatively simple process — but in the production of iron itself; an extremely expensive and labor intensive process until comparatively late in the history of the great civilizations.

It was only with the development of better iron-producing technologies on a large scale that iron (or more accurately steel) began gradually to replace bronze as the preferred metal for weapons.

The Greeks recalled the advent of iron, or, more accurately steel, swords very clearly in a story recounted by Pausanias, which told how a traveller from Sparta was astonished to see a craftsman in Tegea forging a sword of iron.[156] This event is supposed to have occurred during the reign of the Spartan king Anaxandrides, which must therefore place it in the early 6th century. If by the Iron Age we mean the point at which iron (actually steel) replaced bronze as the metal for weaponry, this is when the Iron Age began. Yet it must not be forgotten, for one minute, that steel was, very occasionally, used for weapons before this time. Thus the so-called "iron dagger" (actually of good quality carbon steel) in the tomb of Tutankhamun, is an example of a steel weapon predating the time of Anaxandrides. The prohibition against using iron for weapons was not one of technology or knowledge, but of simple economics.

To summarize, then, the age of metals, properly speaking must have begun around 1100 BC with the Copper Age (wrongly named Early Bronze). This epoch was contemporary with the flowering of the Neolithic, and was characterized by the use of finely-wrought stone tools, with a tiny amount of metal, usually native copper, and usually cold hammered, for a few specialized purposes. Sometime in the 10th century, probably in the latter years, true bronze was discovered, quite possibly in Britain, (which is the only place where ore of mixed copper and tin occurs naturally).[157] From that point on, smelting techniques were developed and improved, and iron, which had been known earlier from meteorites, began to be worked. Yet iron, as a whole, remained subsidiary to bronze for weapons manufacture until more efficient smelting techniques were developed, sometime in the 6th century.

---

156 Pausanias iii, 3, 7 and iii, 11, 8

157 Recent attempts to claim that tin reserves in Anatolia fuelled the Bronze Age long before the Phoenicians discovered Britain display both poor thinking and basic dishonesty, and can only be prompted by a desperate attempt to explain the supposed existence of a Bronze Age a thousand years before the Phoenician voyages. The economics prove the fallacy. If reasonable supplies of tin existed in Anatolia, the incredible cost of journeys to Britain could never have been recovered. People would simply have bought the cheaper Anatolian tin. Herodotus (5th century BC.) casually remarks that in his time the tin employed in the Hellenic world came from the Cassiterides — i.e. the British Isles. (iii,115) The tiny amounts of tin discovered by geologists in Turkey during the 1990s were almost certainly unknown to the ancients.

All during this period, and long afterwards, stone tools of typical Neolithic style continued to be employed by the ordinary peasant farmers the Near East and Europe. All metals were incredibly expensive, due to the obvious difficulties of transporting ore and finished products, as well as the labor-intensive nature of production techniques. For many centuries peasant farmers simply could not afford metal tools. Yet everyday tasks around the farmstead required cutting instruments of various kinds. These were supplied by the local stone-tool manufacturers whose workshops are still very much in evidence throughout the countryside.

Far away from Egypt, the mighty temple-complexes of Stonehenge and Avebury (contemporary with Egypt's pyramids) almost certainly owed their existences to the wealth generated in south-west Britain by the newly-established metallurgical industries of the 9th century BC. Archaeologists were astonished at the opulence exhibited in the tombs of the Wessex people; that branch of the so-called Early Bronze Age responsible for the final phase of Stonehenge. The "unique regional concentration of rich graves in Wessex" provides a contrast to the "general poverty" of other British Early Bronze graves.[158] It is known that "The power and wealth of these chieftains was based on their dynamism and their commercial success, in particular their skill as middlemen in channelling trade from Ireland, Europe and the Mediterranean through their territory."[159]

Thus the wealth and power of Stonehenge's builders was based on trade — their trading links with the eastern Mediterranean are beyond question. Yet the writer of the above words did not venture take the next logical step and connect that Mediterranean traffic with the well-attested tin-trade of nearby Cornwall. Such a step would have been tantamount to admitting that the first flowering of the Bronze Age was directly connected with the first exploitation of Britain's copper and tin resources, and that, as the ancient writers always insisted, Britain was of primary importance as a source of tin. The very motif of a sword emerging from a stone, the central icon of Britain's national myth, is a direct clue to the country's significance in the Bronze Age revolution. However, as everyone always knew (until the application of erroneous Near Eastern chronologies confused the picture) Britain's tin was not exploited till the Phoenicians opened the Atlantic routes around 900 BC.

---

158 Euan MacKie *The Megalith Builders* (Oxford,1977) p.96
159 Colin Burgess "The Bronze Age" in Colin Renfrew ed. *British Prehistory* (1974) p.184

CHAPTER 5. THE ASSYRIAN CONQUEST

THE ASIATIC DYNASTY

According to the king-lists and genealogies, the Fifth Dynasty pyramid-builders from Elephantine were replaced by the Sixth Dynasty, a mysterious line of kings whose seizure of the throne is unrecorded, and whose royal titles are strongly reminiscent of the Asiatic Hyksos kings. Thus for example the two major pharaohs of the time, Pepi I and Pepi II, shared virtually the same name as the two major pharaohs of the Hyksos epoch, Apopi I and Apopi II. Indeed both names have identical meanings, i.e. "Apep's man", or "he of Apep" (Apep of course being the dreaded Serpent of Chaos).

Why, the reader might ask at this stage, should a monarch name himself after the hated and feared dragon-serpent that had earlier apparently threatened to destroy mankind? The answer is no mystery. As a deity of death and destruction, Apop was a god of immense power. Ancient kings, in their wars, sought to emulate the destructiveness of the gods in their battles with the titans. Significantly enough, the kings of Mesopotamia were particularly noted for this. Thus Shalmaneser III, a later king of Assyria, recorded how he left the Hittite land covered in ruined heaps, "like spoil-heaps left by the Flood." Even more pertinently, the kings of Assyria described themselves as "dragons". The same king Shalmaneser III, for example, described himself repeatedly as "the great dragon".

It was Professor Gunnar Heinsohn, in 1987, who first proposed that the Hyksos, the legendary Asiatic conquerors of Egypt, be identified with the Assyrians, conquerors of Egypt in the latter 8th and early 7th centuries BC. In this way he identified the first Hyksos king Sharek (Manetho's Salitis), who appears in the genealogical table of Memphite priests,[160] with the Assyrian empire-builder Sargon (Sharru-kin). In the reconstruction proposed here, the Hyksos are identified not only as Assyrians, but also as the pyramid-builders of Dynasty 6.

The Sixth Dynasty's origin and rise to power are regarded as being shrouded in the deepest mystery. In the early days of Egyptology scholars were frequently undecided whether kings bearing the name "he of Apep" should be placed with the Old Kingdom Sixth Dynasty or the Hyksos Fifteenth.[161] Similarly, they were (and still are) confused as to whether to assign to the First or Second Intermediate Periods a great quantity of material — artifacts and written texts of all kinds — which clearly date from a period of Asiatic domination, but which nevertheless give the names of kings and dignitaries who are otherwise assigned to the Sixth Dynasty.[162]

The kings of the Sixth Dynasty left a number of very substantial pyramids, the inner chambers of which were inscribed with some of the best and most complete examples of the Pyramid Texts. Most of our knowledge of these texts comes from the Sixth Dynasty monuments. By contrast, no tomb of any Hyksos pharaoh has ever been discovered.[163] Yet it seems almost certain that the Hyksos built pyramids, for three pyramids belonging to the Thirteenth Dynasty (which we shall argue was a line of Hyksos clients), two of whom were clearly Asiatic (one called Ameny Amu — Ameny the Asiatic — and another Khendjer), were found at Dahshur and Sakkara.[164] But the tombs of the Great Hyksos pharaohs are entirely missing. This is an enduring mystery to Egyptology, but it is a mystery which is solved if the Sixth Dynasty pharaohs are the Hyksos.

There is in fact an abundance of evidence linking the Sixth Dynasty with Asia. To begin with, the name "Hyksos" (rendered in its proper Egyptian title of *Hikau-*

160 W.C. Hayes "Egypt: From the Death of Ammenemes III to Seqenenre II" in *CAH* Vol.2 part 1 (3rd ed.) p.59

161 H.R. Hall *The Ancient History of the Near East* (3rd ed. London, 1916)

162 Petrie (*A History of Egypt* Vol.1 p.119) noted how scarabs of Khyan, now unequivocally identified as a Hyksos ruler, are stylistically identical to those of Pepi II. Further questions regarding these rulers are posed on pp.238-9 and 245 In his *Making of Egypt* (1939) Petrie notes how two of the most characteristic artifacts brought to Egypt by the Hyksos, daggers with raised ribs and toggle pins, were "similar to the objects brought by the VIIth — VIIIth [7th-8th] dynasties," p.142

163 I.E.S. Edwards *The Pyramids of Egypt* (1961 ed.) p.243

164 Ibid. pp.237-8

khoswet) first appears in documents of the time.[165] Scholars try to suggest that the "Rulers of Foreign Lands" mentioned in these Sixth Dynasty documents are not the same as the later Asiatic Hyksos, but this explanation is strained.

Secondly, personal adornments and artwork of clearly Asiatic (specifically Mesopotamian) provenance makes their first appearance in Egypt at this time. Chief among the personal adornments are so-called "button badges", medallion-like talismans worn on a string round the neck. These amulets, usually inscribed with a cruciform design, were popular with a number of Asiatic peoples. During the Sixth Dynasty such amulets became common in Egypt, though most occur in the burials of the petty kings of Dynasties 7 and 8.[166] (These latter, who had clearly Semitic names, we shall argue were contemporaries and vassals of the Sixth Dynasty). Button badges, although worn in northern Syria, were particularly associated with Mesopotamia. In the words of Petrie; "... the eight-pointed star is figured on a button in Egypt, exactly like the pattern from Bismya in Sumer."[167] Petrie suggested that some of these at least were worn by a bodyguard of foreign soldiers.[168] He regarded the appearance of these ornaments as the material sign of an intrusive population.

Other specific links with Asia are forthcoming: "On a jasper cylinder of Khandy, second king of the VIIth [7th] dynasty, he appears as a Syrian king giving life to the Syrian, while the Egyptian stands in the background holding a papyrus stem. The ibexes and guilloche mark this as Syrian work."[169] The conclusion was inescapable; "It is evident ... that the Syrian had conquered and held Egypt as a joint kingdom with Syria."[170]

There are thus very strong grounds for believing that during the Sixth Dynasty Egypt was part of a much larger political unit encompassing everything from the Nile valley to the Euphrates, at the very least. Scarabs and other artifacts of Pepi I and Pepi II are found in considerable quantities throughout Syria/Palestine: Yet the evidence shows that Egyptians were not the rulers of this political unit, but the ruled; and that the kings of the Sixth Dynasty were themselves Asiatics who took upon themselves the titles and privileges of pharaohs.

When a nation is subjugated by a foreign power there is generally a complete disruption of the established order. New local administrations are established throughout the conquered territory, whose purpose is to impose the will of the

---

165 W.C. Hayes op. cit. p.55

166 F. Petrie, *The Making of Egypt* (London, 1939) p.122

167 Ibid.

168 Ibid.

169 Ibid. p.123

170 Ibid.

invading power. In short, a feudal-type situation evolves. Strange then that one of the most outstanding features of the Sixth Dynasty was its feudalism.[171] From the very beginning there appeared a new class of local rulers, "Great Lords" of the districts, or "Nomes", who were completely unknown before, and whose power and authority vied with that of the pharaoh himself. "These nomarchs," according to Breasted, "...are loyal adherents of the Pharaoh, executing his commissions in distant regions, and displaying the greatest zeal in his cause; but they are no longer his officials merely; nor are they so attached to the court and person of the monarch as to build their tombs around his pyramid. They now have sufficient independence and local attachment to locate their tombs near their own homes."[172]

But the nomarchs were not the only local rulers of the epoch. The dislocation of Egyptian society caused by the Hyksos conquest led to political fragmentation and chaos throughout the Nile Valley. Independent or semi-independent states appeared in the various nomes. This fragmentation may have been exacerbated by periodic rebellions, incited by the vicious exploitation that normally accompanies conquest and colonization. Quite probably, high ranking members of the Hyksos ruling class would have been given lordships in the various regions, to use and exploit as they saw fit; much in the manner of the Norman barons after the conquest of England. These "barons", we shall argue, incited rebellion in the land of the Nile throughout the Hyksos period, rebellions that gave rise to numerous "dynasties" which, although placed in sequence in the textbooks, actually reigned simultaneously. Among these lines of "rulers" we may count all those of the First Intermediate Period (Seventh to Eleventh), as well as those of the Second (Thirteenth to Seventeenth).

AKKADIANS, HYKSOS AND ASSYRIANS

If the pharaohs of the Fourth, Fifth and Sixth Dynasties reigned during the latter 9th and 8th centuries BC, as we claim; and if the Sixth Dynasty was a line of Asiatic kings identical to the Hyksos and originating in Mesopotamia, this would imply that they were one and the same as the Assyrians, whom the classical authors insisted ruled the entire Near East sometime in the 8th century BC. We shall in fact argue that the Sixth Dynasty was Assyrian, yet before doing so another identification has to be established — an identification first proposed by Professor Heinsohn in 1987 — that of the Hyksos with the all-conquering Akkadians of Mesopotamia. In fact, as demonstrated in some detail in Chapter 4, the history of

---

171 J.H. Breasted *A History of Egypt* (1951 ed.) p.132
172 Ibid.

the ancient Near East has been triplicated by scholars, and the actual history of the region, recorded in the classical and Hellenistic authors, was duplicated in the second millennium and again triplicated in the third millennium. Thus "phantom" kingdoms and civilizations occupying two millennia, which never really existed, are described in the textbooks that now fill the libraries of the world.

Like the other nations and rulers of the Near East, the Sixth Dynasty too appears in the textbooks in triplicate. They are, as we shall see, one and the same as the Hyksos, who are nevertheless placed seven centuries after them; and they are likewise identical to the Empire Assyrians, who are placed a further seven centuries after the Hyksos.

We have stated that evidence points to Asia, and more specifically to Mesopotamia, as the probable homeland of the Sixth Dynasty. In addition, even conventional scholarship would agree that the Sixth Dynasty was contemporary with the Akkadians, early Mesopotamia's most famous warrior-nation. The implication is that the Sixth Dynasty was a line of kings established in power by the Akkadians. Is there then any evidence to suggest that the Akkadians conquered Egypt?

The evidence exists in plenty.

To begin with, the Akkadian kings actually claimed to have conquered Egypt, a region they named "Magan". Yet since the Akkadians are supposed to have flourished in the third millennium BC, the conquest of Magan is viewed with the deepest suspicion; and attempts have been made to see in the country some region other than Egypt.[173] Nevertheless, Magan was one of the names normally used to refer to Egypt in later times, and there is one almost incontrovertible piece of evidence to suggest that it also meant Egypt in the Akkadian epoch. This is a series of alabaster vases of rather obviously Egyptian manufacture and inscribed with the name of the Akkadian king Naram Sin. The vases, described as "booty of Magan", initially caused considerable excitement because "Magan was a name undoubtedly applied to Egypt in a later period of Babylonian history, and the vases have a distinct likeness to Egyptian alabaster vases, which more commonly bear inscriptions in the late 5th and 6th Dynasties, the dates of which accord well enough with that of Naram-Sin."[174]

In fact, both Naram-Sin and his grandfather Sargon refer to the subjugation of Magan and Meluhha (the latter usually identified as Ethiopia), and Naram-Sin actually provides the name of the defeated king of Magan — Mannium. This

---

173 C.J. Gadd "The Dynasty of Agade and the Gutian Invasion" in *CAH* Vol.1 part 2 (3rd ed.) p.439 "its name [Meluhha's] was regularly associated with Magan, a land which can now with some confidence be located on the shores of the Gulf of Oman ..."

174 Ibid. p.445

was recognized by a number of authorities as strikingly similar to Min/Menes, the name of the first pharaoh, and seemed to add yet more weight to the belief that the Akkadians had conquered the Nile Kingdom.[175] Nevertheless, the King Mannium defeated by Naram Sin was certainly not the same as the First Dynasty Menes and is much more probably identified with Unas (Wenis) of Dynasty Five. ("w" and "m" are easily confused and often interchangeable). This further supports our contention that the Fifth and Sixth Dynasties did not run in sequence, but were largely contemporaneous.

The genealogy of the Memphite priests has a King Sharek as the first of the Hyksos, a title that sounds very close to that of Sharrukin, Sargon the Conqueror.

The name of Sargon of Akkad was to go down in legend. A usurper on the throne, he termed himself *sharru-kin* ("Legitimate King") almost by way of proclaiming his right to the crown. Within a short period, Sargon had built an empire the likes of which had never been seen before. He conquered the whole of Mesopotamia and his armies reached westwards towards the Upper Sea (the Mediterranean). He did not stop there, however, for he swept northwards into Anatolia and southwards (if our interpretation of Magan is correct) into Egypt.

Sargon thus stamped his authority over much of the known world; and his successors were to adopt the title, used afterwards by the Medes and Persians, "King of the Four Quarters". If this is correct, Sargon can be none other than Sharek (Salitis), the Hyksos invader of Egypt. Manetho provides virtually the only account of the Hyksos conquest, and he emphasizes the ease with which the Egyptians were defeated:

> Tutimaeus. In his reign, for what cause I know not, a blast of God smote us; and unexpectedly, from the regions of the East, invaders of some obscure race marched in confidence of victory against our land. By main force they easily seized it without striking a blow; and having overpowered the rulers of the land, when they burned our cities ruthlessly, razed to the ground the temples of the gods, and treated all the natives with a cruel hostility, massacring some and leading into slavery the wives and children of others. Finally, they appointed as king one of their number whose name was Salitis. He had his seat at Memphis, levying tribute from Upper and Lower Egypt, and always leaving garrisons behind in the most advantageous positions.[176]

Manetho hereby gives the impression that the pharaoh of the invasion was Tutimaeus. Yet we shall argue here that Tutimaeus (actually Teti, the name of the first pharaoh of Dynasty 6) was the Egyptian title adopted by the invader, who can be none other than Sargon I.

Two questions are raised at this point. First and foremost, if the Akkadians had really conquered Egypt we must expect them to have introduced a variety of

---

175 Ibid.

176 Josephus *Against Apion* i,14

cultural and technological features (aside from a few button-badges and small trinkets) into the Nile Kingdom. The peoples of Mesopotamia were highly-civilized, and were responsible for the invention of some revolutionary new techniques and technologies — not least of which was the wheel. If the Akkadians entered Egypt we must expect them to have brought these things with them.

Secondly, in suggesting that "Hyksos" was the name given by the Egyptians to these Akkadian invaders, we must expect Hyksos cultural features to display their Mesopotamia origin. The Hyksos, we should find, actually spoke Akkadian, worshipped Mesopotamian deities such as Marduk and Ishtar, and possessed a material culture indistinguishable from that of Mesopotamia in the Akkadian epoch. In addition, we would expect Hyksos material to be found in the same stratigraphic levels as the Akkadian.

Let us at this stage look at what the Asiatic invaders brought to Egypt.

Historians are agreed that Sargon's empire, universally regarded as the world's first superpower, was built above all with the help of the horse-drawn chariot. The chariot had first appeared amongst the Sumerians in Early Dynastic times, but this was a heavy, cumbersome contraption, four-wheeled and drawn by asses. The evidence is scanty, but it appears fairly clear that the two-wheeled horse-drawn chariot made its appearance in the final stage of Mesopotamia's Early Dynastic Age, immediately prior to the rise of the Akkadians.[177] In the days before cavalry, the chariot was supreme. Foot soldiers simply could not resist an onslaught of massed chariotry.

If the Akkadians used chariots against the infantry of Egypt, that is a fairly straightforward explanation for the ease (emphasized by Manetho) with which they conquered the country.

Yet scholars are unanimous in their belief that the chariot was introduced to Egypt by the Hyksos, who also, supposedly seven hundred years after the Akkadians, used this revolutionary weapon to establish their world empire. That the chariot introduced by the Hyksos was an Akkadian device is strongly suggested by the fact that at least one of the Egyptian words for "chariot", *markabata*, is derived from the Akkadian *narkabat*.[178] This strongly suggests that the Hyksos spoke Akkadian, a suggestion supported by a whole variety of other evidence to be examined shortly. Furthermore, a host of innovations of Mesopotamian origin, mostly of a military nature, were introduced into Egypt during the Hyksos epoch.

---

177 The earliest representation of the two-wheeled chariot is apparently a small copper model, drawn by four onagers, from Tell Agrab in Lower Mesopotamia, and dated to E.D. III. See Sir Max Mallowan "The Early Dynastic Period in Mesopotamia" in *CAH* Vol.1 part 2 (3rd ed.) p.269

178 H.R. Hall *The Ancient History of the Near East* (3rd ed. London, 1916) p.213

The 'Shepherd Kings' of Mesopotamia

Manetho derived the word "Hyksos" from two Egyptian words which translated as "Shepherd Kings". Although this etymology is now rejected, there are good grounds for believing that the Ptolemaic scribe had tapped into a genuine Egyptian tradition about the Hyksos, a tradition which somehow linked them with shepherds.

Why link a nation of military conquerors with the humble occupation of the shepherd?

The land most famous in the ancient Near East for its shepherds and sheep was Assyria. A bas-relief on the stairways of the Apadana at Persepolis portrays the subject peoples of the Achaemenid Empire delivering their tribute to king Xerxes. Each region brings the tribute upon which the economic strength of that nation is based. The Lydians, for example, with their long side-locks, deliver measures of gold-dust to the Great King. The Assyrians are there too. They bring fleeces and live sheep.[179] The Assyrian kings of the Neo-Assyrian epoch were regularly portrayed wearing robes trimmed with woolen fringes and grasping in their right hands the Assyrian symbol of royal authority and power — the shepherd's crook. The pharaohs of Egypt also used the shepherd's crook as a symbol of kingly authority, but its use in this context appears to have been unknown before the Hyksos Age. Who then could have introduced such a royal symbol to Egypt but the sheep-rearing people of northern Mesopotamia, the Assyrian Shepherd Kings?

The links between the Hyksos and Mesopotamia, specifically with the Akkadians of Mesopotamia, are in fact all-pervasive. A granite lion of Khyan, one of the most powerful Hyksos pharaohs, was actually discovered in Baghdad,[180] and during their epoch large numbers of cultural innovations, specifically connected with Mesopotamia, were introduced to the Nile Valley. Thus the bronze scimitar, known to have a Mesopotamian origin, was brought to Egypt by the Hyksos.[181] A very specific type of cylinder-seal, portraying a bull-headed hero, is associated with the Akkadian epoch; yet such seals appear in Hyksos-age strata in Palestine/Syria.[182] Pottery of the Akkadian age offers precise parallels with Hyksos pottery.[183] Architecture of the two peoples, supposedly separated in time

179 John Hicks *The Persians* (Time-Life, 1978) pp.36-7

180 W.C. Hayes "Egypt: From the Death of Amenemmes III to Seqenenre II" in *CAH* Vol.2 part 1 (3rd ed.) p. 60

181 H. Bonnet, *Die Waffen der Volker des alten Orients* (Leipzig, 1926). p. 94

182 See, e.g., Gunnar Heinsohn, "Who were the Hyksos?" *Sixth International Congress of Egyptology* (Turin, 1991) pp. 10-12

183 Ibid. pp. 18-27

by over seven centuries, offers further comparisons. Thus the peculiar defensive triple-gate of the Akkadian Age is copied in exact detail by the Hyksos.[184] In the same way, the cults of Ishtar and Bel made their first appearance in Egypt in the time of the Hyksos, whilst many of the Hyksos rulers and officials had names that were quite evidently Semitic.

One of the most enduring legacies of the Hyksos epoch appears to have been the establishment of the Akkadian language as the *lingua franca* of diplomacy throughout the Near East — a situation that we find already at the beginning of the New Kingdom. The famous Amarna documents, for example, show Syrian vassal kings of Amenhotep III and Akhnaton corresponding with their master by means of letters written in Akkadian — an Akkadian strikingly similar to that used by Sargon I and Naram Sin.[185] Even Mesopotamian diplomatic protocols are preserved, with royal correspondences written in cuneiform upon clay tablets and concealed within clay envelopes.

Amongst Egyptologists the question of who taught the Egyptians the Akkadian language is still one that prompts lively debate. Yet proof positive that the Hyksos used Akkadian, and were therefore almost certainly the nation responsible for making it the language of commerce and diplomacy throughout Palestine/Syria, came with the discovery at Hazor in Israel of some jugs of Hyksos date, one of which bore an inscription in Akkadian cuneiform. "Three jugs belonging to Middle Bronze Age II were found *in situ* in Locus 6175. On one of them (C339/1) an inscription was found incised in cuneiform, the earliest in this script to be discovered hitherto in Palestine."[186] It was understood that "the historical conclusions connected with the fact that the grammatical form of the name is Akkadian and not Western Semitic" would be far-reaching. One scholar noted that "it is instructive that the first element of the name, whose reading is plain, has the Akkadian form *is-me* (i.e., 'he has heard') and not the West Semitic form one would expect: *iasmah*, as in the name Iasmah-Adad known from Mari."[187]

Thus the experts expressed their puzzlement and discomfort at the apparently anomalous and anachronistic appearance of the Akkadian language amongst the Hyksos.

All in all, the evidence increasingly demonstrates that the Hyksos were a mighty and cultured people, closely connected to Mesopotamia, and not the ignorant barbarians portrayed by the Egyptians. They described themselves as

---

184 Ibid. pp.32-5

185 Gunnar Heinsohn loc. cit. p.32

186 Y. Yadin et al. Cited from Heinsohn, loc. cit. p.31

187 A. Malamat "Hazor, 'The Head of all those Kingdoms" *Journal of Biblical Literature* Vol. LXXIX (1960) p.18

"Rulers of Nations" — a term held to be "suggestive of worldwide domination".[188] Strange indeed that such an awesome imperial power should have escaped the attention of everyone but the Egyptians! Not only were they great conquerors, their technological innovations are now justly recognized. "Through their Hyksos adversaries the Egyptians probably first became acquainted with the composite bow, bronze daggers and swords of improved type, and other advances in the equipment and technique of war, as well as with some of the important western Asiatic innovations in the arts of peace which are encountered in Egypt for the first time under the Eighteenth Dynasty."[189] Such benefits of civilization could force only one conclusion about those responsible; "However we may evaluate them, they were evidently not the ruthless barbarians conjured up by the Theban propagandists of the early New Kingdom and the Egyptian writers of later periods."[190]

So the Hyksos epoch was one of high civilization. Fresh ideas from the east flooded into Egypt, and we cannot doubt that international trade, as well as diplomacy, was a characteristic of the age. Literature — in the form of the "Prophetic" and "Pessimistic" treatises — flourished, as did art and architecture. The Hyksos kings (if our identification of the Sixth Dynasty is correct) built great monuments throughout Egypt, and they poured substantial resources into beautifying the nation's temples and shrines. Put simply, the archaeological record demonstrates that Egyptian civilization suffered not at all from the Hyksos occupation, and that, on the contrary, it was greatly enriched by the infusion of Asiatic influence.

Where, it has been asked again and again, could such a powerful and civilized nation have originated? The answer has been given. They were from Mesopotamia. But the Hyksos monarchs did not rule in the 16th century BC, as conventional scholarship supposes; they reigned in the 8th: And their Akkadian language was also that of the mighty nation of warriors whom the classical authors tell us ruled most of the Near East during this epoch: the Assyrians.

PYRAMID-BUILDERS AND ZIGGURAT-BUILDERS

A point to be stressed here is that none of the "Assyrian" (actually "Neo-Assyrian") material so proudly displayed in museums throughout the world actually belongs to the period under discussion at present. The Neo-Assyrians, as I have

---

188 W.C. Hayes "Egypt: From the Death of Ammenemes III to Seqenenre II" in *CAH* Vol.2 part 1 (3rd ed.) p.61

189 Ibid. p.57

190 Ibid. p.55

demonstrated elsewhere, are in reality alter-egos of the Persian Great Kings, with whom they are stratigraphically contemporary. Our epoch, the "Old Assyrian", or Akkadian, is known to us solely from the Akkadian records of Mesopotamia, the Sixth Dynasty and Hyksos records of Egypt, and certain of the classical and Hellenistic authors who refer to the Empire Assyrians.

The appearance of the name Sharek on the genealogical table of the Memphite priests would imply that Sargon I (Sharrukin) had actually led the Hyksos invasion and made himself first pharaoh of a new dynasty. Recalling the conclusions already reached, it is tempting to identify Sargon I with Teti, first of the Sixth Dynasty pharaohs. If such be the case, then we can see why Manetho placed the Hyksos invasion during the reign of a king Tutimaeus. Teti and Tutimaeus are evidently identical. Continuing this line of approach, we would then be compelled to identify Sargon's son Rimush with Teti's son Pepi/Apopi I; Rimush's son Manishtusu with Pepi I's son Merenre I; Manishtusu's son Naram-Sin with Merenre I's son Pepi/Apopi II, and Naram-Sin's son Shar-kali-sharri with Merenre II. Thus we have:

"Old Assyrians"/Akkadians	Sixth Dynasty/Hyksos
Sharrukin (Sargon I)	Sharek/Teti I
Rimush	Apopi/Pepi I
Manishtusu	Merenre I
Naram-Sin	Apopi/Pepi II
Shar-kali-sharri	Merenre II

It must of course be stressed that the above identifications are very tentative. There was a strong tradition in Egypt that pharaoh Teti was murdered in a palace coup and that his assassin, after occupying the throne only a short period of time, was killed by a brother who took the title Pepi I. Similarly, Sargon I seems to have met a violent end. Yet Rimush, who replaced him, may well have been his assassin. For the latter occupied the throne only a short time before being replaced by an elder brother named Manishtusu. Thus it may well be that Manishtusu, not Rimush, is the Mesopotamian alter-ego of Pepi I. Other identifications are just as tentative. The (Hyksos) pharaoh named Khyan, whose lion was found at Baghdad, may well have been yet another alter-ego of Apopi/Pepi I, though there are indications that he is more probably identified with Apopi/Pepi II.

The Hyksos Empire, though commonly believed to have lasted at least a century and a half, is, if the above identifications are correct, revealed to have in reality endured less than a hundred years. The imagined length of the dynasty (actually dynasties) is due to a factor already mentioned. During the Hyksos epoch petty kingdoms sprang up the length of the Nile Valley, and the rulers of these vassal states were frequently permitted to surround their names with the royal cartouche (many of them were probably in any case related by blood to the Great Hyksos pharaohs). But modern scholars, and also ancient ones, believed these kingdoms to have existed in sequence, rather than, as they really did, in concurrence.

Springing to power then shortly after 800 BC, the Hyksos/Akkadian/Assyrian Empire would have dominated the Near East until near the end of the 8th century: For the evidence suggests that shortly before 700 BC the Medes (who in the archaeological record appear as Mitanni) overthrew the Old Assyrians and established themselves as masters of the region. In Egypt, the Hyksos/Old Assyrians were defeated and expelled by a line of Theban rulers who would form the glorious Eighteenth Dynasty, and establish Egypt herself as a military power of the first order. Thus the Mitanni kingdom and the Eighteenth Dynasty rose to power at the same time, and there is every likelihood that they were close allies in the great war against Assyria.

Our new chronology means therefore that the Sixth Dynasty, who are the Great Hyksos, were the kings opposed and eventually defeated by the Eighteenth Dynasty, and that the eleven dynasties believed to come between these two were ephemeral, local, or fictitious. But if the Sixth Dynasty was followed immediately by the Eighteenth, there should be clear indications of this from the world of art, literature, technology and culture in general. Do these suggest a close link?

In fact, a great deal of evidence from these very areas suggests that the Sixth and Eighteenth Dynasties, separated from each other in the textbooks by eight hundred years, belong right next to each other. Scarabs of the two epochs, for example, are "identical in type and workmanship" according to Flinders Petrie.[191] Technology tells a similar tale. Looking at glazing and glassmaking techniques, John Dayton remarked on the fact that certain colors of glaze found in Sixth Dynasty pottery could not have been developed much before the Eighteenth Dynasty; "Green pigments were produced from malachite, but is also appears that an artificial green frit was used as early as the VIth [6th] Dynasty (Lucas 1962). However, in the writer's opinion it is unlikely than an artificial green was used before the Amarna [18th Dynasty] period, when analyses show that the art of modifying the blue effect of copper by the addition of antimony and iron was mastered."[192]

We should not, at this point, forget the almost monotheistic tone of many of the Pyramid Texts (most of which were written in the Sixth Dynasty), and how

191 F. Petrie, *A History of Egypt* Vol.1 (1894)

192 John Dayton *Minerals, Metals, Glazing and Man* (London, 1978) p.33

the words and expressions used in praise of the rising sun Atum are strongly reminiscent of those used in the latter Eighteenth Dynasty by Akhnaton in praise of the sun-disc Aton. Nor should we fail to recall how the plastic arts of the two epochs, especially sculpture, display striking parallels. Thus the copper statue of a naked Pepi II seems to prefigure the artistic revolution of the Amarna Age, where the pharaoh is again portrayed naked. It should be noted here also that such Old Kingdom portrayals of naked kings are strikingly similar to the *kouroi* figures of 7th and 6th century Greece — a similarity often remarked upon, but not understood. Since it is assumed that almost two thousand years separate these two sculptural styles, the parallels are regarded as most mysterious.[193] Yet the parallels between the sculpture of the Sixth and Eighteenth Dynasties, though not spanning so great an historical gap, are equally striking; and the kneeling statue of Hatshepsut could almost have been executed by the same artist who fashioned a statue of Pepi I in precisely the same position.

The burial and mummification customs of Dynasty 6, it appears, were also strikingly similar to those of the Eighteenth Dynasty. The great anatomist Elliott Smith was famously convinced that the mummy of Merenre I (third ruler of Dynasty 6), was prepared in the fashion of the Eighteenth Dynasty, and refused to date the body earlier.[194]

Thus there is an abundance of evidence to support our contention that the Sixth Dynasty, the last rulers of the so-called Old Kingdom, were in reality the Asiatic Hyksos, who were overthrown and expelled by the Eighteenth Dynasty, the first rulers of the so-called New Kingdom. But such a proposition, so startling in its various implications, apparently raises almost as many problems as it solves.

It is just some of these problems that we shall now address.

THE MIDDLE KINGDOM

Our juxtaposition of the last Old Kingdom dynasty with the first New Kingdom dynasty means of course that the entire concept of the Middle Kingdom, a period of roughly seven hundred years that in conventional chronology separates Egypt's Pyramid Age from its Imperial epoch, must be eliminated. But how can this be possible? Surely, it will be said, the Eleventh, Twelfth and Thirteenth Dynasties in particular were great lines of kings who left many monuments. Where

---

193 See e.g. Michael Rice *Egypt's Making* (London, 1990) p.237 note to ill.94 These Old Kingdom figures "anticipate the Greek 'kouroi', which first appear nearly two thousand years later in the sixth century BC. The similarity extends even to the position of the hands, and the right leg advanced."

194 J. Elliott Smith in *American Journal of Archaeology* Vol.1 p.193

do they fit in, if we leave them no room to reign as independent monarchs in their own right?

I would begin by stating that the most important of these dynasties, the Twelfth, never actually ruled, but was a line of priest-kings resident in Middle Egypt, who "reigned" alongside the Eighteenth Dynasty. What evidence do I have for this?

To begin with, stratigraphy never shows any real distance between the Twelfth and Eighteenth Dynasties. On the contrary, they are consistently found at the same level. At Ugarit, for example, Claude Schaeffer found a sphinx of Amen-emhet III (Dynasty 12) next to alphabetic cuneiform tablets, which are known to date from the latter years of the 18th Dynasty.[195] More recently, a building of Eighteenth Dynasty date in Qatna, Syria, revealed, "two serpentine vessels made in Egypt in the 12th dynasty," which, according to the excavators, identified them as "clearly heirlooms, 500 years old at the time of burial."[196] This pattern repeats itself in all the excavated sites. Again and again archaeologists found material of the Twelfth Dynasty, along with that of the Eighteenth, immediately above that of the Hyksos. Where material of the two dynasties are actually found in the same buildings, or tombs, the Twelfth Dynasty material is normally explained away (as above) as "heirlooms"; a favorite method of disposing of uncomfortable anomalies.

The textual evidence agrees. The Karnak List of kings, compiled by Thut-mose III, has the Old Kingdom (ending with Pepi II) followed by some of the kings of the Twelfth Dynasty, which in turn is followed by the Eighteenth (though the early kings of the Eighteenth Dynasty are missing). Scholars of course claim that Thutmose thus failed to mention the Hyksos, whom they imagine reigned between the Twelfth and Eighteenth Dynasties. Yet the Abydos List, compiled during the reign of Seti I of the Nineteenth Dynasty, shows the same thing. Here again we find the monarchs of the Twelfth Dynasty immediately preceding those of the Eighteenth. It is just possible that Thutmose III, reigning shortly after the expulsion of the Hyksos, might have omitted them out of spite. Yet by the time of Seti I the Hyksos threat was part of the fairly distant past. Why then omit them? Even worse, why omit also the great kings of the Thirteenth Dynasty, who are not regarded as Hyksos at all?

But of course, if the Great Hyksos Fifteenth Dynasty (Apepi I and Apepi II) is the same as the Sixth Dynasty of Pepi I and Pepi II and if furthermore the Twelfth Dynasty was more or less contemporary with the Eighteenth (as the stratigraphic evidence seems to suggest), then neither Thutmose III nor Seti I left

---

195 Claude Schaeffer, *Stratigrapie comparée et chonologie de l'Asia occidentale* (Oxford, 1948)

196 *Current World Archaeology*, No.15, February/March, 2006, p.20

out the Hyksos at all; and they are listed in precisely the correct place, i.e. immediately prior to the start of the contemporary Twelfth and Eighteenth Dynasties.

Again, Flinders Petrie was astonished to find numerous scarabs containing the names of Twelfth and Eighteenth Dynasty pharaohs next to each other: "Scarabs bear double cartouches of Usertesen [Senwosret] III and Tahutmes [Thutmose] III ... others read doubly [kha/maat] ka, Usertesen II and Hatshepsut; others have these two names both complete; and other scarabs of Men-ka-ra, Nefer-ka-ra, Amenemhat II, Usertesen III, and Amenhotep I are identical in type and workmanship with the scarabs of Hatshepsut and her brother."[197] These scarabs thus give further weight to the stratigraphic testimony, and call to attention also the fact that typical Twelfth Dynasty names and titles were very popular during the Eighteenth Dynasty. Thus for example Thutmose III's firstborn son was named Amenemhet (one of the two royal titles of the Twelfth Dynasty pharaohs), whilst a family of local rulers from Thutmose III's time carried the name Sebekhotep — a royal title borne by a line of rulers who also reigned during the Twelfth Dynasty.

All this evidence, taken together, would suggest that the two lines of kings, supposedly separated in history by 500 years, reigned jointly, and that most probably the Twelfth Dynasty pharaohs — great devotees of the god Amon, like their Eighteenth Dynasty contemporaries — were a line of priest-kings entitled to surround their names with the royal cartouche. And this interpretation would solve the vexed question of the astonishingly long reigns of the Twelfth Dynasty monarchs — close to forty years. If, as we suggest, they were a line of priestly monarchs, then their "reigns" would probably have begun at their births, not upon the death of the preceding ruler.

But we have as yet only scratched the surface; for a great body of other evidence points to the fact that the Theban kings of the so-called Eleventh Dynasty, the immediate predecessors of the Twelfth were the same as, or at least contemporary with, the Theban rulers of the Seventeenth Dynasty, the immediate predecessors of the Eighteenth. The artwork of the Eleventh Dynasty, for example, is virtually identical to that of the Seventeenth, whilst, as we might expect, the work of the Twelfth Dynasty offers a precise match with that of the Eighteenth.[198]

During the final years of the "Second" Intermediate Age, according to conventional ideas, Thebes and much of Upper Egypt was ruled by the Seventeenth Dynasty, a line composed of kings named Inyotef and Seqenenre. These monarchs were in continual conflict with the Hyksos pharaohs, whose power base was in

---

197 F. Petrie, *A History of Egypt* Vol.2 (London, 1896) pp.94-5

198 Petrie, loc. cit. p.146 Petrie notes that "the works of the 11th and the 17th and the 12th and the 18th dynasties, when compared, are barely distinguishable."

Lower Egypt. Yet here we detect remarkable parallels with the Eleventh Dynasty — a line composed of kings named Inyotef and Mentuhotep — who ruled Thebes during the "First" Intermediate Period; just as the Seventeenth Dynasty fought Asiatics based in the north, so too the Eleventh Dynasty fought enemies based in the north, who appear to have been largely Asiatic. Nebhepetre Mentuhotep, the most illustrious king of the Eleventh Dynasty, was honored in later ages as a great warrior and a unifier of the country. On the monuments his name was frequently associated with that of Ahmose, the renowned warrior who expelled the Hyksos and founded the Eighteenth Dynasty.[199] Yet seven hundred years earlier Nebhepetre Mentuhotep also expelled Asiatics from Egypt, as his temple as Deir El Bahri illustrates. Nebhepetre won great victories over these people, and earned himself the title *Smatowy*, "Uniter of the Two Lands".

As we have said, the artwork of the Eleventh Dynasty bears striking resemblance to that of the Seventeenth. Furthermore, both lines of kings were buried at Deir El Bahri, and, as Maspero noted, the Seventeenth Dynasty monarchs employed precisely the same funerary architecture — the pyramid-topped mastaba — as their Eleventh Dynasty predecessors.[200] Even the design of sarcophagi was remarkably similar during the two epochs, supposedly separated by over six centuries.

We recall now also that Eleventh Dynasty styles, as well as being virtually indistinguishable from those of the Pyramid Age, also strongly prefigure those of the Eighteenth Dynasty. Most spectacular in this respect is Nebhepetre's temple at Deir El Bahri, which closely resembles, and was clearly the model for, Hatshepsut's adjacent and more well-known funerary monument. Furthermore, all the early rulers of the Eighteenth Dynasty were interred in precisely the same manner as the Mentuhoteps: "The tombs of the first pharaohs of the Eighteenth Dynasty, Kames, Aahmes, Amenophis I, were pyramid-mastabas of the same kind as those of Mentu-hetep at Der-el-Bahari."[201]

Thus in terms of art, architecture and religious culture, there is a clear and immediate line of development from the Eleventh Dynasty to the Eighteenth; and it is evident that the six or seven centuries said to separate these two are fictitious. Collating all the evidence, it begins to look fairly certain that the Eleventh Dynasty Inyotefs and Mentuhoteps belonged to the Hyksos period, and were alter-egos of the Seventeenth Dynasty Inyotefs and Seqenenres, the direct predecessors of the Eighteenth Dynasty, who began the war of liberation against the Hyksos. It would seem that Nebhepetre Mentuhotep I of the Eleventh Dynasty,

199 W.C. Hayes loc. cit. p.59

200 G. Maspero, *Art in Egypt* (London,1912) p.148

201 Ibid.

who initiated the war of liberation against the north, was an alter-ego of Kamose of the Seventeenth/Eighteenth Dynasty, who similarly initiated the war of liberation against the Hyksos. Nebtawy Mentuhotep III, who completed the conquest of northern Egypt, must have been an alter-ego of Ahmose, founder of the Eighteenth Dynasty. Nebtawy's vizier and commander-in-chief, largely responsible for his victories, was to become Amenemhet I, founder of the so-called Twelfth Dynasty.

Clearly Amenemhet acquitted himself so well against the Hyksos that he and his descendants were awarded a sort of parallel kingship, or priest-kingship (an office by no means uncommon in Egypt). The priest-kings of this line, though clearly of Theban origin, had their capital at a place called It-tawy, seemingly located near Lisht (just to the south of Memphis), where they built their pyramids.

The Thirteenth Dynasty

According to conventional ideas, the Eleventh, Twelfth, and Thirteenth Dynasties reigned before the Hyksos Invasion, but in the reconstruction proposed here, the Eleventh and Thirteenth Dynasties actually held power during the Hyksos age, and they continued to hold positions of importance throughout much of the Eighteenth Dynasty.

Whilst Asiatic influence is admittedly pronounced during the Twelfth Dynasty, it is even more so during the Thirteenth. One of these rulers actually bore the Semitic name Khendjer, whilst another was known as Ameny Amu (Ameny the Asiatic). In our view then the so-called Thirteenth Dynasty, whose art and culture strongly resembles that of the Hyksos, was little more than a collection of petty princes (over seventy in number), provincial governors who worked first for the Hyksos pharaohs and then, later, for the Eighteenth Dynasty.

There is in fact nothing new in the suggestion that the Thirteenth Dynasty were Hyksos, or at least clients of the Hyksos. Both Maspero and Petrie held this view, and they commented repeatedly on the striking similarities between the artwork of the Thirteenth Dynasty and that of the Hyksos dynasties proper. The work of the two periods, they said, was so close as to be indistinguishable.[202]

The major, and in fact the only important kings of the Thirteenth Dynasty bore the name Sebekhotep. Artifacts of Sebekhotep III have been found as far part as the Third Cataract in Nubia and in Byblos. But who, the question has been asked repeatedly, were these kings who appeared to be Hyksos, yet according to conventional chronology lived before the Hyksos conquest? As early as

---

202 See Maspero, loc. cit. p.124 ; also Petrie's *The Making of Egypt* pp.142-6

1950 a French scholar named Raymond Weill suggested that the Sebekhoteps be understood as a dynasty of nomarchs entitled to surround their names with the royal cartouche,[203] and he further suggested that they were vassals of the Twelfth Dynasty pharaohs. As a matter of fact, a dynasty of nomarchs named Sebekhotep were very prominent during the Twelfth Dynasty, though the same line of rulers seem to have endured right through to the time of the Eighteenth Dynasty, when members of the family built splendid tombs for themselves at Beni Hasan. Scholars of course believe that the Sebekhoteps of the Twelfth Dynasty are separated from those of the Eighteenth by roughly 500 years — an incredibly long period for a single family to retain its power and privilege. Yet evidence presented above would suggest that the Twelfth and Eighteenth Dynasty Sebekhoteps were contemporaries.

During the Twelfth Dynasty — a great "feudal" epoch (like the Sixth Dynasty) — powerful princes, or lords of the nomes, controlled vast areas of the country. These nomarchs, the Sebekhoteps, the Khnumhoteps, the Inyotefs, the Bebys, etc., bore names that recurred again during the Hyksos epoch, and once more during the 18th Dynasty. The evidence however strongly suggests that all these princes rose to power during the Hyksos occupation, and that many managed to hold onto their positions under the new regime of the Eighteenth Dynasty.

It was during the "Middle Kingdom" that the famous Execration Texts — curses inscribed on pots, which were then smashed — were written. These texts frequently allude to the peoples and cities of Palestine/Syria, and many of the names appearing are typically Hebrew.[204] A group of Thirteenth Dynasty papyri published by F.L. Griffith in 1898 mention slaves with Asiatic names.[205] Of even greater significance however is the famous Papyrus Brooklyn, a Thirteenth Dynasty prison-register which bears on its reverse side a list of 95 servants in an Egyptian household. As W.F. Albright noted, thirty of these were Asiatics, many of whom had good Hebrew names. Some of these were domestics (*hry-pr*), just like Joseph in Genesis 39:2 "in the house".

On the list, Albright notes, are a number of names of definite biblical provenance. The name Job ('Ayyabum) for example, occurs. So too do Asher and Issachar. Two names on the list are from the root 'QB, whence is derived Jacob. The title of one of the Hebrew midwives of the Moses story — 'Shiphrah — occurs on the list, "in nearly the same form" as encountered in Exodus. Another known

---

203 R. Weill, *XIIe dynastie royaute de Haute-Égypte et Domination Hyksos dans le Nord* (Cairo, 1953)

204 See e.g. W. Bright, *A History of Israel* (London, 1960) p.70

205 F.L. Griffith, *Hieratic papyri from Kahun and Gorub* (London, 1898) p.LXII; 10-11 cf. Pls. XIII;15-17; XXX; 35

Hebrew name occurring on the list is Dodovah; and it appears that Epher too is represented. According to Albright, the list shows that "virtually all the tribal names of the House of Jacob go back to early times, and the tribes had already a long history at the beginning of the Mosaic Age."[206]

So, once again a faulty chronology has forced the rewriting of history. Since these texts are believed to predate Moses by around 400 years, it has to be assumed that the compilers of Genesis and Exodus got their dates wrong by at least that length of time. From the point of view of the reconstruction proposed here however, the Execration Texts provide not the slightest problem. These Hebrew slaves of the Hyksos were prisoners of war captured during the intermittent wars with the still semi-nomadic Israelites, who at that time were led by the Judges. The occurrence of the name of Moses' midwife 'Shiphrah is not a mystery but entirely to be expected, since by this time the Exodus was already about 100 years old and the epic events surrounding the escape from Egypt were now part of Hebrew mythology.

POLITICAL FRAGMENTATION IN EGYPT

The disturbances of nature which brought the Early Dynastic Age to and end, also initiated a period of political confusion. Whilst the Fourth Dynasty under Sneferu managed to grasp the reins of power and bring some unity and stability, it is clear that all was not as it had been. As well as the major catastrophe that ended the Third Dynasty, there was, throughout the 8th century BC, a series of lesser disasters which, although not on the scale of previous such events, periodically revived the fear of a return to them. So the Pyramid Age was not the epoch of supreme stability and pharaonic authority that it is said to have been.

During the brief interregnum which preceded the coronation of Sneferu, independent or semi-independent statelets, ruled by petty princes and officials with names like Inyotef and Khety, sprang up the length and breadth of the Nile Valley. These local rulers were in essence no more than the equivalent of sheriffs or district magistrates, but for a short time they rose to greater prominence, and many of the Pessimistic treatises, most of which were composed during and immediately after the catastrophe which ended the life of Huni and terminated the Third Dynasty, mention their names. Thus Inyotef (III), ruler of Thebes in this period, speaks of his actions on the day of *Shedyetshya*, or Day of Misery, when it seemed that all the people of the region were threatened with complete destruction by

---

206 W.F. Albright, "Northwest Semitic Names in a List of Egyptian Slaves from the Eighteenth Century BC." *Journal of the American Oriental Society* 74 (1954) p.233

the forces of nature.[207] From the same period a dignitary named Kay records how he offered shelter to "all who came frightened on the day of tumult."[208]

One of the most famous documents of the time, "A Man's Dispute with his Soul over Suicide", clearly describes some form of natural catastrophe. The text speaks of a flood-storm and a darkening of the sun. The narrator's family is lost in the Lake of the Crocodile, a body of water apparently corresponding to the cosmic waters that surround the primeval island, or island of creation.[209] Later we hear how the narrator's children were "crushed in the egg" because they had, "looked into the face of the Double Crocodile before they had lived."[210] The Double Crocodile, or Henti, was a persona of the evil Set, and the picture of the child Horus crushing the heads of the Double Crocodile became a favorite motif of Egyptian art. (Compare also with the child Hercules' strangling of the twin serpents who attacked his cradle).

In the midst of these upheavals of nature, the Egyptians looked for succor to their beloved Horus, the conqueror of Set and restorer of peace to the cosmos.

Having demonstrated their worth during the crisis, the pharaohs of the Fourth and Fifth Dynasties permitted the provincial rulers, the lords of the nomes, to hold onto their privileges. In Upper Egypt, in the district of Thebes, the ruling family, the Inyotefs, were prominent right throughout the Old Kingdom, and in time they were to organize resistance against the Hyksos, who were of course one and the same as the Sixth Dynasty.[211] From them, we shall argue, would arise the kings of the mighty Eighteenth Dynasty. In Middle Egypt the ruling family bore the name Khety, or Akhety. These rulers, whose generic name Manetho Hellenized as Akhthoes, had their home in the city of Heneneswe, which the Greeks of Ptolemaic times called Herakleopolis, the name still in popular use among scholars. The Khety kings are thus known as the "Herakleopolitans", and their dynasties counted by Egyptologists as the Ninth and Tenth. During the Sixth Dynasty, we shall argue, this line of rulers became trusted clients of the Hyksos, and bitter enemies of the Inyotefs.

As has already been stressed, the cosmic events of the 9th and 8th centuries BC were linked in some way by the people of the era to the deity known to the Greeks as Herakles (Hercules), the dragon-slaying hero *par excellence*. The city of

---

207 W.C. Hayes, "The Middle Kingdom in Egypt: Internal History from the Rise of the Heracleopolitans to the Death of Ammenemes III" in *CAH* Vol.1 part 2 (3rd ed.) p.471

208 Ibid. p.470

209 Brendan Stannard, *The Origins of Israel and Mankind* (Lancaster, 1983) p.761

210 Ibid.

211 In his *Making of Egypt* (1939) p.126 Petrie notes how the name Inyotef (Antef) makes its first appearance in Egypt in the time of the 6th Dynasty.

Herakleopolis/Heneneswe was a cult centre of the god Hershuf (an alter-ego of Horus), whom the Hellenes identified with their own Herakles/Hercules. Horus, or Hershuf, was the Divine Child destined by the gods to save mankind from destruction: He it was who battled and overcame the wicked Set, lord of darkness and chaos, just as Hercules rid the world of monsters in the course of his Twelve Labors. The Herakleopolitans were thus the Egyptian equivalents of the Greek Herakleids, a dynasty specially devoted to Hercules, who owed their position to the divine intervention of Hercules.

This is precisely as it should be, since the Greek Age of Hercules, or Heroic Age, was contemporary with the Pyramid Age, which was also contemporary with the so-called First Intermediate Age, the Age of the Herakleopolitans.

Political fragmentation was therefore endemic in Egypt from the end of the 3rd Dynasty right through to the end of the Sixth (Hyksos). Whilst Sneferu and his successors held unquestioned royal authority, the rulers of the nomes were occasionally permitted to appropriate to themselves royal titles and iconography: Hence the confusion.

We recall at this point the striking parallels observed between the artwork of the Inyotef/Mentuhotep dynasty and that of the Fourth Dynasty. Even after the Hyksos (Sixth Dynasty) Invasion, the Inyotef and Khety potentates managed, to some degree, to hold onto their privileges. In time, the Inyotefs would organize resistance to the Hyksos, whilst the Khetys became more and more associated with the invaders. Eventually, open war broke out between Upper and Middle Egypt, though Hyksos pharaohs were initially content to let their Herakleopolitan clients conduct the campaign against the Thebans, who were still, at that point, little more than a nuisance. But things were to change rapidly. The Theban Inyotefs and Mentuhoteps, posing as national liberators, completely trounced the Herakleopolitans.

In conventional history, this Theban victory is used to mark the beginning of the "Middle Kingdom", an event normally dated around 1950 BC. However, for us there is no distinction between the so-called First and Second Intermediate Periods. These events directly preceded the all-out war between the Theban Seventeenth Dynasty and their Hyksos enemies, who however are also Assyrians. With their Herakleopolitan vassals defeated, and with alarming events occurring at the other end of the vast Hyksos/Assyrian Empire, the invaders suddenly realized they had a fight on their hands. By the time of Mentuhotep III's death, the scene was set for the great war of liberation, an endeavor undertaken by Mentuhotep's successor Ahmose (with whose name he is repeatedly associated on the monuments).

Chapter 6. The Wandering Tribes of Israel

Moses and His World

We have stated that the Early Dynastic epoch, both in Mesopotamia and in Egypt, did not end peacefully, but was terminated by a cataclysmic upheaval of nature. It has furthermore been hinted that this cataclysm marked the Exodus of the children of Israel from Egypt.

In another place[212] I have demonstrated in some detail how the biblical patriarchs, from Abraham to Moses, can only be contemporary with the Early Dynastic era. There I have shown that in terms of character and personality Abraham, the father of the Jewish nation, is virtually identical to Menes, the first pharaoh, whilst Abraham's great-grandson Joseph, who brought the Hebrews into Egypt, is identical to Imhotep, the wise vizier who solved the crisis of a seven-year famine in the time of Djoser.

The catastrophic end of the Early Dynastic epoch is echoed in part at least in the Pessimistic treatises of Egypt and in the story of the Exodus. The extraordinary episode of the parting sea is mirrored in a tale from the time of king Sneferu, and more particularly in the El Arish inscription, where the god Horus is credited with expelling Asiatics eastwards, through the Red Sea, after a pharaoh had pur-

---

212 In my *Genesis of Israel and Egypt* (London, 1997)

sued them into the "place of the whirlpool."[213] There is other evidence however which suggests that the story of the Exodus, and the epic events associated with it, became widely known throughout the Near East. Most particularly, there appear to be very clear references to the event in Greek tradition. Thus for example the flight of the Danaids from Aegyptus (Egypt) seems to refer to the flight of the Israelite tribe of Dan, during the escape from bondage.[214] This is confirmed by the story's close link to the legend of Cadmus, the hero credited with introducing the Phoenician alphabet to Greece. In this tradition Agenor, the twin brother of Belus (father of Danaus and Aegyptus), was said to have left Egypt to settle in the land of Canaan. Shortly thereafter, Agenor's daughter Europa was abducted by Zeus, whereupon he ordered his sons, who are named as Cadmus, Thasus, Cilix, Phoenix, and Phineus, to set out in search of her.[215]

The occurrence of the name Phineus in particular provides probably the most direct and unequivocal link with the Exodus. There seems little doubt that the Greek Phineus is one and the same as Phinehas, the grandson of Moses' brother Aaron, who slays the Israelite Zimri along with his Midianite bride in their tent.[216] In the Greek legend Phineus (or Phineas) attacks Perseus along with his bride Andromeda, daughter of the king of Joppa (Jaffa), at their wedding feast, but is slain by the Gorgon's head, which Perseus exposes.[217] Again, in another tradition the Greeks told how Phineus, who had been plagued by harpies, was rescued by two of the Argonauts, Calais and Zetes, who pursued the harpies through the air.[218] This accords with a Jewish tradition about Phinehas which has the flying swordsman Zaliah pursue Balaam through the air, on the orders of Phinehas.[219]

The story of the Danaids, as well as that of Agenor and Phineus, must have arrived in Greece through the same channels as the Phoenician alphabet. After their entry into Canaan the Twelve Tribes were allocated separate territories. Dan's portion was in the very north of the country — regions now comprising eastern

---

213 The El Arish shrine is discussed in some detail by Velikovsky in *Worlds in Collision* and *Ages in Chaos*. The biblical parallels were always apparent, but scholars did not dare draw the obvious conclusions, because it had already been decreed that the Sea of Passage event was totally fabulous.

214 "This myth," says Robert Graves, "records the early arrival in Greece of Helladic [i.e. Pre-Hellenic] colonists from Palestine by way of Rhodes." *The Greek Myths* Vol.1 (1955) p.203

215 Apollodorus, iii,1,1

216 Numbers 25:6-15

217 Ovid *Metamorphoses* v,1-230

218 *Argonautica*, ii,178ff.

219 L. Ginzberg, *The Legends of the Jews* Vol.1 (1961 ed.) p.508

Lebanon.[220] It is known that they became closely associated with the Phoenician kingdoms of the region. Some of the Phoenician traders and settlers who brought the alphabet to Greece must have been from the tribe of Dan.

These characters of Greece's Heroic Age help to illustrate yet another point mooted earlier; namely that the Pyramid Age of Egypt, the Exodus and Judges period of Israel, and the Mycenaean Age of Greece were all contemporary.

The remainder of the present volume will show that the Israelite Exodus and Conquest belong very clearly in the 9th/8th century, and that characters and events of the period share numerous features with characters and events of the Heroic Age of Greece. It will be further demonstrated how events in both these regions tie in with what we know of Egypt in the Pyramid Age.

RA-ATUM AND YAHWEH

The present work has stressed repeatedly that the monotheistic tone of Egyptian religious literature during the Pyramid Age displays striking affinities with the monotheism of the Mosaic code, and that these affinities are not coincidental. They are contemporary (and probably mutually influential) responses to the cosmic events of the period.

To all intents and purposes Moses was the founder of the Jewish religion. Almost all the customs, traditions, rituals and festivals of Judaism go back to him and his age. Most fundamentally, he was the "inventor" of Jewish monotheism. Yahweh was the god of Moses; his name had never been heard before his time. So new was this deity that Moses famously asks him his name at the Burning Bush. True, it is claimed throughout the Torah that he was also the god of Abraham, Isaac and Jacob. But these claims are viewed as merely seeking to legitimize the new cult. The Canaanite/Phoenician "father of the gods", El, who was in fact also originally the Hebrews' chief deity, was later associated with Yahweh; though their separate origins were so evident that modern scholars view the two cults as virtually incompatible, and speak of entirely separate sources for the Torah; one "Yahwist", the other "Elohist". Yahweh however, irrespective of later developments, was the god of Moses, the God whom the children of Abraham to this day pray when they say *Shema Yisrael Adonai Elohenu, Adonai* "Hear O Israel, the Lord our God, the Lord, is One".

Moses' first encounter with Yahweh occurs at the burning bush, during his exile in Midian (Exodus 3); and it is evident that the new deity was in some way or other a fire-god. The meeting occurs near the holy mountain of Horeb, a pinnacle clearly identical to the mountain otherwise known as Sinai — though

---

220 Judges 18:7-28

located in Midian — where some time later the prophet has his second encounter with his god, this time at the summit of the fiery mountain.

On the morning of the third day there were thunders and lightnings, and a thick cloud upon the mountain, and a sound arose as of mighty trumpets. All the people who were in the camp trembled. Then Moses brought the people out of the camp to meet the revelation of God; and they took their stand at the foot of the mountain. And Mount Sinai was wrapped in smoke, because Yahweh revealed himself there in the fire; and the smoke of it went up like the smoke of a kiln, and the whole mountain quaked greatly. (Exodus 19:16-18)

Evidently the god of Moses was no longer a sky-god, though he was still identified with the unleashed forces of nature. How then, it might be asked, does this square with our linking him to that other great deity of the period, Ra-Atum? The latter, whilst monolithic, was still identified with at least one of the heavenly bodies.

The answer to this question is in two parts. Firstly, the Egyptian religion clearly never was identical to the Jewish, not even at the stage of its foundation, which was moreover accomplished by a prince of Egypt. The parallels are there, but they are not exact. Ra-Atum was not a new god; he was a deity who appropriated the functions and powers of earlier gods. The Egyptians had no reason to reject the religion of their forefathers in its entirety. With Moses and the Israelites it was different. Here there was motive, as well as opportunity, to make a fresh start. The slaves and their leader had every reason to totally reject a pantheon and religion which had condemned their children to a premature death on the altar.[221]

Secondly, whilst it is said that at no time did the Jews worship the sun, there is no question that Yahweh was viewed as a god of light — as demonstrated, we said, by his first epiphany at the Burning Bush, and emphasized in various other places throughout the Torah. His very first words, after all, were "let there be light". Both the Pessimistic Texts and the Book of Exodus speak of the traumatic obscuring of the sun (evidently by clouds of ash and dust) during the catastrophe which accompanied the flight of the Hebrew slaves. It is evident that the return of the sun after this episode would have been greeted with great joy by both peoples.

---

221 As I demonstrate elsewhere (*The Genesis of Israel and Egypt*, 2nd ed.), the Age of the Patriarchs, which came to an end with the Exodus, was the Age of Human Sacrifice. This sacrifice is hinted at in various parts of the Patriarch narrative, one of which is the order of the pharaoh of the Oppression to kill the newborn Hebrew boys. (In Jewish legend their blood was mixed with the mud and straw, which the slaves used to fashion bricks and the bodies of child sacrifices were frequently buried in the foundations of temples during the epoch in question)

Strikingly, it seems that the name Yahweh may appear in other cultures far removed from the Near East. Thus the Chinese Emperor Yahu is reported to have reigned during some form of catastrophic disturbance of nature; whilst among one of the Indian tribes of North America the term "Yahu" was used during a ritual chant. Velikovsky theorized that the name could be derived from some form of sound-effects occurring as a result of the cosmic disturbances of the epoch.[222]

In later centuries the Israelites reverted to polytheism on many occasions, and the prophetic books of the Old Testament are full of the words of Yahweh's messengers upbraiding them for the worship of the Baals and Asheroths. In fact, all ancient peoples reverted to polytheistic star and planet worship at some stage or other; some even reverting to that ultimate expression of planet-adoration; human sacrifice. The Egyptians too, after their brief flirtation with monotheism during the Pyramid Age, reverted to full-blown polytheism after the demise of the Sixth Dynasty. One determined attempt, during the time of Akhnaton, was made to recover the pristine purity of the worship of the "One Alone", but this was short-lived.

"Exodus" in the Pyramid Texts

We have already suggested that the Pyramid Texts, carved on the inner chambers of the pyramids of the Fifth and Sixth Dynasties, refer, at least in part, to the catastrophic events surrounding the Exodus. The Texts tell of battles among the gods, of darkness over the earth, of the rebirth of the sun (Ra-Atum) after the darkness, and of general chaos throughout the cosmos.

Although, owing to the dictates of accepted chronology, the idea that these texts could refer to the events described in Exodus has not been widely explored, scholars have nevertheless been struck by the parallels between the two bodies of material. One of the most explicit attempts to link the Texts to the Exodus was made by Walter Warshawky in a 1983 article, "The Exodus in the Pyramid Texts?"[223] Warshawsky held that there "seem to be many references to the Exodus" in the Pyramid Texts,[224] and listed seven specific passages from the Texts as proof. In the article, he concentrated however on only one; the so-called Cannibal Hymn of Unas, of the Fifth Dynasty.

One sentence of the Cannibal Hymn reads; "For it is the King who will give judgment in company with him whose name is hidden on that day of slaying the

---

222 See *Worlds in Collision* (1950)

223 W. Warshawsky, "The Exodus in the Pyramid Texts?" *SIS: Workshop*, 4:4 (1983) pp.5-6

224 Ibid. p.5

Oldest Ones." Thus according to the translation of Faulkner.[225] Other translations have those being slain as "the eldest" or "the elder one" Budge translated; "He weighs words with Him of the hidden name [on] the day of the slaughtering of the first born." The Semsu, according to Budge, may mean either "eldest" or "first born". The term actually occurring in the texts is *ntr smsw*. This implies eldest god, or first-born god. The first-born or eldest are slain, according to another passage, when, "The sky is overcast, the stars are darkened, the celestial expanses quiver, the bones of the earth gods tremble, the planets [?] are stilled...." (Hymn 393) Warshawsky interpreted these phrases as meaning that "the sky is filled with dust and clouds so that the stars cannot be seen, the world shakes, the mountains quake, the world stands still."

Warshawsky admits that he could not yet "fully understand the references to the eating of the dead in this context [though] ... the clues may lie in Micah 3:3 and Ezekiel, which seem to speak in the same language."[226]

Warshawsky held that the killing of the first-born in the Pyramid Texts, as well as the catastrophic events that accompanied the deed, was identical to the killing of the first-born of Egypt as recounted in the Book of Exodus. It is true, he admits, that in the Pyramid Texts the killing of the first-born is primarily a reference to the slaying of the child Horus by Set. Nevertheless, he guessed, it may have been the killing of the first-born in heaven (some type of catastrophic cosmic event) that brought about the plague associated in the biblical passage with the death of Egypt's first-born. Velikovsky, he notes, took great pains to rewrite *bechor* as *bekhor*, "first-born" as "chosen". Warshawsky himself suggested that the term actually derived from the Egyptian *b'ik hor* (the Greek Harpocrates) and that it had both meanings. In other words, the Hebrew term found in the Book of Exodus was actually influenced by the Egyptian name of the child Horus, slain by Set. Warshawsky also saw other events of the Exodus as identical to, or influenced by, events from Egyptian myth. Thus, "The 'Judgment of Thoth' the Hebrews saw as the giving of the Law on Mount Sinai, the punishment of Seth being ridden by Osiris as the story of Balaam and his donkey. The planet involved seems to be Venus."[227]

Warshawsky ends by stating his belief that "the [Cannibal] Hymn was written after the Exodus and this would imply that also most of the Pyramid Texts were written after the Exodus."

The evidence suggests that he was right.

---

225 I Faulkner, *Ancient Egyptian Pyramid Texts* (1969) p.81 Text 399

226 Warshawsky, loc. cit. p.6

227 Ibid.

HERCULES OF ISRAEL

The Egyptians and Hebrews were by no means the only nations that periodically reverted to polytheism following the events of the 9th and 8th centuries BC. In Greece there were prolonged episodes, especially during times of renewed disturbances in nature, when the old sky-gods continued to hold sway. It was in the course of such events that a heroic character, who worked towards ending human sacrifice, was believed to have taken a hand. His name was Hercules.

As has been noted, Hercules was not a human being but a god, begotten by Zeus, a son whose purpose in being was to save both gods and men from destruction. As such, he is clearly identifiable with the cosmic events of the 9th and 8th centuries, the events which brought to an end the catastrophic Age of Sacrifice. Calm in the heavens was restored by the agency of this deity, and thus too calm on the earth.

But calm on the earth did not arrive overnight, and cataclysmic events are recounted throughout the Age of Hercules. Thus for example the hero was credited with pushing apart the Pillars (the two great rocks) which stood at the entrance to the Mediterranean, and which henceforth bore his name. Another tradition stated that he tore Italy from Sicily: others that he changed the courses of rivers and toppled the walls of cities (as for example Troy).

Greek legend spoke — in later years at least — of more than one Hercules. The Phoenician, or Tyrian Hercules was known as Melicertes (Melkarth), and it is clear that Hercules, or a character very similar to him, was honored throughout the Near East. Now scholars have long been aware that in many respects Moses bears close comparison with Hercules. Apart from the fact that both are placed in an epoch of violent upheavals of nature, which they themselves initiate (Moses tears apart the waters of the Sea of Passage, as Hercules tears apart the rock pillars of Europe and Africa), both are also linked with new forms of religious observance and belief (the Ten Commandments of Moses, and the abolishment of human sacrifice by Hercules) and to enmity with the serpent-deity. Here we may cite the fact that Moses' rod consumes the two serpents of the pharaoh,[228] whilst Hercules strangles the two serpents sent to destroy him in the cradle.[229]

It is evident that the personalities and attributes of Moses and Hercules are so similar that it can scarcely be doubted their stories contemporaneous and linked. Moreover, as the founder of the cult of the One God Yahweh, who is resolutely a Father, Moses offers a precise parallel with Hercules; for he was above all a son and servant of Zeus, the Greek Jupiter (Jove) the "Sky Father", whose Latin title

---

228 Exodus 7:8-12
229 Apollodorus ii,4,8 and Pindar *Nemean Odes* I,35ff.

may even be linguistically linked to Yahweh (sometimes reconstructed as Jehovah). Hercules's great enemy was the serpent-like Mother of the Gods, Hera, who sought continuously to destroy him. It was above all to the dreaded goddess of the sky (originally Venus) that human sacrifices were offered. As a true servant of the Father, whose task it is to do away with the bloody gifts dedicated to the Mother, Hercules may be seen as a very precise Hellenic equivalent of Moses. Yet this is not all: as the destroyer of numerous ancient cults and cult-centers devoted to blood-sacrifice the Greek Hercules was viewed by some as a rebel against all the gods — virtually in fact as a monotheist.

When this is combined with the cycle of legends surrounding evidently Hebrew personalities from the age of the Exodus such as Danaus and Phineus, who were placed by the Greeks in the same time and era as Hercules, there seems little doubt that we are correct in placing the Moses and Hercules epochs together.

Hercules was a god — the god Mars, in fact — but the deeds attributed to him were also linked to other great figures of the age. Many of the characters of the Heroic Age share aspects of his personality. Thus one of the major deeds of Hercules, the decapitation of the Cosmic Serpent, the Hydra, is also performed by other figures of the time. For example Perseus mimics the role of Hercules as he decapitates the serpent-headed Gorgon with a sword forged by the gods. By the same token, Hercules's abolishment of human sacrifice is mimicked by Theseus when he slays the bull-headed Minotaur in the Labyrinth.

In the same way, a number of characters of Israelite history from the time of the Exodus and Conquest, and not just Moses, assumed the mantle of Hercules. Most obvious in this regard is Samson. The parallels between this character (a Hebrew version of the Babylonian god Shamash, whose Northwest Semitic name was Samsum) and Hercules are too obvious to need emphasizing. Both were heroes of great physical strength; both men defeated whole armies single-handedly; both killed a fierce lion with their bare hands: both lost their strength, or were emasculated, through their association with a woman; both were linked to a legend of pillars being pushed apart; both were linked to a decapitation myth. In the case of Samson, the decapitation element is present, though it is he who is the victim, when he loses his strength by having his hair cut off by Delilah.[230]

The evidence thus states ever more clearly that Greece's Heroic Age is one and the same as Israel's age of wandering and conquest. Yet even clearer links between the two histories are forthcoming.

---

230 The custom of head — as well as scalp — hunting is rooted in the cosmic events of the 9th/8th century BC, when the Cosmic Serpent was decapitated. Much of mankind's custom and mythology relates back to this event. The whole subject is dealt with insightfully and controversially by Velikovsky in *Worlds in Collision* (1950).

THE AGE OF THE JUDGES

Moses, it was said, was not fated to cross the river Jordan and enter the Land "flowing with milk and honey" which Yahweh had promised to his people. The task of leading the Israelites to their new home he assigned to Joshua, "the savior", who in fact accomplished his mission with a ruthless ferocity. But the violence of the invader was matched by the violence of nature; and the entire Conquest of Canaan was accompanied by intense disturbances in the natural order. Even the crossing of the Jordan bore witness to these events, for it appears that the river suddenly altered its course. In any event, the children of Israel were supposed to have crossed dry shod. At the site of the crossing Joshua erected a circle of twelve standing-stones, and named the spot "Gilgal" — a word that conjures forth a whole wealth of associations, for the term means "wheel of the sun" (Joshua 4:20-24).

The Book of Joshua therefore spells out in no uncertain terms that the Exodus and Conquest occurred during the Megalithic epoch, the epoch of standing-stone circles, the epoch of Mycenae and the pyramids.

Just as the Homeric gods played an active part in the wars and conflicts of the Mycenaean Age, the Jewish Yahweh participated in the conflicts of the Israelites. Arriving at Jericho on the west bank of the Jordan, the Israelites prepared for a siege. But the walls of the city collapsed, apparently as a result of a violent earthquake. Similar incidents are recorded throughout the story of the Conquest, with Yahweh on one occasion hurling great rocks (meteorites) from the sky; and on another arresting the progress of the sun through the firmament. Events of precisely the same category are reported in the epics and traditions of Hellas in the Age of Heroes. But the parallels do not end there. Everything about the Israelite Age of the Conquest, its culture, belief-systems, institutions and military practices underline the similarities with Mycenaean Age Greece. This is particularly the case with regard to military affairs.

The Books of Joshua and the Judges, as well as that of Samuel, which comes immediately afterwards, score a number of firsts in terms of military tactics and technology, tactics and technology strangely reminiscent of that familiar from Homer. Interestingly enough, they are also reminiscent of those employed during the Akkadian epoch in Mesopotamia, which, though placed a thousand years earlier in conventional chronology, is rightfully contemporaneous with the former.

At least four pieces of military equipment, all very much characteristic of Mycenaean Greece, are mentioned (or at least emphasized) for the first time during the period of the Judges. These are: (a) the chariot, (b) swords, (c) body armor, (d) the composite bow.

The chariot is specifically mentioned on numerous occasions in connection with the Philistines, who use it with devastating effect on their enemies. In their wars against the Philistine cities, for example, it is stated that the tribe of Judah could not dislodge their opponents "because they had iron chariots."[231] The iron technology of the Judges epoch corresponds very closely with that described by Homer in the *Iliad*. In both, bronze is the metal of weapons, with iron reserved for tools.[232]

It seems certain that the iron chariots of the Philistines refers to stout iron fittings, which rendered them stable. Indeed the mention of both iron and chariots together strongly implies that both were recent innovations.

Swords are of course linked to iron in the Judges and Early Monarchy period, but this should not be taken to mean that all swords (or indeed any swords) of the period were of iron. Bronze remained the metal of weapon manufacture until the techniques of steel forging were mastered. In Greece this did not occur until the reign of the Spartan king Anaxandrides, sometime in the latter 6th century BC.[233] The Philistines, of course, are the great sword-makers of the period under discussion. During an important battle between them and Saul, the Israelites are reported to have had not a single sword.[234] Obviously Saul's followers could not have gone into battle unarmed, and it is evident that the swords which the Hebrews lacked were new weapons, weapons of a type only possessed by the Philistines. Almost certainly these were true swords, long bronze weapons of European type.

To guard against the new weaponry, both Philistines and Israelites now begin to employ a novel defense: body armor. Thus in the story of David's encounter with the Philistine champion Goliath, he dons a coat of armor donated by King Saul.[235] Yet body armor only became essential in the ancient world when weapons of true bronze first became available. This occurred during the Akkadian age in Mesopotamia and the Mycenaean age in Greece. In Egypt, it occurred when the Hyksos introduced weapons of tin bronze.

The composite bow was yet another innovation of the Hyksos, and, once again, it appears in the time of the Judges[236] — as indeed it appears in the Trojan

231 Judges 1:17-19

232 See e.g. 2 Samuel 12:31

233 Pausanias, iii,3,7 and iii,11,8

234 1 Samuel 13:19

235 Ibid., 17:38

236 In the words of one scholar, "it is the technologically advanced Philistines who first develop massed archery firepower and use it to shoot down Saul and his army in 1 Samuel 31. David, in response, institutes mass archery-training programs in the Israelite army. Later, when David comes up against massed chariots for the first time, he orders their

campaign, where its use is immortalized in the slaying of Achilles, shot in the ankle by Paris. But, again, the composite bow is also associated with the Akkadians, supposedly a thousand years earlier.

In detail after detail then the Age of the Judges is revealed as contemporary with Mycenaean Greece. This even goes for the custom of deciding the outcome of battle by a single combat between two champions; and we need only point here to the famous duel, from the end of the Judges period, between the youthful David and the Philistine champion Goliath. Together with the other characteristics of the two epochs, the personalities of the great figures of the time and the disruptive influence of the forces of nature recorded equally in Hellenic and Hebrew tradition, it becomes increasingly less likely that our juxtaposition of these two seminal periods in the histories of both nations could be mistaken.

THE PHILISTINE-ASSYRIAN ALLIANCE

Even without the archaeological agreement, the traditions relating to Moses and his epoch would in any case necessitate placing him alongside the Akkadians. Thus for example Moses is cast into the Nile in a basket shortly after his birth, whilst Sargon of Akkad is cast adrift in the Euphrates shortly after his birth.[237] Such a striking correspondence is difficult to explain if, as conventional scholarship believes, the historical Sargon and Moses are separated from each other by a thousand years; but if the two characters belong to the same century, the parallels become eminently sensible.

Again, it should be remembered that chariot warfare only appears in the Bible after the death of Joshua. This is exactly as it should be if, as we shall argue, Sargon began his conquest of the Near East at precisely this time.

According to the scheme of things proposed in the present work, the Assyrian (Hyksos/Akkadian) conquest of the Near East must have occurred around 770 BC. Since we date the Exodus around 840 BC, the Israelite conquest of Canaan (under Joshua, a generation after Moses), must be placed roughly between 810 and 780 BC. By this reckoning then Sargon's conquest of Syria/Palestine and

---

horses hamstrung. His son Solomon makes chariots the centre of his army." Martin Sieff, *Theses for the Reconstruction of Ancient History: Egypt, Israel and the Archaeological Record, 2400-330 BC.* (1987) pp.6-7

237 C.J. Gadd "The Dynasty of Agade and the Gutian Invasion" in *CAH* Vol.1 part 2 (3ʳᵈ ed.) p.418 This motif, incidentally, is an echo of the custom of child-sacrifice. The child victim was viewed as sailing through the waters of the underworld to the home of the gods. The parallels here with the story of Osiris, Lord of the Underworld, who was trapped in a casket by his wicked brother Set and cast adrift in the Nile (to be eventually washed ashore at Byblos, i.e. Syria/Palestine), should not be overlooked.

Egypt must have occurred shortly after the death of Joshua. The question that must then be asked is: is there any record of this event in biblical tradition?

As a matter of fact the Bible clearly states that immediately after the death of Joshua the whole of Canaan was made subject to a great conqueror from Mesopotamia:

> The people of Israel did what was evil in the sight of the Lord, forgetting the Lord their God, and serving the Baals and the Asheroths. Therefore the anger of the Lord was kindled against Israel, and he sold them into the hand of Cushan-Rishathaim king of Mesopotamia [Naharim]; and the people of Israel served Cushan-Rishathaim eight years.[238]

Josephus the Jewish historian actually calls Cushan-Rishathaim "king of Assyria". It is just at this time too that chariot warfare, which we associate with the Assyrians, makes its first appearance in the Bible. Shortly after the Mesopotamian conquest, the Israelites were oppressed by king Jabin of Hazor in northern Canaan. Jabin, it is said, had "nine hundred chariots of iron."[239] From this time onward chariots, particularly iron chariots, are a frequent and decisive feature of warfare in the Bible.

We hear that after eight years Othniel the Judge freed Israel from the power of Cushan-Rishathaim. Yet in our reckoning the Assyrian kings remained more or less in control of all Syria/Palestine for fifty years or so. How is their apparent absence to be explained?

During the early years in the Promised Land, the Twelve Tribes battled long and hard against the native Canaanites, who by the end of Joshua's life were more or less wiped out. In subsequent years however the Israelites could not repeat the success of earlier times, and they faced ferocious opposition from a number of formidable opponents. Most powerful of these were the Philistines, a people of the Mediterranean coastlands who were not native to the region, and the Amalekites, an apparently Semitic people of possibly Arabian origin.

Velikovsky wished to associate the Amalekites with the Hyksos.[240] However, given the Arab traditions which spoke of the Amalekites as natives of the region of Mecca, it seems unlikely that they could be the same as the Hyksos, whom we identify with the Assyrians. Nevertheless, it does appear that the Amalekites were to become clients of the Assyrians — a fact illustrated by their alliance with the Philistines, who very definitely became part of the Assyrian confederation.

The Philistines were not natives of Canaan. They were a race of overseas immigrants who settled the coastlands of Canaan and battled for control of the up-

---

238 Judges 3:7-8

239 Ibid. 4:3

240 See Velikovsky, *Ages in Chaos* (1952)

lands. The Scriptures inform us that their original homeland was the island of Caphtor, and hint very strongly that the conquest of central Canaan by Joshua roughly coincided with the arrival of the Philistines on the coastal regions. Certainly they are not mentioned until after Joshua's death. Now Caphtor is usually identified as Crete, so that the Philistines are popularly viewed as a race of Aegean immigrants. However, the great flood of immigration to the Canaanite coastlands during the Palestinian Middle Bronze 2 (i.e. the Hyksos epoch) comes from Cyprus,[241] and for this reason the present writer identifies the Philistines as Cypriots. Nevertheless, this seafaring race did indeed have close links with the Minoan Cretans, as we shall presently see.

Aside from the fact that the Philistines were great exponents of the chariot, two other considerations in particular make us suspect that they became a client nation of the Assyrians. Firstly, Sargon I mentions Kapturu as one of his imperial domains. Kapturu can only be Caphtor, the Philistine homeland, and since a seaborne invasion by the non-maritime Assyrians seems improbable, we can only suspect that the people of Caphtor/Kapturu voluntarily forged an alliance with the Assyrians.

Secondly, the Hyksos kings of Egypt adopted the twin titles "Rulers of the Nations" and "Lords of the Sea".[242] The latter claim always seemed a strange one to make until a scarab of the Hyksos king Khyan was uncovered at Knossos in Crete. In addition to this, scholars began to note that many of the Hyksos scarabs — large numbers of which occur in the Philistine cities of Palestine — bear typically Minoan-style spiral motifs. So pervasive was the Minoan influence upon the Hyksos in Palestine that some scholars even began to suggest a Cretan origin for the dynasty; this in spite of the obviously Semitic names of the kings.

But the problem disappears as soon as we realize that the Philistines, a seagoing nation with connections all over the Levant, were allies and close confederates of the Assyrian/Hyksos Empire.

The Amalekites too apparently became Assyrian clients, as their alliance with the Philistines would suggest: And indeed the final defeat of the Amalekite king Agog seems to record the demise of the Assyrian Empire in the west, when Pepi/Apepi II lost all of Egypt and Syria to an alliance of Egyptians (under Ahmose) and Hebrews (under Saul).

---

241 H.W. Catling, "Cyprus in the Middle Bronze Age" in *CAH* Vol.1 part 2 (3rd ed.) pp.173-4

242 F. Petrie, *The Making of Egypt* (1939) p.143

Chapter 7. Heroic Age Greece

The Mycenaean World

The proto-historic age of Greece, commonly referred to as the Heroic or Mycenaean Age, was contemporary with the pyramid-building epoch. The myths relating to Hercules (from whom the Heroic Age derives its name) are all concerned with the cosmic events which brought the Early Dynastic epoch to a catastrophic end, and inaugurated the Megalith-building era, sometime near the middle of the 9th century.

There is in fact an enormous body of evidence which would suggest a date in the late 8th century for the most famous event of the Heroic Age, the Trojan War. Traditions surrounding the Olympic Games, for example (established in the early 8th century) clearly show that the Games were in existence well before the Trojan campaign. Thus Homer, who must have lived within a century or so of the first Olympiad, describes how both Nestor (a participant in the Trojan campaign) and his father Neleus won prizes at the festival.[243] Another tradition held that it was Pelops, the grandfather of Agamemnon, who founded the Games.[244] Traditions about the alphabet tell a similar tale. Cadmus, who brought the Phoenician script to Greece, was said to have lived four or five generations before the Trojan

---

243 *Iliad,* xi 671 and 761
244 Pausanias, v. 8, 1 and vi. 20, 8

campaign. Yet no one would place the introduction of the alphabetic script to Greece much before 800 BC. Palamedes, who fought at Troy, was credited with adding the letters *x, ph,* and *ch* to the Cadmean alphabet, whilst Herodotus saw, and read, an inscribed tripod at Thebes dedicated by Amphitryon, a contemporary of Pelops.[245]

The genealogical evidence stands in agreement. Numerous genealogies of noble Greek families, such as the one linking Pythagoras to Hippasos of Samos, separate the time of the Trojan War from the Persian War by only eight or nine generations — around 200 years, allowing 25 years to a generation.[246]

Then there is the evidence from Asia Minor linking Midas (an 8th century king of Phrygia) to the Trojan campaign. Greek tradition held that Midas, of the Golden Touch, was a contemporary of Agamemnon. It was Midas's father Gordius, a contemporary of Pelops, who founded the Phrygian kingdom, whilst one ancient source tells us that Midas married a daughter of Agamemnon, an Ionian king based at Cyme.[247] Apparently Midas regarded this alliance with the Greeks as so important that he sent a decorated throne to Delphi to commemorate the event. Why go to such lengths if the alliance was with an obscure Ionian princeling, as is normally believed?

Finally, tradition links refugees from Troy with the founding of Rome, an event placed by the Romans themselves in the middle of the 8th century BC. In his *Aenead* Virgil makes the hero Aeneas visit queen Dido at Carthage on the north African coast. Yet neither tradition nor archaeology knows of any city of Carthage predating the 8th century. Similarly, an investigation of the Aeneas legend in central Italy has shown that it originated with the Etruscan immigrants to the region, whose language was apparently closely related to the Tyrrhenian (or Pelasgian) dialect of the northern Aegean. But archaeology has shown that the Etruscans settled the region in the latter 8th and 7th centuries BC.[248]

This then is a tiny sample of the truly enormous body of evidence relating to the proper dating of the Mycenaean epoch. I do not of course intend to present a detailed reconstruction of this part of Greek history. The wealth of material available means that such a project demands a volume of its own. Nevertheless, I do intend, in the next few pages, to show how our revised chronology for Egypt and Mesopotamia casts new and spectacular light upon the story of archaic Greece.

245 Hyginus, *Fabula* 277

246 For a discussion, see V.R. d'A Desborough, *The Greek Dark Ages* (1972) p.324

247 Julius Pollux, ix. 83, quoting the *Constitution of Cyme* by Herakleides of Pontus.

248 See e.g. R.M. Ogilvie, *Early Rome and the Etruscans* (Fontana, 1976) pp.30ff.

THE PYRAMIDS OF GREECE

Scholars were astonished to discover Pyramid Age material in a Mycenaean context in Greece. According to accepted ideas, Egypt's Pyramid Age had ended roughly seven hundred years before the dawn of the Mycenaean epoch. Nevertheless, the peculiar style of building during Greece's Mycenaean Age, which we know as "Cyclopean" or "Megalithic", involving the use of enormous close-fitting and often polygonal blocks of dressed stone, is strikingly similar to the style of architecture prevalent in Egypt in the Pyramid Age. Even more to the point, very specific architectural features have their precise equivalents in the two countries. In this way, the builders of the Mycenaean tholos tombs (spectacular examples of which occur at Mycenae), used the corbelling technique to roof the larger areas in the central burial chambers. But corbelling was also regularly employed in the pyramids of the Fourth, Fifth and Sixth Dynasties. Furthermore, the tholos tombs were mound-like structures, with an approaching passageway (*dromos*) leading to the central chamber, which was underneath the summit of the mound.

In concept, this is essentially identical to the Egyptian pyramids, with the minor qualification that the passageway approaching the central chamber was concealed within the structure, and that the mound which covered it was higher and more mathematically geometric.

It is perhaps worth noting here that just as pyramid-building survived in the Sudan — on the periphery of the Egyptian world — until the 4th century AD., so tholos-tomb building survived in Thrace — on the periphery of the Greek world — until the 3rd century BC. The idea that the epoch of megalithic-building was remote from the later historical ages, and that little or no cultural continuity can be observed from the earlier to the later periods, must be abandoned.

But that is not all. In Greece there survives, to this day — though in a somewhat ruined state — a number of small pyramids of Mycenaean date in various parts of the country. These structures, never more than a few meters high, might more accurately be described as pyramidions. One well-known example stands at Elliniko near Argos, another at Kampia near Epidauros and yet another at Lygourio near Nafplion. Reports of another at Sicyon have not been confirmed and yet another at Dalamanara seems to have been completely demolished. Everything about these enigmatic buildings, from the cyclopean polygonal stones, to the triangular shape of doorway entrances, tells us that they were raised at the height of the Mycenaean epoch. This in fact is further confirmed by Greek legend, which informs us that one of the structures, at Dalamanara, on the road from Argos to Epidauros, was raised to mark the site of a battle between the Heroic Age characters Proteus and Acrisius for the kingdom of Argos. According to Pausanias, this structure was originally decorated with carved Argive-type shields, and claimed that the battle was the first occasion shields were used in warfare.[249] Nothing of this pyramid now remains, but it clearly must be classed alongside other mini-pyramids still standing at Elliniko, Kampia and elsewhere.

Much more impressive than these pyramidions however is a stepped pyramid discovered at the Ampheion in Thebes by the archaeologist Theodore Spyropoulos and excavated between 1971 and 1973. This hill/tomb is situated at the end of the Kadmeion, the acropolis of ancient Thebes, and exactly behind the Archaeological Museum of Thebes. Tradition holds that within the hill of the Ampheion lies the tomb of the twin brothers Amphion and Zethos, first founders of the city of Thebes. The pyramid consisted, so far as can be discerned, of three steps surmounted by a smallish tumulus. Inside the latter Spyroupolos unearthed some extremely important finds; a double grave (recalling the twins Amphion and Zethos) containing bone and pottery remains and some gold jewelry. There was, in addition, originally a system of passageways penetrating to at least 20m within the hill. The whole structure must a one time have been an impressive structure, and it seems evident that it was intended to be visible from a long way off.

Spyropoulos himself drew parallels between this pyramid and the stepped pyramids of Early Dynastic Egypt. It should be pointed out too that there are apparently clear similarities between this tumulus and various megalithic-age structures throughout Europe, most particularly perhaps the mound of Silbury Hill in England, which also originally was constructed in a series of steps.

So the evidence for placing the Pyramid and Mycenaean Ages together chronologically is extensive. The remainder of the present chapter will show how evidence from Greek tradition fully confirms the discoveries of archaeology; and how the Hellenes of the period interacted with the Egyptians of the epoch, but most especially with the Akkadian/Assyrian conquerors of the Egyptians, the dynasty of kings that has come to be known as the Hyksos.

Pelops and the Trojan Campaign

The Assyrian conquest of virtually the entire ancient east was accomplished with Sargon of Akkad's unstoppable chariotry. The Egyptians dared not venture to offer him battle. One tradition about Sargon, recorded in an epic called *The King of the Battle*, told how he overran much of Anatolia after merchants from the city of Purushkhanda appealed for his assistance against a rival named Nur-daggal. To

---

249 Pausanias, ii. 25, 7-9

the astonishment of everyone, Sargon advanced through the mountainous lands of the west and routed Nur-daggal.[250]

That Anatolia, or at least large parts of it, were incorporated into the Akkadian Empire is now accepted wisdom, with some historians suggesting Akkadian hegemony stretching as far west as the Aegean coast.[251]

Placing both the Akkadian Empire and the Heroic Age of Greece in the 8th century, we might expect Greek tradition to allude in some way to Sargon and his empire. The arrival of chariot warfare, for example, would scarcely have gone unnoticed among the Greeks — particularly if the Greeks actually learned the use of the chariot from the Akkadians.

Before going a step further, it should be remarked that the chariot used in Greece during the Mycenaean period was virtually identical in almost every detail to that employed by the Hyksos invaders of Egypt; and it is commonly surmised that the chariot was introduced to Greece during the Hyksos epoch. Indeed, this is more than a surmise, for it is supported by a wealth of archaeological data. Only one question remains unanswered: by which route did the Hyksos chariot reach Hellas? Was it from Egypt, or did it arrive through Anatolia? Both theories have supporters.[252]

It so happens that the Greeks themselves recalled very clearly the arrival of the chariot. It was brought to the land of the Achaeans by a king of Anatolia named Pelops. This man, whom the Peloponnesian Peninsula was named for, established a mighty dynasty centered in the Argive Plain, a dynasty whose most famous scion, the legendary Agamemnon, was to launch the celebrated war against Ilion two generations later.

Pelops, it was said, had been ruler of the fabulously wealthy kingdom of Paphlagonia, and had been driven from his home by "barbarians". These *barbaroi* (Grk. "foreigners") are not named, but we may hazard a very good guess as to their identity. Pelops and his entourage fled westwards to the Aegean, where they sought refuge with Ilus, the king of Troy. Finding no welcome there, the fugitives crossed the sea to Greece, where Pelops set out to win the hand of Hippodameia, daughter of king Oenomaus of Elis. Before he could wed the girl however Pelops had a test to pass: he had to beat Oenomaus in a chariot race — a

---

250 C.J. Gadd, "The Dynasty of Agade and the Gutian Invasion" in *CAH* Vol.1 part 2 (3rd ed.) p.427

251 Ibid. "If the King of the Battle has any historical foundation, Sargon did not stop short at the mountain barrier [of Cappadocia], but extended his sway deep into Asia Minor."

252 See e.g. Frank Stubbings, "The Rise of Mycenaean Civilisation" in *CAH* Vol.2 part 1 (3rd ed.) p.639 "He [Pelops] does at least represent a dimly remembered event or period of events — the conquest of part of the Peloponnese by invaders from Asia Minor, perhaps indeed owing their success to their war-chariots. Such an event we can hardly place very much later than the era of the Mycenaean Shaft Graves."

race across the Peloponnesian Peninsula. Defeat meant death, and many previous suitors had paid for their ardor with their lives. It was said that Oenomaus boasted he would eventually build a temple of human skulls.[253] With the help of Oenomaus's treacherous charioteer Myrtilus, Pelops duly defeated his rival, and claimed the throne of Ells as his prize.[254]

Myrtilus (whose name is Hittite) had his image set among the stars as the constellation of the Charioteer.[255]

The story of Pelops provides the earliest reference to the chariot in Greek tradition, and the central role of horses and chariots in the narrative has long led scholars to believe that it marks their introduction into the country. However, if we are on the right track, if it was the onward march of Akkadian/Assyrian arms that had forced Pelops westwards, we might expect the Greeks to have recalled it in some way. The presence of such a mighty empire in Anatolia and Asia Minor could scarcely have escaped their attention.

As a matter of fact Greek tradition insisted that during the Trojan campaign (two generations after Pelops) all of Asia Minor was part of the Assyrian Empire. One tradition, recounted by many of the classical authors, stated that after the death of Hector, the Assyrian king Teutamus sent a powerful force of Ethiopian troops, under the leadership of Memnon, to support the Trojans. Memnon, it was said, marched to Troy at the head of a thousand Ethiopians and a thousand Susians, and the people of Phrygia, many centuries afterwards, still showed the rough, straight road by which he travelled.[256]

The assistance was belated and ineffective, and after some initial success, Memnon was slain in single combat by Achilles.[257]

This story of Assyrian and Ethiopian involvement in the Trojan campaign has always seemed puzzling, and has generally been dismissed as little more than a romantic fiction. The very concept of Nubian troops coming to the assistance of Troy is regarded as fantastic, whilst no king of Assyria named Teutamus, it is claimed, existed. However, from the perspective of history outlined in the present work, it will be obvious that with Sargon's conquest of Anatolia, Assyrian participation in the Trojan War is entirely to be expected. Furthermore, having identified the Sixth Egyptian Dynasty as another alter-ego of the Hyksos/Assyrians, it may be possible to name the king who sent Memnon to the ringing plains of Ilion.

---

253 Lucian, *Charidemus* 19

254 Pausanias, viii,14,7

255 Apollodorus. *Epitome* ii,8

256 Diodorus Siculus, ii,22 and Pausanias I,42,2

257 Philostratus *Heroica* iii,4

Teutamus, it should be noted, bears a name reminiscent of Teti, first pharaoh of the Sixth Dynasty, whom we have recognized as an alter-ego of Sargon and who is recalled in Manetho's account of the invasion as Tutimaeus. Nevertheless, the reign of Teti/Sargon must be placed around 770-750 BC, whereas the fall of Troy occurred closer to the end of the 8th century. As such, it is tempting to name the Assyrian monarch of the period as either Naram-Sin or Shal-kali-sharri, either of whom could be Pepi/Apopi II.

It must have been at this time, or shortly thereafter, that the chariot was introduced to western Europe, where it became a favored weapon of the Celts. It would no doubt have reached these regions along the same trade-routes that conveyed tin bronze, a western European invention, to the Near East. King Sargon himself records expeditions to the mysterious "tin lands" of the west. Elsewhere I have argued in great detail (in my *Arthur and Stonehenge: Britain's Lost History* (2001)) how the art of tin-bronze manufacture was developed in Britain towards the end of the 9th century BC, and how it was to gain access to this valuable resource that the Phoenicians opened up the western sea-routes and established their Mediterranean and Atlantic colonies (e.g. Carthage and Gades) to service the trade. But this only occurred at the start of the 8th century BC, which means, in effect, that the Bronze Age begins then. Attempts to suggest that the ancients knew other sources of tin much closer to the Near East founder on the economics. If such sources existed (and there is in any case no evidence of them), Phoenician traders could scarcely have found it profitable to fund the vastly expensive expeditions to Britain, an island 3,000 miles distant.

The folk of Britain's Wessex culture, who raised Stonehenge III, derived their fabulous wealth from the tin and bronze trade; and their rich tombs on Salisbury Plain still yield artifacts (such as faience beads) of Near Eastern manufacture. But the trade in luxuries was not all one-way. Bronze and gold trinkets manufactured in the British Isles at the time found their way to Greece, Phoenicia, Egypt and Mesopotamia. Thus Flinders Petrie discovered a series of gold earrings, of obviously Irish manufacture, in a Hyksos-period Egyptian tomb.[258]

Truly astonishing is the picture that emerges once the chronology of antiquity is put right; unsuspected and even undreamt of connections become apparent. Homer's Achaeans visited not only Egypt at the height of her Pyramid Age, but pushed their dark ships much farther, into the dangerous and mysterious waters of the west, even into the mighty "Sea of Atlas" that lay beyond the brooding Pillars of Hercules. They knew however what they were looking for; the "tin isles", the mysterious archipelago associated with the mystical Hyperboreans, the folk

---

258 F. Petrie, *The Making of Egypt* (1939) p.144 "trade brought products from Persia and from Ireland in the Hyksos age."

said to dwell beyond the North Wind. This race of sorcerers and alchemists, dwellers at the edge of the world, alone held the secret of forging bronze; and the national myth of their island home told how their own Hercules, the Bear hero Artos, pulled a bronze sword from a stone whilst still a young man. The wealthy Hyperboreans were known also to be astronomers of the highest order, in virtue of which they had raised, not far from the tin-bearing regions, a great circular temple to the heavenly deities.

MENELAUS IN EGYPT

According to Herodotus, the first Greeks to arrive in Egypt came in the time of Psammetichus, a king normally dated to the early 7th century. The Father of History tells us how a band of bronze-clad Ionians and Carians landed in the Nile Delta and commenced plundering the countryside. Realizing their potential, Psammetichus recruited them as mercenaries; and with the assistance of these troops overcame his rival Dodecarchs, and wrested Egypt from the Assyrian Empire.[259]

In conformity with this picture, Greek pottery and other artifacts of the early 7th century are discovered with great frequency in the Delta, especially at those sites specifically associated with the Greeks. However, in apparent contradiction of these facts, both archaeology and tradition record contact between Hellenes and Egyptians in an earlier epoch.

In his history of Egypt Herodotus informs us that the Egyptians of his time were well acquainted with the story of the Trojan War. They also told of a violent incursion into Egypt by Menelaus, husband of Helen, immediately after the sack of Ilion.[260] Although that tradition is now dismissed as fantasy, it apparently finds a vague echo in the very real contacts between Mycenaean Greece and Egypt discovered by archaeology. Scholars have found that links between early Greece and Egypt were strongest during the Eighteenth Dynasty. During that period great quantities of Mycenaean pottery were imported into Egypt, as were Mycenaean-looking weapons and other artifacts. Furthermore, Mycenaean or Minoan-type characters were frequently portrayed in Eighteenth Dynasty art. Conversely, Egyptian artifacts of Eighteenth Dynasty date were discovered with great frequency in a Mycenaean context in Greece, whilst Eighteenth Dynasty style weaponry was also found in Mycenaean Greece.

It appears that regular Mycenaean contacts with Egypt were established just before the beginning of the Eighteenth Dynasty. Indeed, the Mycenaeans seem to

---

259 Herodotus ii,54
260 Ibid ii, 119

have been particularly linked to the rise of the Eighteenth Dynasty. Inlaid daggers, for example, found in the coffin of Ahhotep, mother of Ahmose (founder of the Eighteenth Dynasty), were almost identical in design to the daggers taken from the Shaft Graves at Mycenae. Ah-hotep herself is of the greatest interest. On a number of inscriptions she is identified as a princess of the Haunebu (or Haunebt), the "Lords of the North".[261] Now, as we noted in Chapter 3, on the Canopus Decree, the Rosetta Stone, and other documents of the Ptolemaic epoch, the name Hellenes is translated as Haunebu;[262] and is apparently a direct translation of the Greek term "Hellenic coast". Indeed the word now transcribed as "Haunebu" was originally given as "Helou-nebut". However, with the discovery of the term in documents of the early Eighteenth Dynasty (to say nothing of its occurrence in texts of the Fourth and Fifth Dynasties), supposedly in the middle of the second millennium BC, the phrase Helou-nebut was quietly dropped and replaced with Haunebut. Nevertheless, the use of the term to denote the lands of the Greeks in the Ptolemaic documents is unequivocal, and scholars are thus compelled, notwithstanding the name change, to link the earlier, Eighteenth Dynasty occurrence of the name, to the Mycenaean Greeks.[263] Such a conclusion has been underlined by the Mycenaean-style weapons associated with Ah-hotep. Could it be then that Ahhotep, a founding member of the Eighteenth Dynasty, was a Greek princess?

On the Karnak stela of Ahmose her son, Ah-hotep is described as "one who cares for Egypt. She has looked after her soldiers; she has guarded her; she has brought back her fugitives, and collected together her deserters; she has pacified Upper Egypt, and expelled her rebels."[264] According to T G H James: "These words suggest that Ahhotpe [sic] had at some critical moment seized the initiative in restoring order in Egypt when control had been lost, possibly on the death of Seqenenre or of Kamose. The terms of her praise are unusually precise and they may well signify that her behavior had been crucial to the establishment of the unified kingdom at the time of the expulsion of the Hyksos."[265] The evidence then, in the words of Frank Stubbings, seems to suggest that "forces from Greece may have served in Egypt, against the Hyksos, as mercenaries."[266]

---

261 Frank H. Stubbings, loc. cit.

262 Cecil Torr. *Memphis and Mycenae* (Isis, 1988) p.50

263 Stubbings, loc. cit.

264 T.G.H. James, "Egypt: From the Expulsion of the Hyksos to Amenophis I" in *CAH* Vol.2 part 2 (3rd ed.) p.306

265 Ibid. pp.306-7

266 Stubbings, loc. cit.

But to state that the Eighteenth Dynasty rose to power with Greek help raises enormous problems for orthodox chronology. Quite apart from the fact that Greek intervention in Egypt at the beginning of the conventionally dated Eighteenth Dynasty (16th century BC) is historically impossible, there seem to be strange — indeed incredible — parallels between this early Greek intervention and the later intervention in the time of Psammetichus. For whilst Psammetichus, in the 7th century, used Greek mercenaries to overcome internal enemies, expel the Assyrians, and establish a great empire, so the Eighteenth Dynasty apparently used Greek mercenaries to overcome internal enemies, expel the mighty Hyksos (whom we have already identified with the Assyrians), and establish a great empire.

Could it be then, as conventional scholarship believes, that these parallels are mere coincidence, and that Greek soldiers did indeed campaign in Egypt centuries before Psammetichus employed his Ionian mercenaries? Or was Herodotus correct; did the first Greeks truly arrive in Egypt in the latter 8th or early 7th century, and were these the Mycenaean warriors who helped the Eighteenth Dynasty to power?[267]

In view of what we have already discovered about both the Eighteenth Dynasty and the Mycenaean epoch, it is clear that Psammetichus's Ionian mercenaries were identical to the Mycenaean soldiers who helped expel the Hyksos. These events, then, must be dated to the last quarter of the 8th century BC, probably around 720 BC, very close to the period of the Trojan campaign. As such, it seems virtually certain that Ahhotep's Greek warriors probably arrived in Egypt fresh from the sack of Ilion, and she may well have formed part of Menelaus's entourage. Since these Greeks were of such crucial importance in the war to liberate Egypt from the Hyksos/Assyrians, it is little wonder that the Egyptians were familiar both with the story of the Trojan War and the wanderings of Menelaus.

This fresh perspective has exciting consequences for Greek history. Most importantly, it means that the whole question of the Shaft Graves in Mycenae must be re-examined. Heinrich Schliemann fervently believed these to represent the actual burials of Agamemnon and his attendants who were murdered by Aegisthus and Clytemnestra upon their return from Troy. Although backed by ancient tradition, and producing much other circumstantial evidence in support, Schliemann's interpretation of the Shaft Graves was subsequently dismissed. The major, and probably the only real reason for this was the fact that stylistically

---

267 It can in fact be shown that Herodotus was mistaken in placing a king Psammetichus (Psamtek) in the 7th century — he actually belonged in the 5th. Nevertheless, the events of which Herodotus speaks are real enough. An 8th century king or noble really did employ Greek mercenaries to drive out the Assyrians. Why the two episodes became confused is discussed in detail in my *Ramessides, Medes and Persians* (2001)

the material in the Shaft Graves (e.g. the inlaid daggers) had to be placed near the beginning of the Eighteenth Dynasty, or even earlier. Since it was believed that the Eighteenth Dynasty came long before the Trojan War (conventionally dated to 1184 BC), it was assumed that the Shaft Graves could not possibly belong to Agamemnon and his followers.

Thus the Shaft Graves are now said to have been the resting places of unknown kings who lived centuries before the dynasty of Atreus.

Armed with our new knowledge such ideas can at last be "laid to rest". The Eighteenth Dynasty did not precede the Trojan campaign, it followed it by a couple of decades. The Shaft Graves must date to around 720 BC and are almost certainly the final resting places of Agamemnon and his unfortunate entourage. Who knows, it may even be that the so-called "Mask of Agamemnon" does indeed portray the legendary lord of Mycenae and that the face behind the mask, which had lain undecayed in its airtight tomb all those centuries before being uncovered by an astonished Heinrich Schliemann, really was that of Atreus's famous son.

A more fitting end to the tale of Troy could not have been imagined by Homer himself.

Mopsus

Shortly after the sack of Ilion, the Assyrian Empire collapsed under the combined assault of Chaldaeans, Medes and Scythians. Out of its ruins in Anatolia, there arose the mighty Hittite (actually Lydian) state, whose capital city Hattusas was discovered on the banks of the Halys River just over a century ago.

To the delight of archaeologists, vast numbers of cuneiform documents, many of them written in Akkadian, were discovered at Hattusas. These documents were to provide fascinating insights into Hittite life, and enabled scholars to piece together a fairly comprehensive history of this "forgotten empire". Many of the documents dealt with relations between the Hittite rulers and various kings in western Asia Minor. With mounting excitement, scholars began to decipher names of individuals and places already known from Greek tradition.

One of the most sensational discoveries had to wait a number of decades after initial translation to be fully appreciated.

A document named the Madduwattash Text, dealing with events during the reign of a Hittite king named Tudkhaliash, as well as his successor Arnuwandash, caused great excitement initially because of its mention of characters apparently connected with Greece, specifically Heroic Age Greece. Thus, for example, the document complains of the activities of a king of Ahhiya (Achaea?) named Attarshiyash (Atreus?) in the land of Zippashla Khariyata, identified as north-western Asia Minor — the region of Troy.

Such an interpretation was perfectly legitimate, but failed to gain widespread acceptance because of the chronology. Scholars accepted unquestioningly the "traditional" date for the fall of Troy (1184 BC), whereas this document was confidently placed (by cross-referencing with Egypt) in the 13th century BC. Thus Attarshiyash of Ahhiya could not possibly be Agamemnon (Son of Atreus) of Achaea. Scholars had thus placed this and related documents near the end of the Hittite Empire (contemporary with the Nineteenth Dynasty of Egypt), but the trend in recent years, apparently even more damning for any attempt to synchronies with Greek history, has been to "backdate the whole of this group of texts to the 15th century BC," owing to the fact that they "exhibit certain archaic features of language and orthography."[268] The writer of these words suggested dating the Madduwattash Text to the time of Tudkhaliyash II, a great-grandfather of Suppiluliumas I, and thus a contemporary of the early Eighteenth Dynasty kings. As such, the Madduwattash Text would describe events very close to the defeat and expulsion of the Hyksos. Since we have already placed the Trojan campaign very close in time to the rise of the Eighteenth Dynasty, it is clear that the Madduwattash Text must refer to events immediately following the sack of Ilion.

This conclusion was dramatically illustrated by the mention in the Madduwattash document of a freebooter named Mukshush. The significance of this name only became apparent with Bossert's discovery of the famous bilingual Karatepe inscription, where the name Mukshush is rendered in the Hittite hieroglyphic version as Muksas, but in the alphabetic Phoenician as Mps. This caused something of a sensation, for it meant that the Mukshush of the Madduwattash Text was "identical in name with Mopsus, a strange figure of Greek legend."[269]

Greek tradition stated that a year before the end of the Trojan War, Mopsus, one of Agamemnon's lieutenants, set off southwards with a band of followers, accompanied by Amphilocus and two Lapith chiefs named Leonteus and Polypoetes. Arriving in Pamphylia, Mopsus founded its most notable cities, Aspendus and Phaselis. Shortly afterwards, he set out for Cilicia, where he established Mallus and Mopsou-hestia (Mopsus' hearth). According to the Lydian historian Xanthus, he ended his days in Ashkelon, where he threw the statue of the goddess Astarte into her own lake.

Mopsus was indeed well known to Lydian tradition, where his name is recorded as Moxus; and the Karatepe monument illustrates very clearly how he was honored as the forefather of the kings of Adana. But the occurrence of his

---

268 O.R. Gurney, "Anatolia, c.1600-1380 BC." in *CAH* Vol.2 part 1 (3rd ed.) p.678

269 R.D. Barnett, "The Sea Peoples" in *CAH* Vol.2 part 2 (3rd ed.) p.364

name on the Madduwattash Text has transformed "for the first time a figure of Greek legend ... into an undeniable historical personality."[270]

From our point of view, the Madduwattash Text adds yet another welcome detail to the picture built up in the preceding pages. Once more, this is confirmation for our proposal that the Trojan campaign, ending around 720 BC, directly preceded the collapse of the Hyksos/Assyrian Empire and the rise of Egypt's Eighteenth Dynasty. Those scholars who wished to identify Attarshiyash of Ahhiya with Agamemnon were absolutely correct. The term Attarshiyash almost certainly denotes "son of Atreus" or "descendant of Atreus", and it is precisely under this title (Atreides) that he is named repeatedly in the *Iliad*. We may well imagine a Hittite scribe hearing the name Atreides as Atreises, since the "s" sound is easily confused with "d" or "t" (consider the pronunciation of any English word ending in "tion"). Similarly, the king Mita of Pahhuva (or Piggaya), who also occurs in the Madduwattash Text, is of course Agamemnon's famous contemporary, Midas of Phrygia.

One final point. The name Madduwattash illustrates in a remarkable way the proper cultural milieu of the so-called Hittite Empire; for it is rather obviously Lydian. Greek writers would have written the word Madyattes, and it is clearly in the same genre as the names of the Lydian kings provided for us by the classical authors; namely Alyattes, Sadyattes, etc. But Lydia only became a great power in the 7th and 6th centuries BC, when the empire fought a long-standing war against the Medes.

---

270 Ibid., p.365

Epilogue

The reconstruction of history proposed in the foregoing pages has sought to demonstrate the necessity of subtracting two thousand years from the length of civilization. Yet this is much more than simply a numbers game, a question of chronology and dates. For a true understanding of mankind's early history cannot ignore the fact that much more than the dating system is at stake. In reality, modern scholarship has fundamentally misunderstood the forces involved both the development of life itself, and the emergence and growth of civilization.

This was a fact that Immanuel Velikovsky vainly tried to bring to the attention of modern scholarship. Our planet, said Velikovsky, is not the safe and tranquil world which conventional ideas of the past would have us believe. On the contrary, as the ancients themselves never tired of stating, the earth has been devastated by vast upheavals of nature many times in the past. The last of these cataclysms occurred well within the span of recorded history; and ancient man himself testified to these events, in his art, literature, legend, religion, and indeed in virtually every sphere of his culture. It is only modern man, of the 20th century, who has ignored what the ancients stated in the most clear and graphic terms possible.

The chronology of early human history, which we find in the textbooks, states that ancient civilizations emerged first around 3000 BC, and that they developed in comparative peace and tranquillity from then onwards. Yet the evidence in the ground speaks of a planet in turmoil as recently as the 9th and even 8th centuries BC. Why, Velikovsky was asked, do the pyramids still stand, and why are they still aligned accurately to the movements of the sun, moon, and planets, if, as you say, our planet suffered the events of which you write in the latter second and early first millennium BC? Such an argument of course only has validity so long as we accept the conventional chronology, which places the pyramids and the other megaliths in the third millennium. However, as we have seen, the pyramids did not exist in the third millennium, nor indeed did civilization. Not only that, far from being a problem for catastrophism, the pyramids were raised as a direct result of the cataclysms, the final series of them.

The megaliths, we have seen, were erected in thanksgiving and in celebration for the ending of the disasters. The great comet, the Cosmic Serpent, which in the mythologies of every nation had rained destruction upon the earth, was now tamed. A titanic clash with another cosmic body "decapitated" the comet, and diverted it from its collision course with the earth. A veritable Sword of Damocles had been removed from over the head of mankind. Humanity celebrated. Immense works were undertaken whose only purpose was to honor the heavenly gods. Pyramids and mounds, "sacred mountains", as well as various types of stone circles, were raised in every part of the globe. There is no need to postulate vast migrations in order to explain the simultaneous appearance of these structures throughout the planet. Simultaneous experience of the same cosmic events is more than adequate explanation.

The catastrophic end to the Early Dynastic Age is almost certainly the event alluded to in the notorious Atlantis legend. Whether or not a civilization inhabiting a continent-sized island ever existed in the midst of the ocean which shares its name is probably of minor importance. What is significant is that the destruction of an Early Bronze civilization is so unequivocally linked to a universal natural cataclysm, a cataclysm equally vouched for in the archaeological record.

Much has been written over the past few years on the nature and age of the great Sphinx at Giza. Evidence of a very compelling nature has been brought forward to suggest that the Sphinx predates the nearby pyramids of Cheops, Chephren, and Mycerinus, and was not erected by Chephren, as Egyptology now insists. Some of the wilder theorists have even suggested a link with the Atlantis legend.

Whilst ideas of this sort may be safely dismissed, it is evident that the Sphinx does not belong to the same epoch as the pyramids, and that the climate of Egypt was very different when the Sphinx was erected. This is confirmed by the clear marks of water erosion on the body of the Sphinx itself and on the rock walls of the pit excavated around the sculpture to separate it from the outcrop. It seems clear too that the head of the Sphinx, which is on a much smaller scale than the body, and is not damaged by water erosion, was recarved at a time when the entire statue was already badly worn. Yet in the thousands of years that have passed since the recarving, very little appreciable erosion of the new head has occurred. This means that Egypt's climate must have been much wetter when the Sphinx was first carved.

Now it is known that the final cataclysm of the Early Bronze epoch (which in Syria/Palestine however is termed Middle Bronze 1) was marked by a dramatic change in the climate of the Near East. The evidence suggests that the climate of Egypt was much wetter during the Early Dynastic Age, and what is now the Sahara Desert was then a vast savannah supporting herds of typical African fauna. Interestingly, ancient tradition, as recalled for example in the story of Phaeton, tells of a time when the Sahara was not arid, and specifically indicates that the desert was formed very suddenly, as a result of a natural cataclysm involving the heavenly bodies.

Almost certainly then the Sphinx, whose cult was known to be of great antiquity, was carved in the Early Dynastic epoch, probably during the 3rd Dynasty. We have shown how the Early Dynastic Age, in Egypt and Mesopotamia, and throughout the earth, was the Age of Sacrifice, an epoch during which the religious impulses of men were directed specifically towards performing ritual bloodletting, bloodletting aimed at appeasing the wrath of the gods and expiating the sins of the community. More often than not, these bloody rituals, performed by the priest-kings, including human sacrifice. So long as the Great Comet, the Dragon monster, threatened the globe, it had to be appeased with blood, and the sphinx-monster, Sekhmet, represented the destructive power of the gods. It is known that human beings were offered in sacrifice both to the Sphinx at Giza as well as to sphinx-deities in other parts of Egypt.

The disaster which ended the Early Dynastic Age also brought an end to the Age of Sacrifice. The heroes of the time, Horus, Moses, and Hercules, became famous for their abolition of human sacrifice.

The catastrophist interpretation of history thus opens exciting possibilities for us. Having already synchronized the Exodus of the Israelites with the beginning of the Pyramid Age, we may also link the same event to the Atlantis story. Certainly it seems that some Early Bronze civilization either in the western Mediterranean, or in the Atlantic as tradition insists, was completely destroyed at this time. As the children of Israel escaped from their bondage in Egypt, a great island civilization was consigned to the depths of the sea in the west.

The true history of our planet, which is only now beginning to emerge, will be shown to be infinitely more exciting and dramatic than the "history" currently found in the textbooks.

Yet much work remains to be done. We have now reached the confines of what is thought to be well-documented history. With the end of the Pyramid Age of Egypt, the Age of the Judges in Israel, and the Age of Heroes in Greece, mythic elements begin to disappear, with hard history taking its place. According to us, this occurs near the end of the 8th century and the beginning of the 7th century BC — comparatively recent times, by any standard. Yet how much do we really know of this and subsequent periods? Not as much, we will find, as was thought. All of Egypt's dynasties, from the Eighteenth to the Thirtieth, need to be placed in the seven centuries remaining before the start of the Roman period. Is it possible that we can find space for them?

Appendix

The Technology of Carving Granite

Whilst it is true that the Iron Age, *per se*, saw the introduction of steel as the preferred metal for weapons-manufacture, and whilst it has been shown conclusively that the Egyptians of the Pyramid Age knew about and exploited iron for tool manufacture, it has to be admitted, without going a step further, that iron itself, or wrought iron, still cannot explain the achievements of the pyramid-builders. For neither iron nor bronze would make any impact upon the types of materials used in the construction of the great monuments of the Fourth Dynasty, as well as in the creations of the sculptors. The central burial chamber of the Great Pyramid has walls, a ceiling (or rather multiple ceilings), and a floor of granite. The stones used were cut with great precision and the fine serrated marks of the saw which did the work can be seen to this day. Granite is an immensely hard substance, and it is admitted by all that a saw of bronze would be completely inadequate to the task. Such a tool would be blunted after only a few strokes, without having made any impact on the stone. In the words of A. Lucas, "bronze chisels, no matter to what extent they have been hardened, will not cut such hard stones as diorite, granite, and schist."[271] A saw of wrought iron would produce a similar result. Indeed, Stephen L. Sass informs us that "bronze . . . is stronger than

---

271 Quoted by C. Ginenthal, *Pillars of the Past* (New York, 2004).

wrought iron."[272] Being softer than bronze, wrought iron clearly cannot be called upon to cut and engrave the hard rocks that bronze is unable to cut.

But the problem goes beyond that. For the Egyptians carved stone of even harder quality than granite. Numerous statues, for example, are executed in basalt; and not a few are in the almost diamond-hard diorite. How, it has been asked again and again, could Egyptian artisans have chiselled these stones into the exquisitely sharp lines of eyelids, lips, and ears that we see today in the museums?

Over the years, there have in fact been many attempts to replicate the techniques and tools used by the Egyptians; and a fairly comprehensive overview of these attempts was provided by Charles Ginenthal in his 2004 book, *Pillars of the Past*. In the discussion to follow, I shall make liberal use of this volume, as it contains perhaps the most thorough and honest examination of the topic yet published.

As Ginenthal notes, the debate on the technology employed by the Egyptians began at an early stage. Both I.E.S. Edwards and Flinders Petrie put forward their own suggestions. Petrie's was as follows:

> The granite and hard stones were also sawn and cut with tubular drills. The saws were blades of copper, which carried [in the copper] the hard cutting points. The material was sand for working the softer stones, and emery for harder rocks. As far back as prehistoric times blocks of emery were used for grinding beads, and even a plummet [weight on a string] and a vase were cut out of emery rock (now in University College). There can be no doubt, therefore, of emery being known and used.

The difficult question is whether the cutting material was used as loose powder, or was set in metal tools as separate teeth. An actual example was found at the pre-historic Greek palace at Tiryns. The hard limestone there had been sawn, and I found a broken bit of the saw left in a cut. The copper blade had rusted away to green carbonate; and with it were some little blocks of emery about a sixteenth of an inch long, rectangular, and quite capable of being set, but far too large to act as a loose powder with a plain blade. On the Egyptian examples there are long grooves in the faces of the cuts of both saws and drills; and grooves may be made by working a loose powder. But, further, the groove certainly seems to run spirally around a core, which would show that it was cut by a single point; and where quartz and softer feldspar are cut through the groove floor runs on one level, and as the feldspar is worn down by general rubbing, the quartz is actually cut through to a greater depth than the softer feldspar. This shows that a fixed cutting point ploughed the groove, and not a loose powder. Also, the hieroglyphs on diorite bowls are ploughed out with a single cut of a fixed point, only one

---

272 Stephen L. Sass, *The Substance of Civilization* (NY 1988), p. 86; see also H.W.F. Saggs, *Everyday Life in Babylon and Assyria* (NY 1965), p. 65

hundred and fiftieth of an inch wide, so it is certain that fixed cutting points were used for hand-graving. There is no doubt that sawing and grinding with loose powder was the general method, but the use of fixed stones seems clearly shown by the instances above.[273]

Ginenthal goes on to note that, "Petrie adds that 'large hieroglyphs on hard stone were cut by copper blades fed with emery, and sawn along the outline by hand.' Elsewhere, he states: 'The material of these cutting points is yet undetermined, but only five substances are possible: beryl, topaz, chrysoberyl, corundum or sapphire and diamond.'"[274] Petrie thus believed that the Egyptian artisans employed tools of hard gemstones to work granite and diorite. These he saw as generally being used as abrasive powders, set in copper saws. Yet this was problematic. In the words of Ginenthal: "Petrie has made it quite clear that the saw markings are indicative of blades that cut, not with powder, but with hard teeth. He also offered that diorite, an extremely hard rock, was engraved by an extraordinarily thin point, 1/150 of an inch thick. His list of minerals to accomplish these tasks includes 'beryl, topaz, chrysoberyl, corundum or sapphire and diamond.' But did the Old Kingdom craftsmen possess these necessary materials as teeth for saws or points for punches or graving tools?"[275] This was a question also considered by Barbara Mertz:

> Saw marks have been found on the granite sarcophagus from the Great Pyramid and on basalt pavement blocks from the temple of that pyramid, and drills were certainly used for hard stone statues and vases. It is true that cutting basalt with a plain copper saw would be somewhat difficult. Nowadays we sometimes cut hard stones by using points of even harder stones which are set into drill or saw. The use of diamond points in industry is well known. Diamonds rank 10 on a measuring device known as the Mohs scale; it can cut just about anything, including quartzite, the hardest stone the Egyptians quarried (7 on the Mohs scale). But sad to say, the Egyptians did not have diamonds. Neither did they have topaz (8) or rubies and sapphires (9) or even beryl (8) before the Greek period. We must conclude, then, that the Egyptians did not use hard stone points, or teeth to cut their granite and quartz.

There is another method of cutting hard stone: with an abrasive powder. Diamond dust is used to cut diamonds. Having no diamonds, the Egyptians had no diamond dust, either, nor, so far as we can tell, did they use pumice or emery powder.[276]

Ginenthal then quotes A. Lucas, who wrote in a similar vein:

273 F. Petrie, *The Arts and Crafts of Ancient Egypt* (London, 1909), pp. 72-73

274 C. Ginenthal, *Pillars of the Past* (New York, 2004), p. 199

275 Ibid., p. 200

276 Barbara Mertz, *Red Land, Black Land*, revised ed. (NY 1978), p. 217

Although beryl occurs in Egypt, there is no evidence that it was known before the Greek epoch. It is highly improbable that it was ever obtained in the large quantities that would have been required had it been [used] for cutting stones. The other stones enumerated are not found in Egypt, and there is neither evidence not probability that they were used in Egypt for any purpose, or even that they were known, if at all, until a very late period.[277]

It is fairly evident then that copper saws equipped with teeth fashioned from these types of gemstones cannot be invoked as a method of cutting granite and diorite. But, perhaps in desperation, historians have proposed copper saws fixed with abrasive powders as a solution (in spite of the clearly observed saw-teeth marks on many of the monuments). I.E.S. Edwards, along with several others, suggested that copper saws with quartz sand and gypsum as abrasives, which can in fact cut limestone, could also have been used on harder stones. Thus Lehner writes: "It is most likely that a copper drill or saw was employed in conjunction with an abrasive slurry of water, gypsum and quartz sand. The copper blade simply acted as a guide while the quartz sand did the actual cutting."[278] On this suggestion, Ginenthal writes, "The problem with this method is that copper is actually softer than quartz sand and also softer than granite, schist, basalt, and diorite. Rather than cutting into these stones the quartz sand will destroy the copper blade. While this method will work with soft limestone, it is not possible to use it with these harder stones."[279] The impossibility of using an emery abrasive attached to a copper saw was demonstrated years ago by the mineralogist H. Garland;

A consideration of the [abrasive cutting] process would seem to give support to the idea that a copper-emery [or other abrasive material] process might have been used by the first Egyptians, but the author has proved by experiment the impossibility of cutting granite or diorite by any similar means to this. By the use of emery powder anointed with oil or turpentine, no measurable progress could be made in the stone, whilst the edge of the copper blade wore away and was rendered useless, the bottom and sides of the groove being coated with particles of copper. For some of these experiments a start was made by sawing a small groove with a steel saw, whilst for others an attempt, devoid of satisfactory results, was made to start a way for the copper blade by scratching with flint points, as it was thought that the latter might have been a method employed by the ancients, and it was quite impossible to start a passage way [a groove] with the copper tool itself.[280]

In Ginenthal's words, "The test proved that the copper-abrasive method will not cut granite or diorite using emery powder or, as Garland stated, 'by any simi-

277 A. Lucas, *Ancient Egyptian Minerals and Industries*, 4th. ed. (London 1962), p. 70

278 Mark Lehner, *The Complete Pyramids* (London, 1977), p. 210

279 C. Ginenthal, loc. cit.

280 H. Garland, C.O. Bannister, *Ancient Egyptian Metallurgy* (London 1927) p. 95

lar means.' Thus, sand-quartz will also destroy the copper blade and will fail to cut the hard stone."[281] Flint too is useless for the purpose.

Another hypothesis, one put forward regularly to this day, is that the Egyptian craftsmen pounded the granite with a hammer made of an even harder stone, such as diorite; and that this method, though extremely slow and laborious, would produce results. The softer granite, it is believed, crumbling under the hammer-blows, then simply had to be smoothed with a rough stone which acted as an abrasive. But, "Garland has shown that if one attempts to employ this method, say, on a granite sarcophagus, one will not be able to cut straight vertical corners inside the coffin; yet the insides of granite coffins exhibit straight vertical corners where the walls meet. 'Any rubbing process would surely have robbed the corners [of any stone] of all sharpness.'"[282] Denys Stocks further notes that, "The use of stone mauls for pounding calcite, granite, basalt, quartzite and graywacke from the interiors of sarcophagi is impracticable: the force of the blows would soon have cracked the shaped stone blocks."[283]

How then were the fine lines found on Pyramid Age sculptures achieved? Again, it was suggested that some form of hardened copper was used. It is true that hammering will harden copper, but the hardness achieved is quite insufficient to cut through granite, never mind diorite. In the words of Christopher Dunn, a master craftsman and engineer thoroughly familiar with metals and their qualities notes,

> I.E.S. Edwards, British Egyptologist and the world's foremost expert on pyramids, said "Quarrymen of the Pyramid age would have accused Greek historian Strabo of understatement as they hacked at the stubborn granite of Aswan. Their axes and chisels were made of copper hardened by hammering."
>
> Having worked with copper on numerous occasions, and having hardened it in the manner suggested above, I was struck that this statement was entirely ridiculous. You can certainly work-harden copper by striking it repeatedly or even by bending it. However, after a specific hardness has been reached, the copper will begin to split and break apart. This is why, when copper is worked to any great extent, it has to be periodically annealed, or softened, in order to keep it in one piece. Even after being hardened in this manner, the copper is not capable of cutting granite. The hardest copper alloy in existence today is beryllium copper. There is no evidence to suggest that the ancient Egyptians possessed this alloy, but even if they did this alloy is not hard enough to cut granite.[284]

---

281 Ginenthal, loc. cit.

282 H. Garland and C. O. Bannister, loc. cit. p. 96

283 Denys A. Stocks, "Stone sarcophagus manufacture in ancient Egypt," *Antiquity*, vol. 73 (1999), p. 919

284 Christopher Dunn, *The Giza Power Plant* (Santa Fe NM 1998), p. 74

Yet some form of sharp, pointed tools *were* used. Petrie has described engraved diorite cut to "one hundred and fiftieth of an inch wide." Copper chisels will simply not do the job. Lucas is frank about the magnitude of the problem;

> In connexion with the working of hard stone, too much stress is usually laid upon the use of chisels [and pointed tools], and those who think they still must have been used point out that copper and bronze chisels, no matter to what extent they have been hardened by hammering, will not cut such hard stones of diorite, granite and schist, and that they cannot be used with an abrasive powder. This is fully admitted.[285]

But the true scale of the problem only becomes apparent when we remember that not only granite, but the much harder diorite, was used extensively during the Pyramid Age:

> It is a striking fact that diorite—one of the most difficult stones to carve—was worked almost exclusively during the Fourth Dynasty, when according to present accepted theories copper was the only base metal in use. We may quote the statue of Cephren [sic] in the Cairo Museum as an example of which Sir Gaston Maspero says — "It is most surprising that the Egyptian artists were able to model with so much delicacy and skill such a hard and difficult material as diorite."[286]

The early historians fully understood that steel was the only material capable of carving and engraving such hard stones. However, being unable to free themselves from the shackles of conventional chronology, they were incapable of even making an approach to a solution. Sir Gardiner Wilkinson long ago realized this but could not disentangle the problem because he also supported the long chronology:

> the hieroglyphs on obelisks and other granitic monuments and sculptures with a minuteness and finish which is surprising, even if they had used steel as highly tempered as our own.

> Some are cut to the depth of more than two inches, the edges and all the most minute parts of the intaglio presenting the same sharpness and accuracy; and I have seen the figure of a king in high relief, reposing on the lid of a granite coffin, which was raised to the height of nine inches above the level of the surface. What can be said, if we deny to men who executed such works as these the aid of steel, and confine them to bronze [or copper] implements? Then, indeed, we exalt their skill in metallurgy far beyond our own, and indirectly confess that they had devised a method of sculpting stone of which we are ignorant. In vain should we attempt to render copper, by the addition of certain alloys, sufficiently hard to sculpture granite, basalt, and stones of similar quality. No one who has tried to perforate or cut a block of Egyptian granite will scruple to acknowledge that our best steel tools are turned [blunted] in a very short time, and require to be re-tempered: and the labor experienced by the French engi-

---

285 A. Lucas, *Ancient Egyptian Minerals and Industries*, 3rd ed. (London 1948), p. 85

286 H. Garland and C. O. Bannister, op. cit. p. 187

neers, who removed the obelisk of Luxor from Thebes, in cutting a space less than two feet deep, along the face of its partially decomposed pedestal, suffices to show that, even with our excellent modern implements, we find considerable what to Egyptians would have been one of the least arduous tasks.[287]

Wilkinson quotes Sir R. Westmacott that chisels "of strong tempered iron, about three-quarters of an inch in diameter ... [can] resist the heat [of being pounded into granite before becoming blunted] sometimes half an hour, seldom longer ... Tools of less diameter ... of steel ... will not resist 300 strokes. ..."[288] Yet, as Ginenthal notes, "we are expected to believe that copper chisels with edges much thinner than these engraved diorite with exquisite hieroglyphs."

Notwithstanding all this, scholars have not abandoned their attempts to explain the achievements of the Egyptians in terms of copper tools. This of course is inevitable, so long as the conventional chronology is unquestioned. Thus as recently as 1999, Denys A. Stocks attempted to explain how to carve sarcophagi of granite employing such tools. Stocks is a member of the Department of Art History and Archaeology at the University of Manchester, England. His work is said to be based upon actual experiments with the materials believed to have been used by the Egyptians. Yet, in the words of Ginenthal, "a careful reading will disclose that his statements that copper and quartz-sand abrasive will accomplish these tasks are filled with provisos such as 'probably represents,' 'experiment indicated' (not that it *proved*), 'experiments suggest' (not that they *prove*), 'stone-cutting saws were probably ...' (not stone-cutting saws *actually did* ...), 'holes were probably drilled' (not holes *were* drilled), 'the true number of holes in the central mass [of stone to hollow it out] can never be known,' 'polishing was probably done with' (not polishing *was* done with)."[289]

It is quite evident that Stocks never actually carved a granite sarcophagus using copper tools. According to him, the Egyptians could nevertheless have performed such a task, as they had plenty of time on their hands. Yet here too he ignores the facts. "The problem he failed to address," says Ginenthal, "is the stone-working anomaly mentioned by Petrie regarding tool marks that left a spiral groove on a core removed from a hole drilled into granite." Petrie had stated, "On the granite core No. 7, the spiral of the cut sinks 0.1 inch in the circumference of 6 inches, or 1 in 60, a rate of ploughing out of quartz and feldspar which is astonishing."[290] In short, the tool-marks indicate that a mere 100 turns of the drill allowed

---

287 Sir J. Gardiner Wilkinson, *A Popular Account of the Ancient Egyptians* (revised and abridged) vol. II (NY 1988), p. 156

288 Ibid. p. 157

289 Ginenthal, loc. cit. quoting Denys A. Stocks, *op. cit.*, pp. 918-922

290 William Flinders Petrie, *Pyramids and Temples of Gizeh* (London 1883), p. 13

it to go one inch into the rock. Petrie was, as he said, astonished by this evidence and attempted to explain it at three different places in his book."[291] Wilkinson, for one, believed that only a diamond-headed drill could do the work:

> although we do not know the precise method adopted by the Egyptians for cutting . . . hard stones, we reasonably conclude they were acquainted with the diamond and adopted it.[292]

Ginenthal notes that, as a rule, whenever an engineer, metallurgist or sculptor is asked to comment on the belief of the Egyptologists that granite and diorite were carved with copper tools, the result is always the same: Incredulity. Thus stonemason Roger Hopkins wrote:

> I am a stone mason by trade and in 1991 the PBS [Public Broadcasting System] series NOVA invited me to go to Egypt to experiment with building a pyramid; I quickly got bored with working the soft limestone and started to ponder the granite work. Here in Massachusetts my specialty is working in granite....
>
> When I was asked by the Egyptologists how the ancients could have produced this work with mere copper tools, I told them they were crazy.[293]

Ginenthal summarizes the situation thus:

> The fact of the matter is that they cannot replicate the experiment. They have replicated ... experiments to show how obelisks are stood upright, how great heavy stones could be moved, etc., but no one has ever been able to carve a large diorite statue and engrave hieroglyphics onto it with fixed points of copper or copper chisels. What has been put forth is a mountain of words, suggestions, hypotheses, all unproven and improvable. They are improvable because they will not work; "there is no evidence" means precisely what it says, "no evidence" that this can be accomplished. The critical tests have been carried out. Their entire procedure is dysfunctional.[294]

So it would seem that carving such materials without good quality steel tools is a straightforward impossibility. But this then raises a couple of other very serious questions. To begin with: Whence came this steel? From which part of the world was it derived, and who were the smiths who forged it? Secondly: If the Egyptians of the 9th and 8th centuries BC, in which time we place the Pyramid Age, were aware of steel-making, why did they fail to utilize this for military purposes? Many centuries after the Pyramid Age Egyptian soldiers were still equipped with bronze scimitars, daggers and spear-heads. Why should this be the case?

To address the first question first; iron ore is rather common in Egypt. It is not of particularly good quality, but it is present. Better sources of the material

---

291 Ibid. pp. 75, 76, 78

292 Sir J. Gardiner Wilkinson, op. cit. p. 67

293 Cited from Ginenthal, loc. cit.

294 Ginenthal, loc. cit.

however are found in lands not too far from the Land of the Nile. It would appear that some of the ore, as well as other metallic alloys used to harden iron, may have come from Greece. An inscription of the Twentieth Dynasty pharaoh Ramses III refers to "ore" he caused to be brought to Egypt from the land of Atika. Now, as early as 1977 Immanuel Velikovsky identified Atika with the region of Attica in Greece, an identification fully supported by the present writer. In his inscription, Ramses III refers to this ore as *hmt*, a word translated as "copper" by Breasted, though with reservations, since *hmt* is not the usual word for copper. In another text *hmt* is in fact used for three different varieties of ore or alloy, all of which cannot be identified, though the hardness of the metal is stressed.[295]

As Velikovsky noted in *Peoples of the Sea*, Greece is not a copper-producing country, though mineral ores are high on its export list. At the top of the list are pyrite and chromite. Now chromite is composed of iron and chromium, and this latter element is surpassed in hardness only by boron and by diamonds. In the modern steel industry chromium is widely used for hardening the alloy.

Since, as we have already shown, the Egyptians of the Fourth, Fifth and Sixth Dynasties were well-acquainted with the Aegean world, it is possible, even likely, that *hmt*, or chromite ore, was being exported to Egypt at this time, and that alloys of iron and chromium were forged into stone-cutting tools.

But if this be the case it raises the second question posed above: if the Egyptians of the Pyramid Age employed such high-quality steel for cutting tools, why then did they fail to employ it for weaponry and thus establish an insurmountable military superiority over their neighbors?

To this there is only one possible answer.

In antiquity the production of iron was a vastly laborious process. Homer hints at such when he repeats the formulaic phrase, "bronze, gold, and iron, wrought with much toil". The production of pure, or wrought iron, was labor-intensive. From the hot slag, which would be recovered from the bottom of the furnace, the smith had to remove all impurities. The only method by which this could be done was repeated heating and hammering over an anvil. To produce even a tiny quantity of good-quality iron, a smith might expend many days of hard, backbreaking labor. The *Encyclopaedia Britannica* puts it thus:

> During most of its history, iron was not recovered in a molten state but reduced from a spongy aggregate of iron and slag formed at a temperature well below the melting point of pure iron ($1,535°$ C, or $2,795°F$). This plastic metallic sponge was consolidated by hammering to squeeze out slag and weld the iron particles into a compact and ductile mass; thus it is called wrought iron, essentially pure iron with remnants of unexpelled slag coating the iron particles.

295 See e.g. Alan Gardiner "The Tomb of a much traveled Theban Official", *Journal of Egyptian Archaeology* IV (1917) pp. 28ff

> Wrought iron contains so little carbon that it does not harden usefully when cooled rapidly (quenched [in water or oil]). [Only w]hen iron containing 0.4 to 1.25 percent carbon is heated to 950°C, or 1,740°F, and then plunged into water or oil, is it hardened.[296]

Historian C.G. Starr makes a further telling comment:

> While iron ores can be melted and refined at a lower temperature than that required for copper, the process takes a longer time, and truly useful weapons and tools of iron involve a complicated technique of repeated heating, quenching, and hammering. Iron objects have turned up even in fifth-millennium levels (sometimes of meteoric source); Hittite smiths in Asia Minor went further in working metal; but the adequate methods of hardening iron products became commonly known only after 1000 [BC].[297]

By contrast, bronze was rather easily produced and modelled into tools and weapons. A sword of bronze was manufactured simply by pouring the molten alloy into a mould of stone or clay; from which form the completed sword was extracted a short time later (as in the British Arthurian legend). A sword of iron, however, or of steel, required prolonged toil over a forge and anvil. Iron tools were extremely expensive. This is a point stressed by the following writer, an adherent to the conventional chronology:

> Innovation in the metallurgy of iron had a drastic effect on its price. In the nineteenth century B.C.E. [sic], forty ounces of silver [2 $\frac{1}{2}$ pounds] bought one ounce of iron, a ratio of forty to one. By the seventh century B.C.E., technology had advanced so far that one ounce of silver now purchased 2,000 ounces [125 pounds] of iron, a ratio of 1 to 2,000. In other words, over a period of one thousand two hundred years [probably more like two hundred years], the price of iron plummeted by a factor of 80,000 (assuming silver kept a constant value).[298]

It is evident then that in antiquity producing tools and weapons of iron and steel was no easy thing. But what is important to remember is that it was not the production of steel, but of iron, that was difficult. Once the iron existed, it was very easy, almost childishly easy, to carbonize it. Among some ancient societies, this was done simply by placing the heated iron onto a goat or sheepskin. Carbon easily migrated from the animal skin into the hot iron, which was then simply tempered (quenched) in water or oil, leaving good-quality mild steel. High-carbon steel was no more difficult to produce. Yet first, one had to have the required iron; and this was difficult to produce. So difficult in fact that in the time of the Old Babylonians iron was worth eight times as much as silver; virtually equivalent in value to gold. Yet there is something we must emphasize again, since it is a point which has never really been understood; iron was expensive, it was

---

296 *Encyclopedia Britannica, Macropedia*, vol. 8, vol. 17 (Chicago 1982) p. 661

297 C.G. Starr, *A History of the ancient World* (New York, 1999) p.129

298 Sass, op. cit., p. 93

not unknown. And as soon as any society could produce pure iron, it could also produce steel. But the smelting of iron began simultaneously with the smelting of copper. The two technologies are virtually identical. Thus the age of steel began at the very beginning of the Bronze Age.

There is therefore no reason whatever to doubt that the Egyptians were well acquainted with good quality carbon steel with which they could cut and fashion granite and diorite. They did not however equip their armies with weapons of this material for a very simple economic reason. Armies required vast quantities of swords, spear-heads and arrowheads. These were quite easily made from bronze; and bronze was more than adequate to penetrate the armor and shields that enemy troops of the time might possess. It would have been economically and logistically impossible to equip an army with steel weapons, given the knowledge of iron-smelting at that time.

It would not however have been impossible to produce a small quantity of good-quality steel implements for the specialized use of the royal stone-masons and sculptors. The saws and chisels employed by these men were precious artifacts, worth their weight in gold, which were carefully husbanded and passed from one generation to another. They were never, or very rarely, discarded, and carefully repaired when damaged.

The peoples of the Americas too, who also understood the technology of bronze smelting, must likewise have possessed very small quantities of steel tools with which they carved the hard stones sometimes used in their great monuments.

REVISED CHRONOLOGY

EARLY DYNASTIC EPOCH			
850 BC	Huni/Ka-nefer-re		
NATURAL CATASTROPHE			
	Sneferu		
	Khufu (Cheops)		
800 BC	Khafre (Chephren)		
	Menkaure	ELEPHANTINE KINGS	
		Userkaf	ASSYRIAN (HYKSOS) KINGS
		Sahura	Teti/Sargon I
			Pepi I/Manishtusu
		Menkuhor	
750 BC		Unas	
			Pepi II/Naram-Sin
			Merenre II/Shar-kali-Sharri
THEBAN KINGS			
	Ahmose		
700 BC	Amenhotep I		

BIBLIOGRAPHY

BOOKS

Aldred, C. *Egypt to the End of the Old Kingdom* (London, 1965)

Bienkowski, P. and A. Millard eds. *Dictionary of the Ancient Near East* (British Museum Press, London, 2000)

Biot, J. B. *Études sur l'astronomie indienne et sur l'astronomie chinoise* (Paris, 1862)

Bonnet, H. *Die Waffen der Völker des alten Orients* (Leipzig, 1926)

Breasted, J. H. *A History of Egypt* (2nd ed. 1951)

Breasted, J. H. *Ancient Records of Egypt* 5 Vols. (Chicago, 1906)

Breasted, J. H. *Development of Religion and Thought in Ancient Egypt* (London, 1912)

Bright, W. *A History of Israel* (London, 1960)

Cerny, J. *Ancient Egyptian Religion* (London, 1952)

Clube, V. and B. Napier *The Cosmic Serpent: A Catastrophist View of Earth History* (London, 1984)

Coldstream, N. J. *Greek Geometric Pottery* (London, 1968)

Cottrell, L. *The Mountains of Pharaoh* (London, 1956)

Cuvier, Georges *Essay on the Theory of the Earth* 5th ed. (1827)

Dalley, S. *Myths from Mesopotamia* (Oxford, 1989)

Dayton, J. *Minerals, Metals, Glazing, and Man* (London, 1978)

Desborough, V. R. d'A. *The Greek Dark Ages* (1972)

Desroches-Noblecourt, C. *Tutankhamun* (London, 1963)

Dunn, Christopher *The Giza Power Plant* (Santa Fe, New Mexico, 1998),

Edwards, I. E. S. *The Pyramids of Egypt* (Pelican Books, 1972)

Gardiner, A. *Egypt of the Pharaohs* (1961)

Garland, H. and C. O. Bannister *Ancient Egyptian Metallurgy* (London, 1927)

Ginenthal, Charles. *Pillars of the Past* (New York, 2004)

Ginzberg, L. *The Legends of the Jews* 7 vols. (1961 ed.)

Graves, R. *The Greek Myths* 2 Vols. (1955)

Griffith, F. L. *Hieratic papyri from Kahun and Gorub* (London, 1898)

Hall, H. R. *The Ancient History of the Near East* (3rd ed. London, 1916)

Heinsohn, G. *Die Sumerer gab es nicht* (Frankfurt, 1988)

Heinsohn, G. *Perserherrscher gleich Assyrerkönige?* (Frankfurt, 1992)

Herzfeld, E. *The Persian Empire; Studies in Geography and Ethnography of the Ancient Near East*, edited from the posthumous papers of Gerald Walser (Wiesbaden, 1968)

Hicks, John. *The Persians* (Time-Life, 1978)

Kamil, J. *The Ancient Egyptians: How they Lived and Worked* (1976)

Kovacs, M. G. *The Epic of Gilgamesh* (Stanford, 1989)

Kramer, S. N. *History Begins at Sumer: Thirty-Nine Firsts in Man's Recorded History* (Pennsylvania, 1981)

Lehner, Mark. *The Complete Pyramids* (London, 1997)

Lepsius, C. R. "Saqqarah" *Denkmäler aus Aegypten und Aethiopien* (Leipzig, 1897)

Lucas, A. *Ancient Egyptian Minerals and Industries*, (4th ed. London, 1962)

MacKie, Euan. *The Megalith Builders* (Oxford, 1977)

Martin, Geoffrey T. *The Hidden Tombs of Memphis* (London, 1991)

Maspero, Gaston. *Art in Egypt* (London, 1912)

Maspero, Gaston. *A History of Egypt, Chaldea, Syria, Babylonia, and Assyria* 13 Vols. (London, 1906)

Mertz, Barbara. *Red Land, Black Land*, (revised ed. New York, 1978)

Meyer, E. *Geschichte des Altertums* 5 vols. (9th ed. Stuttgart, 1952-59)

Murray, Margaret. A. *Egyptian Temples* (Sampson Low, Maston and Co.)

Ogilvie, R. M. *Early Rome and the Etruscans* (Fontana, 1976)

Peet, T. Eric. *A Comparative Study of the Literatures of Egypt, Palestine and Mesopotamia* (London, 1931)

Petrie, F. *A History of Egypt* 3 Vols. (London, 1905)

Petrie, F. *Egyptian Architecture* (London, 1938)

Petrie, F. *Pyramids and Temples of Gizeh* (London, 1883)

Petrie, F. *The Arts and Crafts of Ancient Egypt*, (1909; reprint, London, 1996)

Petrie, F. *The Making of Egypt* (London, 1939)

Pritchard, J. *Ancient Near Eastern Texts* (Princeton, 1950)

Rice, Michael. *Egypt's Making* (London, 1990)

Rickards, Thomas Arthur. *Man and Metals*, 2 Vols. (New York, 1932)

Saggs, H. W. F. *Everyday Life in Babylon and Assyria* (New York, 1965)

Sass, Stephen L. *The Substance of Civilization* (New York, 1988)

Schaeffer, C. *Stratigrapie comparée et chonologie de l'Asia occidentale* (Oxford, 1948)

Schliemann, H. *Tiryns* (London, 1886)

Schultz, Gwen. *Ice Age Lost* (New York, 1974)

Shaw, I. and P. Nicholson. *British Museum Dictionary of Ancient Egypt* (London, 2002)

Spence, Lewis. *Mexico and Peru: Myths and Legends* (1920)

Stannard, Brendan. *The Origins of Israel and Mankind* (Lancaster, 1983)

Starr, C. G. *A History of the Ancient World* (New York, 1999)

Sweeney, E. *Ramessides, Medes and Persians* (New York, 2001)

Sweeney, E. *The Genesis of Israel and Egypt* (London, 1997)

Sweeney, E. *Arthur and Stonehenge: Britain's Lost History* (2001)

Tompkins, P. *Secrets of the Great Pyramid* (London, 1977)

Torr, Cecil. *Memphis and Mycenae* (Isis ed. 1988)

Velikovsky, I. *Ages in Chaos* (1952)

Velikovsky, I. *Peoples of the Sea* (1977)

Velikovsky, I. *Ramses II and his Time* (1978)

Velikovsky, I. *Worlds in Collision* (1950)

Von Beckerath, J. *Handbuch der Aegyptischen Königsnamen* (Berlin, 1984)

Vyse, R. W. H. *Operations Carried on at the Pyramids of Gizeh in 1837* (London, 1840-1842)

Weigall, Arthur. *A History of the Pharaohs: The First Eleven Dynasties* (London, 1925)

Weill, R. *XIIe dnastie royaute de Haute-Égypte et Domination Hyksos dans le Nord* (Cairo, 1953)

Whiston, William. *New Theory of the Earth* (1696)

Wilkinson, Sir J. Gardiner. *A Popular Account of the Ancient Egyptians* (revised and abridged) 2 vols. (New York, 1988)

Wilson, David. *The New Archaeology* (New York, 1974)

Woldering, I. *Egypt: The Art of the Pharaohs* (Baden-Baden, 1963)

Woolly, Leonard. *Ur of the Chaldees* (2nd ed. 1983)

Articles

Albright, W. F. "Northwest Semitic Names in a List of Egyptian Slaves from the Eighteenth Century BC," *Journal of the American Oriental Society* 74 (1954)

Barnett, R. D. "The Sea Peoples" in *Cambridge Ancient History* Vol.2 part 2 (3rd ed.)

Bretschneider, Joachim. "Nabada: The Buried City", *Scientific American* (October, 2000)

Burgess, "The Bronze Age" in Colin Renfrew, ed. *British Prehistory* (1974)

Catling, H. W. "Cyprus in the Middle Bronze Age" in *Cambridge Ancient History* Vol.1 part 2 (3rd ed.)

Drower, Margaret S. "Syria Before 2200 BC," in *Cambridge Ancient History* Vol.1 part 2 (3rd ed.)

Edwards, I. E. S. "The Early Dynastic Period in Egypt" in *Cambridge Ancient History* Vol.1 part 2 (3rd ed.)

Gadd, C. J. "The Dynasty of Agade and the Gutian Invasion" in *Cambridge Ancient History* Vol.1 part 2 (3rd ed.)

Gadd, C. J. "The Dynasty of Agade and the Gutian Invasion" in *Cambridge Ancient History* Vol.1 part 2 (3rd ed.)

Gardiner, A. "The Tomb of a much traveled Theban Official", *Journal of Egyptian Archaeology* IV (1917)

Gardiner, A. H. "New Literary Works from Egypt", *Journal of Egyptian Archaeology* 1 (1914)

Ginenthal, Charles "The Extinction of the Mammoth" *The Velikovskian* (special edition) Vol.III 2 and 3 (1999)

Gurney, O. R. "Anatolia, c.1600-1380 BC," in *Cambridge Ancient History* Vol.2 part 1 (3rd ed.)

Hayes, W. C. "Egypt: From the Death of Ammenemes III to Seqenenre II" in *Cambridge Ancient History* Vol.2 part 1 (3rd ed.)

Hayes, W. C. "The Middle Kingdom in Egypt: Internal History from the Rise of the Heracleopolitans to the Death of Ammenemes III" in *Cambridge Ancient History* Vol.1 part 2 (3rd ed.)

Heinsohn, Gunnar. "Egyptian Chronology: A Solution to the Hyksos Problem," *Aeon* Vol.1 (1988) no.6

Heinsohn, Gunnar. "Old-Akkadians and Hyksos: Stratigraphic room-mates only or identical nations also?" (Paper presented at *Society for Interdisciplinary Studies* Ancient History Study Group Meeting, Nottingham, November, 1990)

Heinsohn, Gunnar. "The Rise of Blood Sacrifice and Priest-Kingship in Mesopotamia: A 'Cosmic Decree'?" *Religion* (1992) 22

Heinsohn, Gunnar. "Who were the Hyksos?" *Sixth International Congress of Egyptology* (Turin, 1991)

Helck, W. "Manetho" in *Der kleine Pauly* Vol.3 (Munich, 1979)

Helck, W. "Zur Lage der aegyptischen Geschichtsschreibung" (résumé) in S. Schoske, ed. *4 Internationaler Aegyptologenkongress, 26/8 — 1/9/1985, München, Resümees der Referate* (Munich, 1985)

James, T. G. H. "Egypt: From the Expulsion of the Hyksos to Amenophis I" in *Cambridge Ancient History* Vol.2 part 2 (3rd ed.)

Kenyon, K. M. "Syria and Palestine c.2160-1780 BC: The Archaeological Sites" in *Cambridge Ancient History* Vol.1 part 2 (3rd ed.)

Lewy, Hildegard "Assyria c. 2600 — 1816 BC" in *Cambridge Ancient History* Vol.1 part 2 (3rd ed)

Malamat, A. "Hazor, 'The Head of all those Kingdoms" *Journal of Biblical Literature* Vol.LXXIX (1960)

Mallowan, Max. "The Early Dynastic Period in Mesopotamia" in *Cambridge Ancient History* Vol.1 part 2 (3rd ed.)

Martin, T. H. "Mémoire sur la date historique d'un rénouvellement de la période sothiaque" in *Mémoires presentés par divers savants a l'Academie des Subscriptions et Belles-Lettres*. Serie 1 Vol.8 part 1 (Paris, 1869)

Olshausen, Otto, in *Zeitschrift für Ethnologie* (1907)

Oppenheim, A. L. "The Babylonian Evidence of the Achaemenian Rule in Mesopotamia" in *The Cambridge History of Iran* Vol.1 (Cambridge, 1985)

Sieff, Martin *Theses for the Reconstruction of Ancient History: Egypt, Israel and the Archaeological Record, 2400-330 BC,* (1987)

Smith, J. Elliott, in *American Journal of Archaeology* Vol.1 (1897)

Smith, W. Stevenson. "The Old Kingdom in Egypt and the Beginning of the First Intermediate Period" in *Cambridge Ancient History* Vol.1 part 2 (3rd ed.)

Stocks, Denys A. "Stone sarcophagus manufacture in ancient Egypt," *Antiquity*, vol. 73 (1999)

Stubbings, Frank. "The Rise of Mycenaean Civilization" in *Cambridge Ancient History* Vol.2 part 1 (3rd ed.)

Warshawsky, Walter. "The Exodus in the Pyramid Texts?" *Society for Interdisciplinary Studies: Workshop* 4:4 (1983)

Ancient Authors

Apollodorus, *Chronicle*

Censorinus, *Liber de Die Natali*

Diodorus Siculus, *History of the World*

Herodotus, *The Histories*

Hesiod, *Theogony*

Homer, *Iliad*

Hyginus, *Fabulae*

Josephus, *Against Apion*

Lucian, *Charidemus*

Ovid, *Metamorphoses*

Pausanias, *Guide to Greece*

Philostratus, *Heroicus*

Pindar, *Nemean Odes*

Plato, *Timaeus*

Pliny, *Natural History*

Tacitus, *Annals of Imperial Rome*

INDEX